Secondhand Time

Voices from Chernobyl

Zinky Boys

Last Witnesses

The Unwomanly Face of War

LAST WITNESSES

LAST
WITNESSES

AN ORAL HISTORY OF
THE CHILDREN OF WORLD WAR II

SVETLANA
ALEXIEVICH

TRANSLATED BY

Richard Pevear and Larissa Volokhonsky

RANDOM HOUSE

NEW YORK

Translation copyright © 2019 by Penguin Random House LLC

All rights reserved.

Published in the United States by Random House,
an imprint and division of Penguin Random House LLC, New York.

RANDOM HOUSE and the HOUSE colophon are registered
trademarks of Penguin Random House LLC.

Originally published in Russian as
Последние свидетели: сто недетских колыбельных
by Molodaya Gvardiya, Moscow, in 1985.
Copyright © 1985 by Svetlana Alexievich

This English translation is published in the
United Kingdom by Penguin, London.

LIBRARY OF CONGRESS CATALOGING-IN-PUBLICATION DATA

Names: Aleksievich, Svetlana, author. | Pevear, Richard, translator. |
Volokhonsky, Larissa, translator.
Title: Last witnesses: an oral history of the children of World War II /
Svetlana Alexievich; translated by Richard Pevear and Larissa Volokhonsky.
Other titles: Poslednie svideteli. English
Description: First edition. | New York: Random House, [2019]
Identifiers: LCCN 2018034984 | ISBN 9780399588754 | ISBN 9780399588778 (ebook)
Subjects: LCSH: World War, 1939–1945—Children—Soviet Union. |
World War, 1939–1945—Personal narratives, Soviet.
Classification: LCC D810.C4 A44313 2019 | DDC 940.53/4709253—dc23
LC record available at lccn.loc.gov/2018034984

Printed in the United States of America on acid-free paper

randomhousebooks.com

246897531

First Edition

Book design by Barbara M. Bachman

CONTENTS

——

INSTEAD OF A PREFACE

———

. . . ONE QUOTATION

In the course of the Great Patriotic War (1941–1945) mil-
lions of Soviet children died: Russians, Belorussians,
Ukrainians, Jews, Tatars, Latvians, Gypsies, Kazakhs, Uzbeks, Armenians, Tadjiks . . .

People's Friendship magazine, 1985, No. 5

. . . AND ONE QUESTION BY A RUSSIAN CLASSIC

Dostoevsky once posed a question: can we justify our
world, our happiness, and even eternal harmony, if in its
name, to strengthen its foundation, at least one little tear
of an innocent child will be spilled? And he himself answered: this tear will not justify any progress, any revolution. Any war. It will always outweigh them.

Just one little tear . . .

LAST WITNESSES

"HE WAS AFRAID TO LOOK BACK . . ."

Zhenya Belkevich

SIX YEARS OLD. NOW A WORKER.

June 1941 . . .

I remember it. I was very little, but I remember everything . . .

The last thing I remember from the peaceful life was a fairy tale that mama read us at bedtime. My favorite one—about the Golden Fish. I also always asked something from the Golden Fish: "Golden Fish . . . Dear Golden Fish . . ." My sister asked, too. She asked differently: "By order of the pike, by my like . . ." We wanted to go to our grandmother for the summer and have papa come with us. He was so much fun.

In the morning I woke up from fear. From some unfamiliar sounds . . .

Mama and papa thought we were asleep, but I lay next to my sister pretending to sleep. I saw papa kiss mama for a long time, kiss her face and hands, and I kept wondering: he's never kissed her like that before. They went outside, they were holding hands, I ran to the window—mama hung on my father's neck and wouldn't let him go. He tore free of her and ran, she caught up with him and again held him and shouted something. Then I also shouted: "Papa! Papa!"

My little sister and brother Vasya woke up, my sister saw me crying, and she, too, shouted: "Papa!" We all ran out to the porch: "Papa!" Father saw us and, I remember it like today, covered his head with his hands and walked off, even ran. He was afraid to look back.

The sun was shining in my face. So warm . . . And even now I can't believe that my father left that morning for the war. I was very little, but I think I realized that I was seeing him for the last time. That I would never meet him again. I was very . . . very little . . .

It became connected like that in my memory, that war is when there's no papa . . .

Then I remember: the black sky and the black plane. Our mama lies by the road with her arms spread. We ask her to get up, but she doesn't. She doesn't rise. The soldiers wrapped mama in a tarpaulin and buried her in the sand, right there. We shouted and begged: "Don't put our mama in the ground. She'll wake up and we'll go on." Some big beetles crawled over the sand . . . I couldn't imagine how mama was going to live with them under the ground. How would we find her afterward, how would we meet her? Who would write to our papa?

One of the soldiers asked me: "What's your name, little girl?" But I forgot. "And what's your last name, little girl? What's your mother's name?" I didn't remember . . . We sat by mama's little mound till night, till we were picked up and put on a cart. The cart was full of children. Some old man drove us, he gathered up everybody on the road. We came to a strange village and strangers took us all to different cottages.

I didn't speak for a long time. I only looked.

Then I remember—summer. Bright summer. A strange woman strokes my head. I begin to cry. I begin to speak . . . To tell about mama and papa. How papa ran away from us and didn't even look back . . . How mama lay . . . How the beetles crawled over the sand . . .

The woman strokes my head. In those moments I realized: she looks like my mama . . .

"MY FIRST AND LAST CIGARETTE . . ."

Gena Yushkevich

TWELVE YEARS OLD. NOW A JOURNALIST.

The morning of the first day of the war . . .

Sun. And unusual quiet. Incomprehensible silence.

Our neighbor, an officer's wife, came out to the yard all in tears. She whispered something to mama, but gestured that they had to be quiet. Everybody was afraid to say aloud what had happened, even when they already knew, since some had been informed. But they were afraid that they'd be called provocateurs. Panic-mongers. That was more frightening than the war. They were afraid . . . This is what I think now . . . And of course no one believed it. What?! Our army is at the border, our leaders are in the Kremlin! The country is securely protected, it's invulnerable to the enemy! That was what I thought then . . . I was a young Pioneer.*

We listened to the radio. Waited for Stalin's speech. We needed his voice. But Stalin was silent. Then Molotov† gave a speech. Everybody listened. Molotov said, "It's war." Still no one believed it yet. Where is Stalin?

---

* The All-Union Pioneer Organization, for Soviet children from ten to fifteen years old, was founded in 1922. It was similar to Scout organizations in the West.

† Vyacheslav Molotov (1890–1986), an Old Bolshevik and close collaborator with Stalin, served in several high offices of the Soviet Union. From 1939 to 1949 he was Minister of Foreign Affairs. On August 23, 1939, he signed the Molotov-Ribbentrop pact of nonaggression between the Soviet Union and Nazi Germany, which was broken by Germany in June 1941.

Planes flew over the city . . . Dozens of unfamiliar planes. With crosses. They covered the sky, covered the sun. Terrible! Bombs rained down . . . There were sounds of ceaseless explosions. Rattling. Everything was happening as in a dream. Not in reality. I was no longer little—I remember my feelings. My fear, which spread all over my body. All over my words. My thoughts. We ran out of the house, ran somewhere down the streets . . . It seemed as if the city was no longer there, only ruins. Smoke. Fire. Somebody said we must run to the cemetery, because they wouldn't bomb a cemetery. Why bomb the dead? In our neighborhood there was a big Jewish cemetery with old trees. And everybody rushed there, thousands of people gathered there. They embraced the monuments, hid behind the tombstones.

Mama and I sat there till nightfall. Nobody around uttered the word *war*. I heard another word: *provocation*. Everybody repeated it. People said that our troops would start advancing any moment. On Stalin's orders. People believed it.

But the sirens on the chimneys in the outskirts of Minsk wailed all night . . .

The first dead . . .

The first dead I saw was a horse . . . Then a dead woman . . . That surprised me. My idea was that only men were killed in war.

I woke up in the morning . . . I wanted to leap out of bed, then I remembered—it's war, and I closed my eyes. I didn't want to believe it.

There was no more shooting in the streets. Suddenly it was quiet. For several days it was quiet. And then all of a sudden there was movement . . . There goes, for instance, a white man, white all over, from his shoes to his hair. Covered with flour. He carries a white sack. Another is running . . . Tin cans fall out of his pockets, he has tin cans in his hands. Candy . . . Packs of tobacco . . . Someone carries a hat filled with sugar . . . A pot of sugar . . . Indescribable! One carries a roll of fabric, another goes all wrapped in blue calico. Red calico . . . It's funny, but nobody laughs. Food warehouses had been bombed. A big store not far from our house . . . People rushed to take whatever was left there. At a sugar factory several men drowned in vats of sugar syrup. Terrible! The whole city cracked sunflower seeds. They found a stock of sunflower seeds somewhere. Before my eyes a woman came running to a store . . . She had nothing with her: no sack or net bag—so she took off her slip. Her leggings. She stuffed them with buckwheat. Carried it off. All that silently for some reason. Nobody talked.

When I called my mother, there was only mustard left, yellow jars of mustard. "Don't take anything," mama begged. Later she told me she was ashamed, because all her life she had taught me differently. Even when we were starving and remembering these days, we still didn't regret anything. That's how my mother was.

In town . . . German soldiers calmly strolled in our streets. They filmed everything. Laughed. Before the war we had a favorite game—we made drawings of Germans. We drew them with big teeth. Fangs. And now they're walking around . . . Young, handsome . . . With handsome grenades tucked into the tops of their sturdy boots. Play harmonicas. Even joke with our pretty girls.

An elderly German was dragging a box. The box was heavy. He beckoned to me and gestured: help me. The box had two handles, we took it by these handles. When we had brought it where we were told to, the German patted me on the shoulder and took a pack of cigarettes from his pocket. Meaning here's your pay.

I came home. I couldn't wait, I sat in the kitchen and lit up a cigarette. I didn't hear the door open and mama come in.

"Smoking, eh?"

"Mm-hmm . . ."

"What are these cigarettes?"

"German."

"So you smoke, and you smoke the enemy's cigarettes. That is treason against the Motherland."

This was my first and last cigarette.

One evening mama sat down next to me.

"I find it unbearable that they're here. Do you understand me?"

She wanted to fight. Since the first days. We decided to look for the underground fighters—we didn't doubt that they existed. We didn't doubt for a moment.

"I love you more than anybody in the world," mama said. "But you understand me? Will you forgive me if anything happens to us?"

I fell in love with my mama, I now obeyed her unconditionally. And it remained so for my whole life.

"GRANDMA PRAYED . . . SHE ASKED THAT MY SOUL COME BACK . . ."

Natasha Golik

FIVE YEARS OLD. NOW A PROOFREADER.

I learned to pray . . . I often remember how during the war I learned to pray . . .

They said: it's war. I—understandably—being five years old, didn't picture anything specific. Anything frightening. But I fell asleep from fear, precisely from fear. I slept for two days. For two days I lay like a doll. Everybody thought I was dead. Mama cried, and grandma prayed. She prayed for two days and two nights.

I opened my eyes, and the first thing I remember was light. Very bright light, extraordinarily bright. So bright it was painful. I heard someone's voice, I recognized it: it was my grandma's voice. Grandma stands before an icon and prays. "Grandma . . . Grandma . . ." I called her. She didn't turn. She didn't believe it was me calling her . . . I was already awake . . . I opened my eyes . . .

"Grandma," I asked later, "what did you pray for when I was dying?"

"I asked that your soul come back."

A year later our grandma died. I already knew what to pray for. I prayed and asked that her soul come back.

But it didn't come back.

"THEY LAY PINK ON THE CINDERS . . ."

Katya Korotaeva

THIRTEEN YEARS OLD. NOW AN ENGINEER
IN HYDROTECHNOLOGY.

I'll tell about the smell . . . How war smells . . .

Before the war I finished sixth grade. At school the rule was that beginning from the fourth grade there were final exams. And so we passed the last exam. It was June, and the months of May and June in 1941 were cold. Usually lilacs blossom some time in May, but that year they blossomed in mid-June. The beginning of the war for me is always associated with the smell of lilacs. And of bird cherry. For me these trees always smell of war . . .

We lived in Minsk, and I was born in Minsk. My father was a military choirmaster. I used to go to the military parades with him. Besides me, there were two older brothers in the family. Of course, everybody loved me and pampered me as the youngest, and also as the little sister.

Ahead was summer, vacations. This was a great joy. I did sports, went to the swimming pool in the House of the Red Army. The children in my class envied me very much. And I was proud that I could swim well. On Sunday, June 22, there was to be a celebration marking the opening of the Komsomol Lake.* They spent a long time dig-

---

* An artificial lake built on the Svisloch River in the Minsk district of Belorussia. "Komsomol" was the acronym of the Communist Youth League, founded by Lenin in 1918.

ging it, building it, even our school went to the *subbotniks*.* I planned
to be one of the first to go and swim in it. For sure!

In the morning we had a custom of going to buy fresh rolls. This
was considered my duty. On the way I met a friend, she told me that
war had begun. There were many gardens on our street, houses
drowned in flowers. I thought, "What kind of war? What's she in-
venting?"

At home my father was setting up the samovar . . . I had no time
to say anything before neighbors came running, and they all had one
word on their lips: *War! War!* The next morning at seven o'clock my
older brother received a notice from the recruiting office. In the afternoon he ran over to his work, got paid off. He came home with
this money and said to mama, "I'm leaving for the front, I don't need
anything. Take this money. Buy Katya a new coat." I had just finished
sixth grade and was supposed to start secondary school, and I dreamed
that they'd have a dark-blue woolen coat with a gray Astrakhan collar
made for me. He knew about it.

To this day I remember that, on leaving for the front, my brother
gave money for my coat. Yet we lived modestly, there were enough
holes in the family budget. But mama would have bought me the
coat, since my brother asked. She just didn't have time.

The bombing of Minsk began. Mama and I moved to our neighbors' stone cellar. I had a favorite cat, she was very wild and never
went anywhere beyond our yard, but when the bombing started, and
I ran from the yard to our neighbors, the cat followed me. I tried to
chase her away: "Go home!" But she followed me. She, too, was
afraid to stay alone. The German bombs made some ringing, howling
noise. I had a musical ear, it affected me strongly . . . Those sounds . . .
I was so scared that my palms were wet. The neighbors' four-year-old
boy sat with us in the cellar. He didn't cry, his eyes just grew bigger.

First separate houses burned, then the whole city. We like looking

---

* *Subbotniks,* from the Russian word for Saturday (*subbota*), were Saturdays devoted to vol-
unteer work for the community.

at a fire, at a bonfire, but it's frightening when a house burns, and here fire came from all sides, the sky and the streets were filled with smoke. In some places it was very bright . . . From the fire . . . I remember three open windows in a wooden house, with magnificent Christmas cactuses on the windowsill. There were no people in this house anymore, only the blossoming cactuses . . . The feeling was that they weren't red flowers, but flames. Burning flowers.

We fled . . .

In villages on the way people fed us with bread and milk—that was all they had. We had no money. I left the house with nothing but a kerchief, and mama for some reason ran out in a winter coat and high-heeled shoes. We were fed for free, no one made a peep about money. Refugees came pouring in crowds.

Then someone in front sent word that the road ahead had been cut by German motorcyclists. We ran back past the same villages, past the same women with jugs of milk. We came to our street . . . Several days ago it was still green, there were flowers, and now everything was burned down. Nothing was left even of the centennial lindens. Everything was burned down to the yellow sand. The black earth on which everything grew disappeared somewhere; there was only yellow sand. Nothing but sand. As if you were standing by a freshly dug grave . . .

Factory furnaces were left. They were white, baked by the strong flame. Nothing else was recognizable . . . The whole street had burned. Grandmothers and grandfathers and many small children had burned. Because they didn't run away with the others, they thought they wouldn't be touched. The fire didn't spare anybody. We walked and if you saw a black corpse, it meant a burned old man. If you saw something small and pink from a distance—it meant a child. They lay pink on the cinders . . .

Mama took off her kerchief and covered my eyes with it . . . So we reached our house, the place where our house had stood several days ago. The house wasn't there. We were met by our miraculously spared cat. She pressed herself to me—that was all. No one could speak . . .

even the cat didn't meow. She was silent for several days. Everybody became mute.

I saw the first fascists, not even saw but heard—they all had iron-shod boots, they stomped loudly. Stomped over our pavement. I had the feeling that it even hurt the earth when they walked.

But how the lilacs bloomed that year . . . How the bird cherry bloomed . . .

"I STILL WANT MY MAMA . . ."

Zina Kosiak

EIGHT YEARS OLD. NOW A HAIRDRESSER.

First grade . . .

I finished first grade in May of '41, and my parents took me for the summer to the Pioneer camp of Gorodishche, near Minsk. I came there, went for a swim once, and two days later the war began. We were put on a train and taken somewhere. German planes flew over, and we shouted "Hurray!" We didn't understand that they could be enemy planes. Until they began to bomb us . . . Then all colors disappeared. All shades. For the first time the word *death* appeared; everybody began to repeat this incomprehensible word. And mama and papa weren't there.

When we were leaving the camp, we each had something poured into a pillowcase—some of us grain, some of us sugar. Even the smallest children weren't passed over, everybody got something. They wanted us to take as much food as possible for the road, and this food was used very sparingly. But on the train we saw wounded soldiers. They moaned, they were in pain. We wanted to give everything to these soldiers. We called it "feeding the papas." We called all military men papas.

We were told that Minsk had burned down, burned down completely, that the Germans were already there, but that we were going to the rear. Where there was no war.

We rode for over a month. They'd direct us to some town, we'd come there, but they couldn't keep us there, because the Germans were already close. And so we arrived in Mordovia.

The place was very beautiful, there were churches standing around. The houses were low, and the churches high. There was nothing to sleep on, we slept on straw. Winter came, and we had one pair of shoes for the four of us. Then we began to starve. Not only the orphanage was starving, but also the people around us, because we gave everything to the front. There were 250 children living in our orphanage, and once we were called to dinner and there was nothing to eat at all. The teachers and the director sat in the dining room, looked at us, and their eyes were full of tears. We had a horse, Maika . . . She was very old and gentle, and we used her to carry water. The next day this Maika was killed. We were given water with a small piece of Maika in it . . . But they concealed it from us for a long time. We wouldn't have been able to eat her . . . Not for anything! She was the only horse in our orphanage. We also had two hungry cats. Skeletons! Good, we thought later, it's lucky they were so skinny, we didn't have to eat them. There was nothing there to eat.

We went around with swollen stomachs. I, for instance, could eat a bucket of soup, because there was nothing in this soup. I'd eat as much as they gave me. We were saved by nature, we were like ruminant animals. In spring not a single tree for several miles around the orphanage would sprout . . . We ate all the buds, we even peeled off the young bark. We ate grass, we ate everything. They gave us pea jackets; we made pockets in them and carried grass around and chewed it. Summer saved us, but in winter it was very hard. Small children—there were some forty of us—were placed separately. During the night there was howling. We called mama and papa. Our house parents and teachers tried not to say the word *mama* before us. They told us fairy tales and found books without this word in them. If anyone suddenly said "mama," howling began. Inconsolable howling.

I repeated first grade in school. It happened like this: I had graduated from first grade with a certificate of honor, but when we came to the orphanage they asked us who had been reexamined, I said I had, because I decided that reexamination meant the certificate of honor.

In the third grade I ran away from the orphanage. I went looking for mama. Grandpa Bolshakov found me in the forest, hungry and exhausted. He learned that I was from an orphanage and took me into his family. He and grandma lived together. I grew stronger and began to help them with the chores: gathered grass, weeded potatoes—did everything. We ate bread, but there was little bread in it. It was very bitter. The flour was mixed with everything that could be ground: goosefoot, filbert blossoms, potatoes. To this day I cannot look calmly at healthy grass, and I eat a lot of bread. I can't have enough of it . . . After dozens of years . . .

Anyhow, I remember a lot. There's much more that I remember . . .

I remember a mad little girl who would get into someone's kitchen garden, find a hole, and start waiting for a mouse. The girl was hungry. I remember her face, even the sundress she wore. Once I came up to her and she . . . told me . . . about the mouse . . . We sat together and looked out for that mouse . . .

All through the war I waited so that, when the war ended, grandpa and I could harness a horse and go in search of mama. Evacuated people stopped at our house, and I asked them all whether they had met my mama. There were many evacuated people, so many that in every house there stood a cauldron of warm nettles. In case people came, there should be something warm for them to eat. We had nothing else to give them. But there was a cauldron of nettles in every house . . . I remember it well. I gathered those nettles.

The war ended . . . I waited for a day, for two days. No one came to get me. Mama didn't come for me, and papa, I knew, was in the army. I waited for two weeks like that, and couldn't wait any longer. I got under a seat on a train and rode . . . Where? I didn't know. I thought (this was still my child's mind) that all trains went to Minsk. And in Minsk mama was waiting! Then papa would come . . . A hero! With orders, with medals.

They had perished somewhere under the bombs. The neighbors told me later—they had both gone looking for me. They had rushed to the train station.

I'm already fifty-one years old. I have children of my own. But I still want my mama.

"SUCH PRETTY GERMAN TOYS . . ."

Taisa Nasvetnikova

SEVEN YEARS OLD. NOW A TEACHER.

Before the war . . .

How I remember myself . . . Everything was good: kindergarten, children's theater, our courtyard. Girls and boys. I read a lot, was afraid of worms and loved dogs. We lived in Vitebsk. Papa worked in construction management. Of my childhood I remember most of all how papa taught me to swim in the Dvina.

Then there was school. The impression I have kept from school is: very wide stairs, a transparent glass wall, and lots of sun, and lots of joy. The feeling was that life is a feast.

In the first days of the war papa left for the front. I remember saying goodbye to him at the train station . . . Papa kept telling mama that they'd drive the Germans away, but he wanted us to evacuate. Mama couldn't understand why. If we stayed at home, he would find us sooner. At once. And I kept repeating, "Papa dear! Only come back soon. Papa dear . . ."

Papa left, and a few days later we also left. On the way we were bombed all the time. Bombing us was easy, because the trains to the rear ran just five hundred yards apart. We traveled light: mama was wearing a sateen dress with white polka dots, and I a red cotton jumper with little flowers. All the adults said that red was very visible from above, and as soon as there was an air raid and we rushed for the bushes, they covered me with whatever they could find so that my red jumper wouldn't be seen. Otherwise I was like a signal light.

We drank water from swamps and ditches. Intestinal illnesses set in. I also fell ill. For three days I didn't regain consciousness . . . Afterward mama told me how I was saved. When we stopped in Briansk, a troop train arrived on the next track. My mama was twenty-six, she was very beautiful. Our train stood there for a long time. She got out of the car and an officer from that train complimented her. Mama said, "Leave me alone, I cannot look at your smile. My daughter is dying." The officer turned out to be a field paramedic. He jumped into our car, examined me, and called his comrade: "Quickly bring tea, rusks, and belladonna." Those soldiers' rusks . . . a quart bottle of strong tea, and a few belladonna pills saved my life.

Before we reached Aktyubinsk the whole train had been sick. We children were not allowed where the dead and killed lay; we were protected from that sight. We only heard the conversations: so many buried here, and so many there . . . Mama would come with a very pale face, her hands trembled. And I kept asking, "Where did these people go?"

I don't remember any landscapes. That's very surprising, because I loved nature. I only remember the bushes we hid under. The ravines. For some reason it seemed to me that there was no forest anywhere, that we traveled only through fields, through some sort of desert. Once I experienced fear, after which I wasn't afraid of any bombing. We hadn't been warned that it would be a short stop of ten or fifteen minutes. The train started and I was left behind. Alone . . . I don't remember who picked me up . . . I was literally thrown into the car . . . Not our car, but the one before the end. For the first time I had a scare that I would be left alone and mama would go off. While mama was near me, I wasn't afraid. But here I went mute with fright. And until mama came running to me and threw both arms around me, I was mute, and no one could get a word out of me. Mama was my world. My planet. When I had pain somewhere, I would take mama's hand and the pain would go away. At night I always slept next to her, the closer the less fear there was. If mama was near, it seemed that everything was as it used to be at home. You close your eyes—there isn't any war. Only mama didn't like to talk about death. And I kept asking her . . .

From Aktyubinsk we went to Magnitogorsk, where papa's brother lived. Before the war they had been a big family, with many men, but when we arrived there were only women in the house. All the men had gone to the war. At the end of 1941 two death notices came—my uncle's sons had been killed . . .

Of that winter I also remember chicken pox, which everybody at school came down with. And red trousers . . . Mama got a length of dark red flannelette for her coupons, and she made me a pair of trousers. The children teased me: "Fancy pants, go back to France." I was very hurt. A bit later we got galoshes for our coupons. I tied them up and ran around. They rubbed at my little bones, and I had to put something under the heels so that the heels were higher, to avoid getting blisters. The winter was so cold that my hands and feet kept freezing. The heating system at school often broke down, the water on the floor in the classroom turned to ice, and we could slide between the desks. We sat there in our coats and mittens, only we cut the tips off so that we could hold a pen. I remember that we were forbidden to offend and tease those whose papas had been killed. For that we were severely punished. We also all read a lot. As never before or after . . . We read all the children's books, all the adolescent books. They started giving us adult books. The other girls were afraid . . . even the boys didn't like the pages where death was written about and skipped over them. But I read them.

Heavy snow fell. All the children ran outside and made a snowman. I was perplexed: how was it possible to make a snowman and be happy, if there was a war?

The adults listened to the radio all the time; they couldn't live without the radio. Neither could we. We rejoiced at every salute fired off in Moscow, we were excited over each piece of information: how are things at the front? In the underground? Among the partisans? Films were produced about the battles of Stalingrad and Moscow, and we watched them fifteen or twenty times. If they showed them three times in a row, we watched them three times in a row. The films were shown at school, there was no special movie theater, they showed them in the corridor with us sitting on the floor. We sat for two or three hours. I memorized death . . . Mama scolded me for that. She consulted doctors about why I was like that . . . Why was I interested in such an unchildlike thing as death? How to teach me to think about children's things . . .

I reread fairy tales . . . Children's fairy tales . . . Again, what did I notice? I noticed how much killing there was in them. A great deal of blood. That was my discovery . . .

At the end of 1944 . . . I saw the first German prisoners . . . They walked in a wide column down the street. I was struck that people came up to them and gave them bread. I was so struck that I ran to mama at work to ask: why do our people give the Germans bread? Mama said nothing, but only wept. Then I also saw my first dead man in a German uniform. He was marching in the column and fell down. The column paused, then moved on, and next to him one of our soldiers was stationed. I ran to them . . . I was drawn to look at death close up, to be near it. Whenever the radio announced enemy losses, we always rejoiced . . . But now . . . I saw . . . The man was as if asleep . . . He didn't even lie down, but sat huddled up, with his head leaning on his shoulder. I didn't know: should I hate him or pity him? He was the enemy. Our enemy! I don't remember if he was young or old. He was very tired. Because of that it was hard for me to hate him. I told mama about that, too. And again she wept.

On May 9 we woke up in the morning, because by the entrance someone was shouting loudly. It was still very early. Mama went to find out, and came running back bewildered: "Victory! Can it be Victory?" This was so unexpected: the war ended, such a long war. Some wept, some laughed, some shouted . . . Those who had lost their loved ones wept, but still they rejoiced, because even so it was

Victory! One had a handful of grain, another some potatoes, yet another some beets—it was all taken to one apartment. I'll never forget that day. That morning . . . By evening it was already not the same . . .

During the war everybody spoke softly for some reason, even in a whisper as it seemed to me, but now suddenly everybody began to speak loudly. We were with the grown-ups all the time, they gave us good things, caressed us, told us to go out: "Go outside. Today is a holiday." Then they called us back. We had never been embraced and kissed so much as on that day.

But I was a lucky one, my papa came back from the war. Papa brought beautiful children's toys. German toys. I couldn't understand how such beautiful toys could be German . . .

I tried to talk about death with papa, too. About the bombings, when mama and I were evacuated . . . How our dead soldiers lay along both sides of the road. Their faces were covered with branches. Flies buzzed over them . . . Huge swarms of flies . . . About the dead German . . . I told him about my friend's papa, who came back from the war and died a few days later. Of a heart attack. I couldn't understand: how could someone die after the war, when everybody was happy?

Papa said nothing.

"A HANDFUL OF SALT . . . ALL THAT WAS LEFT OF OUR HOUSE . . ."

<u>Misha Maiorov</u>

FIVE YEARS OLD. NOW A DOCTOR OF AGRONOMY.

During the war I liked dreams. I liked dreams about peaceful life, about how we lived before the war . . .

First dream . . .

Grandma has finished her household chores . . . I've been waiting for this moment. Now she moves the table to the window, spreads the fabric on it, puts cotton wool on top of it, covers it with another piece of fabric, and begins to quilt a blanket. I, too, have a job: on one side of the blanket grandma hammers in little nails, to each one of them ties a piece of string, rubs it with chalk, and I hold it tight on the other side. "Tighter, Mishenka," grandma asks. I pull more tightly, grandma lets go—snap!—and there's a chalk line on the red or blue satin. The lines crisscross forming rhombs, the black thread stitches will go along them. The next operation: grandma lays out paper patterns (they're called stencils now) and a design appears on the quilted blanket. It's very beautiful and interesting. My grandma is an expert at stitching shirts; she's especially good at the collars. Her Singer sewing machine goes on working even when I'm already asleep. And grandpa is asleep, too.

Second dream . . .

Grandpa is making shoes. Here, too, I have something to do. I whittle wooden pegs. Now all soles are held by metal pins, but they rust, and the sole quickly falls off. Maybe at the time they already used metal pins, but I remember the wooden ones. A smooth, knot-less log of old birch should be sawed into rounds, which are left to dry under an old rag. Then they are split into pieces about an inch thick and four inches long, and they, too, are left to dry. Eighth-inch-thick splints can easily be cut off these pieces. A shoemaker's knife is sharp, it's easy to cut edges off this splint on two sides: you prop it against the worktable—*zhik-zhik*—and the splint becomes sharp, and then you just split it into nail-shaped pins. With a shoemaker's awl, grandpa makes a hole in the boot sole, puts the peg in, taps it with a shoemaker's hammer—and the pin is in the sole. The pegs were inserted in double rows, which is not only pretty, but also very strong: the dry pins will swell from moisture and hold the sole in place still more fast, and it won't fall off until it's worn out.

Grandpa also puts soles on felt boots, or rather a second sole, they serve longer then and you can wear them without galoshes. Or else he doubles the back of the heel with leather, so that the felt shoe doesn't wear out inside the galosh. My task is to twist a linen thread, tar it, wax it, and thread it through a needle. But a shoemaker's needle is very valuable, and therefore grandpa very often uses bristles, the most ordinary bristles from a wild boar's scruff, or maybe a domestic boar, only the bristles are softer. Grandpa has a whole bunch of these bristles. They can be used to sew on a sole or a small patch in an awk-ward place: bristles are flexible and will get in anywhere.

Third dream . . .

Older children organized a theater in the neighbors' big barn. The show is about border patrol and spies. A ticket costs ten kopecks. I don't have it, they don't let me in, I begin to howl: I, too, want "to see the war." I peek into the barn on the sly—the "border patrol" wore real army shirts. The show was terrific . . .

Then my dreams broke off . . .

Soon I saw soldiers' army shirts in our home . . . Grandma gave meals to the tired and dust-covered soldiers, and they kept saying,

"The Germans are barging ahead." I started badgering grandma: "What are the Germans like?"

We load bundles onto a cart, I'm seated on them. We go somewhere. Then we come back . . . There are Germans in our house! They're like our soldiers, only in a different uniform and merry. Mama, grandma, and I now live behind the stove, and grandpa—in the barn. Grandma doesn't quilt blankets anymore, grandpa doesn't make shoes. Once I pushed aside the curtain: a German with earphones was sitting in the corner by the window, turning the handle of the radio set. There was music, then distinct Russian speech . . . The other German was spreading butter on bread at the moment. He saw me and waved the knife right in front of my nose. I hid behind the curtain and didn't come out from behind the stove anymore.

A man in a charred shirt is being led down the street past our house, barefoot, his hands bound with wire. The man is all black . . . Later I saw him hanged next to the village council building. They said he was one of our pilots. At night I dreamed about him. In my dream he was hanging in our yard . . .

I remember everything in black: black tanks, black motorcycles, German soldiers in black uniforms. I'm not sure that it was really only black, but that's how I remember it. A black-and-white film . . .

. . . I'm wrapped in something and we hide in the swamp. All day and all night. The night is cold. Strange birds cry in frightening voices. It seems that the moon shines very, very bright. Scary! What if the German shepherds see or hear us? Occasionally their hoarse barking reaches us. In the morning we go home! I want to go home! Everybody wants to go home, to the warmth! But there is no more home, only a heap of smoking embers. A smoldering place . . . Like after a big bonfire . . . We find in the ashes a lump of salt that always lay on our hearth. We carefully collected the salt, and also the clay mixed with the salt, and poured it into a jar. That was all that was left of our house . . .

Grandma was silent all the while, but at night she began to lament,

"Ah, my cottage! Ah, my cottage! I was a young girl in i-i-i-it . . . Here the matchmakers ca-a-a-ame . . . Here the children were bo-o-o-orn." She went around our black yard like a ghost.

In the morning I opened my eyes. We slept on the ground, in our kitchen garden.

"AND I KISSED ALL THE PORTRAITS IN MY SCHOOLBOOK . . ."

<u>Zina Shimanskaya</u>

ELEVEN YEARS OLD. NOW A CASHIER.

I look back with a smile . . . With astonishment. Can this have happened to me?

The day the war began we were at the circus. Our whole class. At the morning performance. We didn't suspect a thing. Not a thing . . . The adults already knew, but we didn't. We clapped our hands. Laughed. There was a big elephant there. A huge one! A monkey danced . . . And then . . . We poured out into the street gaily—and people were going around all in tears: "War!" The children all shouted: "Hurray!" We were glad. We pictured war as people in *budenovki** on horseback. Now we'll show ourselves, we'll help our fighters. Become heroes. I loved war books most of all. About battles, about feats of courage. All sorts of dreams . . . Myself bending over a wounded soldier, carrying him out of the smoke. Out of the fire. At home the whole wall over my desk was covered with newspaper photographs of war scenes. Here was Voroshilov,[†] there Budenny . . .

---

* A *budenovka* was a distinctive woolen hat with a pointed top and earflaps, worn by Red Army soldiers during the Russian Civil War (1917–1922), named for Semyon Budenny (1883–1973), a Russian cavalry officer who became the leader of the Red Cavalry during the Civil War and was later a close ally of Stalin.

† Kliment Voroshilov (1881–1969) was a prominent military figure, one of the first five Marshals of the Soviet Union, and a member of the Central Committee of the Communist Party from 1921 to 1961. He played a major role in Stalin's Great Purge of 1937.

My girlfriend and I tried to escape to the Finnish War, and the boys we knew to the Spanish War.* We pictured war as the most interesting event in life. The greatest adventure. We dreamed of it, we were children of our time. Good children! My girlfriend always went around in an old *budenovka*. I forget where she found it, but it was her favorite hat. How did we run away to the war? I don't even remember which one it was, probably the Spanish one. I'll tell you in a moment . . . She stayed with me overnight on purpose, and at dawn we quietly left the house together. On tiptoe . . . Shh . . . We took along some food. My older brother probably watched us, because in the last few days we kept whispering and putting things in little bags. He caught up with us in the courtyard and brought us back. He scolded us and threatened to throw out all my war books. I spent the whole day crying. That's how we were!

But now it was real war . . .

A week later German troops entered Minsk. I don't remember the Germans themselves then, but I do remember their technology. Big cars, big motorcycles . . . We didn't have and had never seen any like that. People became deaf and dumb. They all had frightened eyes . . . Foreign posters and leaflets appeared on the fences and posts. Foreign orders. "New rules" came. After a while the school reopened. Mama decided that war is war, but I shouldn't interrupt my studies and had to go to school. At the first lesson the same teacher of geography who had taught us before the war began to speak against Soviet power. Against Lenin. I said to myself: I'm not going to study in such a school. No-o-o . . . I don't want to! I came home and kissed all the portraits in my schoolbook . . . All my favorite portraits of our leaders.

The Germans used to burst into apartments all the time, looking for someone—now for Jews, now for partisans . . . Mama said, "Hide

---

* The Finnish War, also known as the Winter War, was fought between Finland and the Soviet Union in the winter of 1939–1940. In the Spanish Civil War (1936–1939), Soviet troops were sent ostensibly to support the Spanish Republic against the military revolt led by Francisco Franco.

your Pioneer neckerchief." During the day I did, but at night when I went to bed I put it on. Mama was afraid: what if the Germans come knocking at night? She tried to persuade me, she wept. I waited till mama fell asleep and it was quiet at home and outside. Then I took my red tie from the wardrobe, got my Soviet books out. My friend slept in her *budenovka*.

I'm still glad we were like that . . .

"I GATHERED THEM WITH MY HANDS . . . THEY WERE VERY WHITE . . ."

Zhenia Selenia

FIVE YEARS OLD. NOW A JOURNALIST.

That Sunday . . . June 22 . . .

My brother and I went to pick mushrooms. It was the season for the best boletuses. Our wood was not big, we knew every bush in it, every clearing, and where what mushrooms grew, and what berries, and even flowers. Willow herb, Saint-John's-wort, pink heather . . . We were already going home, when we heard a thundering noise. The noise came from the sky. We raised our heads: there were some twelve or fifteen planes over us . . . They flew high, very high; I thought our planes never flew so high. We heard the noise: *rrrrr*!

Just then we saw our mama, she was running toward us—weeping, in a broken voice. This is the impression that remained from the first day of the war—mama, instead of calling us gently as usual, cries, "Children! My children!" Her eyes are big, instead of a face—just eyes . . .

Some two days later a group of Red Army soldiers stopped at our farmstead. Dust-covered, sweaty, with caked lips, they greedily drank water from the well. How revived they became . . . How their faces brightened when four of our planes appeared in the sky. We made out distinct red stars on them. "Ours! Ours!"—we shouted along with the soldiers. But suddenly small black planes popped up from somewhere. They circled around ours, and something was rattling and booming. The strange noise reached the ground . . . as if someone was tearing oilcloth or linen fabric . . . So loud. I didn't know yet that this was machine-gun fire heard from a distance or from high up. Our planes were falling and after them followed red streaks of fire and smoke. *Ba-bang!* The soldiers stood and wept, unashamed of their tears. For the first time I saw . . . for the first time . . . Red Army soldiers weeping . . . They never wept in the war films I used to go to watch in our settlement.

After another few days . . . Mama's sister, Aunt Katia, came running from the village of Kabaki. Black, ghastly-looking. She told us that the Germans had come to their village, rounded up all the activists, led them outside the village, and shot them all with machine guns. Among those shot was mama's brother, the deputy of the village council. An old Communist.

To this day I remember Aunt Katia's words: "They smashed his head, and I gathered his brains with my hands. They were very white."

She lived with us for two days. And told about it all the time . . . Her hair turned white in those two days. And when my mother sat with Aunt Katia, embracing her and weeping, I stroked her hair. I was afraid.

I was afraid that mama also would turn white . . .

"I WANT TO LIVE! I WANT TO LIVE! . . ."

Vasia Kharevsky

FOUR YEARS OLD. NOW AN ARCHITECT.

These pictures, these lights. My riches. The treasure of what I lived through . . .

No one believes me, even mama didn't believe me. After the war, when we began to remember, she kept wondering, "You couldn't recall that yourself, you were little. Somebody told you . . ."

No, I myself remember . . .

Bombs are exploding, and I'm clutching at my older brother: "I want to live! I want to live!" I was afraid to die, though what could I have known about death? What?

I myself . . .

Mama gave me and my brother the last two potatoes, and just looked at us. We knew that those potatoes were the last ones. I wanted to leave her . . . a small piece . . . And I couldn't. My brother also couldn't . . . We were ashamed. Terribly ashamed.

No, I myself . . .

I saw our first soldier . . . I think he was a tankist, I can't say exactly . . . I ran to him: "Papa!" He lifted me to the sky: "Sonny!"

I remember everything . . .

I remember the adults saying, "He's little. He doesn't understand." I was surprised: "They're strange, these adults, why have they decided that I don't understand anything? I understand everything." It even seemed to me that I understood more than the adults, because I didn't cry and they did.

The war is my history book. My solitude . . . I missed the time of childhood, it fell out of my life. I'm a man without a childhood. Instead of a childhood, I have the war.

The only other shock like that in my life came from love. When I fell in love . . . Knew love . . .

"THROUGH A BUTTONHOLE . . ."

Inna Levkevich

TEN YEARS OLD. NOW A CONSTRUCTION ENGINEER.

In the first days . . . From early morning . . .

Bombs were exploding over us . . . On the ground lay telephone poles and wires. Frightened people ran out of their houses. They ran out to the street, constantly warning each other, "Watch out—there's a wire! Watch out—there's a wire!" so that no one would get snared and fall. As if that was the most terrible thing.

In the morning of June 26 mama still handed out the salaries, because she worked as an accountant at a factory, but by evening we were already refugees. As we were leaving Minsk, we saw our school burn. Flames raged in every window. So bright . . . So . . . so intense, right up to the sky . . . We wept that our school was burning. There were four of us, three went on foot, and the fourth "rode" in mama's arms. Mama was nervous, because she took the key, but forgot to lock the apartment. She tried to stop the cars, cried and begged, "Take our children, and we'll go and defend the city." She refused to believe that the Germans were already in the city. That the city had surrendered.

Everything that was happening before our eyes and with us was frightening and incomprehensible. Especially death . . . Pots and pans lay about around the killed people. Everything was burning . . . It seemed as if we were running over burning coals . . . I always made friends with boys, and was myself a tomboy. I was interested to see how the bombs came flying, how they whined, how they fell. When mama shouted, "Lie down on the ground!" I peeked through a buttonhole . . . What was there in the sky? And how were people running . . . Something was hanging from a tree . . . When I realized that this something was a man, I was stunned. I closed my eyes . . .

My sister Irma was seven; she carried a Primus stove and mama's shoes. She was terribly afraid to lose those shoes. They were new, of a pale-rose color, with a faceted heel. Mama had taken them by chance, or maybe because they were her most beautiful thing.

With the key, and with the shoes, we soon returned to the city, where everything had burned down. Soon we began to starve. We gathered goosefoot and ate it. Ate some sort of dry flowers! Winter was coming. Fearing the partisans, the Germans burned a big kolkhoz* orchard outside the city, and everybody went there to cut some wood from the stumps, to have at least a little. To heat the stove at home. We made liver out of yeast: we fried yeast in a pan and it acquired the taste of liver. Mama gave me money to buy bread at the market. An old woman there was selling kid goats, and I imagined that I'd save the whole family by buying a kid. The kid would grow up—and we'd have a lot of milk. So I bought the kid, paying all the money mama had given me. I don't remember mama scolding me, but I do remember us sitting hungry for several days: we had no money. We cooked some sort of mixture to feed the kid, and I took him with me to bed, to keep him warm, but he was cold anyway. Soon he died. This was a tragedy. We wept very much, didn't want mama to take him away. I wept the most, considering myself guilty. Mama took him away by night, and told us that the mice ate the kid.

Yet under the occupation we celebrated all the May and October holidays.† Our holidays! Ours! We always sang songs, our family all

---

*   *Kolkhoz* was a Soviet acronym for "collective farm."

†   May 1 is International Workers' Day, also known as Labor Day or May Day, adopted at the Second Socialist International in 1889, in part to commemorate the Haymarket massacre in Chicago on May 4, 1886. The October holiday commemorated the start of the Bolshevik Revolution on October 25, 1917 (November 7 by the Gregorian calendar).

liked to sing. We could eat potatoes in skins, maybe one piece of sugar for us all; still on that day we tried to prepare something a bit better than usual, even if the next day we'd go hungry—we still celebrated all the holidays. In a whisper, we sang mama's favorite song: "The morning paints in tender hues / The ancient Kremlin walls . . ." That was a must.

A neighbor baked some little pies to sell and offered them to us: "Take them wholesale, and go and sell them piecemeal. You're young, light-footed." I decided to do it, because I knew how hard it was for mama alone to feed us. The neighbor brought the pies, my sister Irma and I sat and looked at them.

"Irma, don't you think that this pie is bigger than that one?" I said.

"Seems so . . ."

You can't imagine how I wanted to try a little piece.

"Let's cut a tiny bit, and then go selling."

We sat like that for two hours till there was nothing to take to the market. Then the neighbor started making candy, the kind they stopped selling in the stores for some reason. She gave some to us to go and sell. Again Irma and I sat over them.

"One is big, bigger than the others. Let's lick it a little bit, Irma."

"Let's . . ."

We had one coat for the three of us, one pair of felt boots. We often stayed home. We told fairy tales to each other . . . read some books . . . But that wasn't interesting. The interesting thing was to dream how the war would end and we'd live after that. Eating only pies and candy.

When the war was over, mama put on a little crepe de chine blouse. I don't remember how it was she still had it. We had exchanged all nice things for food. This blouse had black cuffs, and mama unstitched them so that there was nothing dark, only light.

We went to school at once and from the first days began to learn songs for a parade.

"ALL I HEARD WAS MAMA'S CRY . . ."

Lida Pogorzhelskaya

EIGHT YEARS OLD. NOW A DOCTOR OF BIOLOGY.

All my life I'll remember that day . . . The first day without papa . . .

I wanted to sleep. Mama got us up early in the morning and said: "It's war!" Who could sleep? We were getting ready to leave. There was no fear yet. We all looked at papa, and papa was calm. As always. He was a party worker. Each of you, mama said, has to take something along. I couldn't choose anything to take, but my younger sister took a doll. Mama carried our little brother. Papa caught up with us when we were already on our way.

I forgot to tell you that we lived in the town of Kobryn. Not far from Brest. That was why the war reached us on the very first day. We had no time to collect our senses. The adults almost didn't talk, they walked silently, rode on horseback silently. It was becoming frightening. People are walking, many people, and all of them silent.

When papa caught up with us we calmed down a little. In our family papa was the head in everything, because mama was very young, she had married at the age of sixteen. She didn't even know how to cook. But papa was an orphan, he knew how to do everything. I remember how we loved it when papa had time and could prepare something tasty for us. It was a feast for everybody. Even now I think there's nothing tastier than the farina that papa used to cook. All the while we rode without him we waited for him. To remain in the war without papa—that we couldn't imagine. That's the sort of family we were.

Our wagon train was big. It moved slowly. Occasionally everybody stopped and looked at the sky. Searching for our planes . . . Searching in vain . . .

At midday we saw a column of some sort of soldiers. They were on horseback and dressed in new Red Army uniforms. Well-fed horses. Big. Nobody guessed that these were saboteurs. We decided: they're our men. And rejoiced. Papa came out to meet them, and I heard mama's cry. I didn't hear the shot . . . Only mama's cry: "A-a-a . . ." I remember that these soldiers didn't even dismount . . . When mama cried out, I broke into a run. Everybody ran somewhere. We ran silently. I only heard how mama cried. I ran till I got tangled and fell in the tall grass . . .

Our horses stood there till evening. Waiting. And we all returned to that place when it was getting dark. Mama sat there alone and waited. Somebody said, "Look, she's turned gray." I remember the adults digging a hole . . . pushing me and my sister: "Go. Take leave of your father." I went two steps and couldn't go farther. Sat down on the ground. My little sister sat next to me. My brother slept, he was very little and didn't understand anything. Mama lay on a cart unconscious; we weren't allowed to go to her.

So none of us saw my father dead. Or remembered him dead. Whenever I remembered him, I always saw him in a white uniform jacket. Young and handsome. Even now, and now I'm already older than our papa.

In the Stalingrad region, where we were evacuated, mama worked on a kolkhoz. Mama, who didn't know how to do anything, didn't know how to weed vegetables, couldn't tell oats from wheat, became a top worker. We had no papa, and there were others who had no papa. Some others had no mama. Or brother. Or sister. Or grandfather. But we didn't feel we were orphans. Everybody pitied us and

took care of us. I remember Aunt Tanya Morozova.* Her two children had been killed, she lived alone. And she gave us all she had, as
our mama did. She was a total stranger, but over the time of the war
she became our family. My brother, when he grew up a bit, used to
say that we had no papa, but instead—two mamas: our own and Aunt
Tanya. That's how all of us were growing up. With two or three
mamas.

I also remember how we were bombed on the way to evacuation,
and we ran to hide. We didn't run to hide with mama, but to the soldiers. When the bombing was over, mama scolded us for running
away from her. But still, as soon as there was another bombing, we
ran to the soldiers.

When Minsk was liberated, we decided to go back. Home. To Belarus. Our mama was a native of Minsk. But when we got off at the
Minsk train station, she didn't know where to go. It was a different
city. Only ruins . . . Crushed stone . . .

Later I studied in the Goretsk agricultural academy . . . I lived in a
dormitory, there were eight girls in our room. All orphans. No one
selected us specially or gathered us together—there were many of us.
More than one roomful. I remember how we all shouted during the
night . . . I might just leap out of my cot and start banging on the
door . . . Trying to go somewhere . . . The girls would catch me. Then
I'd begin to cry. They would do the same. The whole room would
cry together. And in the morning we would have to go to class and
listen to the lectures.

Once I met a man in the street who looked like papa. I followed
him for a long time. Since I hadn't seen my papa dead . . .

---

* Russians (and others) use the terms *aunt* and *uncle* loosely, referring to neighbors or people
one is close to, or to grown-ups in general.

"WE PLAYED,
AND THE SOLDIERS WEPT . . ."

Volodia Chistokletov

TEN YEARS OLD. NOW A MUSICIAN.

It was a beautiful morning . . .

Morning sea. Blue and calm. The first days since my arrival at the Soviet-Kvadge children's sanatorium on the Black Sea. We heard the noise of the airplanes . . . I dove into the waves, but there, under the water, the noise could still be heard. We weren't frightened, but began to play "war," not suspecting that somewhere war was already going on. Not a game, not a military exercise, but war.

A few days later we were sent home. Mine was in Rostov. The first bombs were already falling on the city. Everybody was preparing for street fighting: digging trenches, building barricades. Learning to shoot. We children guarded the boxes for storing bottles of explosive mixture, delivering sand and water in case of a fire.

All the schools were turned into hospitals. Our school No. 70 housed the field army hospital for the lightly wounded. Mama was assigned there. She was allowed to take me along, so that I didn't stay at home alone. And when there was a retreat, we went wherever the hospital went.

After one bombing I remember a pile of books among the rubble. I picked one up that was called *The Life of Animals,* a big book with beautiful pictures. I didn't sleep all night, reading it, unable to tear myself away . . . I remember I didn't take any war books, I didn't want to read about war. But about animals, about birds . . .

In November 1942 . . . The head of the hospital ordered that I be issued a uniform, but to tell the truth, it had to be urgently made over to fit. And they spent a whole month looking for boots for me. So I became the foster child of the hospital. A soldier. What did I do? The bandages alone could drive you crazy. There was never enough of them. I had to launder, dry, and roll them up. Try rolling up a thousand a day! I got the hang of it and did it quicker than the adults. My first rolled up cigarette also came out well . . . On my twelfth birthday the first sergeant, smiling, handed me a package of shag, as if I was a full-grown soldier. I did smoke it . . . On the sly from mama. I showed off, of course. Well . . . it was also scary . . . I had a hard time getting used to blood. Was afraid of burned men. With black faces . . .

After a train transporting salt and paraffin was bombed, the one and the other proved useful. The salt went to the cooks, the paraffin to me. I had to master a skill unspecified in any lists of military professions—making candles. That was worse than the bandages. My task was to make sure the candles burned for a long time, because they were used whenever there was no electricity. Doctors didn't stop surgery either under the bombs or under shelling. During the night the windows were curtained with sheets or blankets.

Mama wept, but all the same I dreamed of escaping to the front. I didn't believe I could be killed. Once I was sent to get bread . . . We had just set out when artillery shelling began. It was mortar fire. The sergeant was killed, the coachman was killed, and I got a concussion. I lost speech, and when after a while I began to speak again, I stuttered. I still stutter. Everybody was surprised that I was still alive, but I had a different feeling—how could I be killed? I went with the hospital through the whole of Belarus, through Poland . . . I learned some Polish words . . .

In Warsaw . . . A Czech turned up among the wounded—a trombonist from the Prague Opera. The head of the hospital was glad of him, and when the man began to recover, he asked him to go around the wards and look for musicians. He came to us with an excellent orchestra. He taught me to play the viola, and I taught myself to play the guitar. We played and the soldiers wept. We played merry songs . . .

So we reached Germany . . .

In the ruins of a German village I saw a child's bicycle lying about. I was happy. I got on it and rode. It rode so well! During the war I hadn't seen a single child's thing. I forgot they existed. Children's toys . . .

"IN THE CEMETERY THE DEAD LAY ABOVE GROUND . . . AS IF THEY'D BEEN KILLED AGAIN . . ."

Vania Titov

FIVE YEARS OLD. NOW A SPECIALIST IN LAND RECLAMATION.

Black sky . . .

Fat black airplanes . . . They roar down very low. Just over the earth. That's war. As I remember it . . . I remember separate glimpses . . .

There was a bombardment, and we hid in the garden behind the old apple trees. All five of us. I had four brothers, the oldest one was ten. He taught us how to hide from the planes—behind the big apple trees, where there were lots of leaves. Mama rounded us up and led us to the cellar. It was frightening in the cellar. Rats with small piercing eyes that glowed in the dark lived there. They glowed with an unnatural brightness. And the rats kept squeaking all night. They frolicked.

When the German soldiers came to our cottage, we hid on the stove.* Under some old rags. We lay with our eyes closed. From fear.

They burned our village. Bombed the village cemetery. People went running there: the dead lay above ground . . . They lay there as

* The traditional Russian tile stove was a large and complex structure that served for heating, cooking, and washing, and even included shelves for sleeping.

if they'd been killed again . . . Our grandfather, who had died recently, lay there. They were reburied . . .

During the war we played "war." When we were tired of playing
"Whites and Reds" or "Chapaev,"* we played "Russians and Germans." We fought. Took prisoners. Shot them. Put on soldiers' helmets, our own and German ones. Helmets lay about everywhere—in
the woods, in the fields. Nobody wanted to be a German, we even
squabbled over it. We played in real dugouts and trenches. We fought
with sticks, or hand-to-hand. Our mothers scolded us . . .

That surprised us, because earlier . . . before the war . . . they didn't
scold us for that . . .

---

* The Whites were Russian forces loyal to the emperor during the revolution. Vasily Chapaev (1887–1919) was a distinguished Red Army commander during the Russian Civil War.

"I REALIZED—THIS WAS MY FATHER . . . MY KNEES TREMBLED . . ."

Lenya Khosenevich

FIVE YEARS OLD. NOW A DESIGNER.

What has stayed in my memory is color . . .

I was five years old, but I remember very well . . . My grandfather's house—yellow, wooden, some beams on the grass behind the paling. The white sand we played in—as if it was laundered. White as could be. I also remember mama taking me and my little sister to be photographed somewhere in town, and Ellochka crying and me comforting her. The photograph has survived; it's our only prewar photograph . . . For some reason I remember it being green.

Then all the memories are in dark colors . . . If these first ones are in light tones—the green grass, like a light watercolor, and the white sand, and the yellow paling . . . then later everything is in dark colors. I'm carried somewhere, choking from the smoke, our things are in the street, bundles, for some reason one chair . . . People are crying. And mama and I go down the street for a long time. I hold on to her skirt. To everybody mama meets, she repeats the same phrase: "Our house has burned down."

We spend the night in some entryway. I'm cold. I warm my hands in the pocket of mama's jacket. I feel something cold in it. It's the key to our house.

Suddenly mama's not there. Mama disappears, grandma and grandpa remain. I now have a friend two years older—Zhenia Savochkin. He's seven, I'm five. I'm taught to read with a book of fairy tales by the Grimm brothers. Grandma teaches by her own method, and I can even get a rude flick on the brow from her: "Eh, you!" Zhenia also teaches me. He reads a book and shows me the letters. But most of all I like to listen to the fairy tales, especially when grandma reads. Her voice resembles mama's. One evening a beautiful woman comes and brings something very tasty. From what she says I understand that mama is alive, and, like papa, is fighting. I'm happy and I shout: "Mama will come back soon!" I want to run outside and share the news with my friend. I get it with a belt from grandma. My grandfather defends me. When they went to bed, I collected all the belts in the house and threw them behind the wardrobe.

I'm hungry all the time. Zhenia and I go to pick rye, which grows right behind the houses. We rub the ears and chew the grains. The field now belongs to the Germans . . . and so do the ears of rye . . . We see a car, we run away. An officer in a green uniform with gleaming epaulettes pulls me literally from our gate. He beats me either with a swagger stick or with a belt. I'm petrified with fear and don't feel any pain. Suddenly I see grandma: "Dear sir, give me back my grandson. In God's name, I beg you!" Grandma kneels before the officer. The officer leaves, I lie on the sand. Grandma carries me into the house. I can barely move my lips. After that I'm sick for a long time.

I also remember carts going down the street, many carts. Grandpa and grandma open the gates. Refugees come to live with us. After a while they get sick with typhus. They're taken to a hospital, as it's explained to me. After some time grandpa gets sick. I sleep with him. Grandma grows thin and barely moves about the room. In the afternoon I go out to play with the boys. I come back in the evening and don't find either grandpa or grandma at home. The neighbors tell me they have also been taken to the hospital. It frightens me, being alone. I already guess that nobody comes back from the hospital where the refugees—and now my grandparents—have been taken. It's frightening to live alone in the house. At night the house is big and unfamiliar. Even in the daytime it's frightening. Grandpa's brother takes me to live with him. I have a new grandpa.

Minsk is being bombed, we hide in a cellar. When I come out from it, the sun dazzles my eyes, and I go deaf from the roar of the motors. Tanks are moving down the street. I hide behind a post. Suddenly I see a red star on the turret. Ours! I run to our house at once: if our tanks have come, mama has also come! I approach the house—some women with rifles are standing by the porch, they pick me up and begin to ask questions. One of them looks somewhat familiar. She reminds me of somebody. She comes closer to me and embraces me. The other women begin to cry. I shout "Mama!" Then I just collapse . . .

Soon mama brought my little sister from the orphanage, but she refused to recognize me—she forgot me completely during the war. But I was so glad to have a little sister again.

I came home from school and found my father, who had returned from the war, asleep on the sofa. He was asleep, and I took the papers out of his map case and read them. And I realized—this was my father. I sat and looked at him until he woke up.

My knees trembled all the time . . .

"CLOSE YOUR EYES, SONNY . . .
DON'T LOOK . . ."

Volodia Parabkovich

TWELVE YEARS OLD. NOW A PENSIONER.

I grew up without mama . . .

I've never remembered myself as a child . . . My mama died when I was seven. I lived with my aunt. I was a cowherd, I stocked firewood, drove horses to the night pastures. There was enough to do in the kitchen garden. Then in winter we went sliding on wooden sleds and skating on homemade skates, also wooden, edged with metal and tied to our bast shoes with strings, and also went skiing on skis made of planks and discarded coopers' rivets. I made it all myself.

To this day I remember the first ankle boots my father bought me. And how upset I was when I scratched them with a twig in the forest. I was so sorry that I thought: it would be better if I cut my foot—it would heal. I wore those boots leaving Orsha with my father when the fascist airplanes bombed the city.

Outside the city they shot at us point-blank. People fell to the ground . . . In the sand, in the grass . . . "Close your eyes, sonny . . . Don't look," my father begged. I was afraid both to look up—the sky was black with planes—or at the ground—the dead lay everywhere. A plane passed close to us . . . Father also fell and didn't get up. I sat over him: "Papa, open your eyes . . . Papa, open your eyes . . ." Some people shouted, "Germans!" and pulled me after them. And I couldn't grasp that my father would never get up again and that I had to leave him like that in the dust on the road. There was no blood on him anywhere, he simply lay silently. People pulled me away by force, but for many days I walked and kept looking back, waiting for father to catch up with me. I woke up during the night, awakened by his voice . . . I couldn't believe I had no father anymore. So I was left alone, in my one woolen suit.

After wandering for a long time . . . I rode a train, went on foot . . . I was taken to an orphanage in the town of Melekess in the Kuibyshev region. I tried to escape to the front several times, but each time it failed. They caught me and brought me back. But, as they say, no luck can be good luck. While cutting firewood in the forest, I lost control of the ax, it bounced back and hit me on a finger of my right hand. The teacher bandaged me with her kerchief and sent me to the town clinic.

On our way to the orphanage, along with Sasha Liapin, who had been sent to accompany me, I noticed a man in a sailor's cap with ribbons, who was hanging an announcement on the board next to the town Komsomol Committee. We came closer and saw that it was the rules of application to the navy's cadet school on the Solovetsky Islands.* This school was open only to volunteers. Priority of acceptance was given to the children of sailors and the wards of orphanages. I can hear that sailor's voice as if it was happening today: "So you want to become sailors?"

"We're from an orphanage," we said.

"Then go in to the Komsomol Committee and write an application letter."

I can't describe to you our rapture at that moment. It was the direct way to the front. By then I didn't believe I'd be able to avenge my father! That I'd have time to get to the war.

We went in to the town Komsomol Committee and wrote applications. A few days later we were already standing before a medical commission. One of its members looked me over: "He's very small and skinny."

---

* The Solovetsky Islands (also known collectively as Solovki), in the White Sea, were the location of a fortified monastery founded in 1436, then of a notorious Soviet hard-labor camp from 1926 to 1939. A naval academy was set up there just prior to the start of WWII.

Another, in an officer's uniform, sighed. "Never mind, he'll grow up."

They changed our clothes, having some trouble finding the right sizes. When I saw myself in the mirror in a sailor's uniform, in a sailor's cap, I was happy. A day later we were already sailing on a boat to the Solovetsky Islands.

Everything was new. Unusual. It's late at night . . . We stand on deck . . . The sailors urge us to go to bed.

"Go to the crew's quarters, boys. It's warm there."

Early in the morning we saw the monastery shining in the sun and the golden hues of the forest. These were the Solovetsky Islands, where the first school of naval cadets in the country was about to open. But before beginning to study, we had to build the school—more precisely, the dugouts. The ground of Solovki is nothing but stone. We didn't have enough saws, axes, shovels. We learned to do everything by hand: dig hard soil, cut centennial trees, root up stumps, do carpentry. After work we went to rest in cold tents, with beds lined with fir branches, with mattresses and pillows stuffed with grass. We covered ourselves with overcoats. We did our own laundry, the water was mixed with ice . . . We wept—our hands hurt so.

In 1942 . . . We took a military oath. We were issued sailors' caps with the inscription "Naval Cadet School," but, to our great regret, not with shoulder-length ribbons, but with a little bow on the right side. They gave us rifles. In the beginning of 1943 . . . I was assigned to serve on the guards destroyer *Intelligent*. Everything was new to me: the crests of the waves the ship's bow cut through, the "phosphorus" stripe left by the propellers . . . It was breathtaking . . .

"Are you scared, sonny?" the commander asked.

"No," I said, not thinking for a second. "It's beautiful!"

"It would be beautiful, if it weren't for the war," the commander said and looked away for some reason.

I was fourteen years old . . .

"MY LITTLE BROTHER CRIES, BECAUSE HE WASN'T THERE WHEN PAPA WAS THERE . . ."

Larissa Lisovskaya

SIX YEARS OLD. NOW A LIBRARIAN.

I remember my papa . . . And my little brother . . .

Papa was with the partisans. The fascists captured him and shot him. Some women told mama where they had been executed—papa and several other people. She ran to where they lay . . . All her life she remembered that it was cold, the puddles were glazed with ice. They lay in their stocking feet . . .

Mama was pregnant. She was expecting our little brother.

We had to hide. The families of the partisans were arrested. They seized them with the children. Took them away in canvas-covered trucks . . .

We stayed for a long time in our neighbors' cellar. Spring was already beginning . . . We lay on potatoes, and the potatoes sprouted . . . You fall asleep and during the night a sprout pops up and tickles you near the nose. Like a little bug. I had bugs living in my pockets. In my socks. I wasn't afraid of them—either by day or by night.

We got out of the cellar and mama gave birth to our little brother. He grew, began to speak, and we used to remember papa:

"Papa was tall . . ."

"Strong . . . How he used to toss me in his arms!"

That was me and my sister talking, and our little brother would ask, "And where was I?"

"You weren't there yet . . ."

He begins to cry, because he wasn't there when papa was there . . .

"THAT GIRL WAS THE FIRST TO COME . . ."

Nina Yaroshevich

NINE YEARS OLD. NOW TEACHER OF
PHYSICAL EDUCATION.

There was a big event in our home . . .

In the evening a suitor came to propose to my eldest sister. There was a discussion well into the night about when the wedding would take place, where the couple would register their marriage, how many guests to invite. And early in the morning my father was summoned to the recruiting office. The noise spread over the village—war! Mama was at a loss—what were we to do? I thought of just one thing: living through that day. No one had explained to me yet that war was not for a day or two, but maybe for a very long time.

Now it's summer, a hot day. I'd like to go to the river, but mama prepares us for the road. We also had a brother who was just discharged from the hospital; he had had an operation on his foot, and he came home on crutches. But mama said, "We all must go." Where? Nobody knew anything. We walked some three miles. My brother hobbled and cried. How could we go with him? We turned back. At home our father was waiting for us. The men who went to the recruiting office in the morning all came back; the Germans had already taken our regional center. The town of Slutsk.

The first shells came flying. I stood and watched them before they hit the ground. Someone taught us that you should open your mouth so as not to be deafened. So we opened our mouths, stopped our ears, and could still hear them coming. Whining. It's so frightening that the skin on your face and your whole body gets taut. There was a bucket hanging in our yard. When everything became quiet, we took it down: we counted fifty-eight holes. The bucket was white, they thought someone was standing there in a white kerchief, and they shot at it . . . Just for fun . . .

The first Germans rode into the village in big trucks adorned with birch branches. The way we did when there was a wedding. We used to break a lot of birch branches . . . We watched them through the wattle fences. We didn't have fences then, but wattle fences. Made of vines. We tried to get a look at them . . . They seemed like ordinary people . . . I wanted to see what kind of heads they had. For some reason I had this idea that they had inhuman heads . . . Rumors were already going around that they killed people. Burned them. But they rode about laughing. Pleased, suntanned.

In the morning they did exercises in the schoolyard. Doused themselves with cold water. Rolled up their sleeves, got on their motorcycles—and off they went.

A few days later they dug a big pit outside the village next to the milk factory. Every day at around five or six in the morning shots were heard from there. Whenever they started shooting, even the cocks stopped crowing and hid themselves. One evening my father and I were riding in the cart, and he stopped the horse not far from that pit. "I'll go and have a look," he said. His cousin had been shot there. He went, and I followed him.

Suddenly father turned and stood so as to hide the pit from me: "Go back. You mustn't go farther." I only saw, when we crossed the brook, that the water in it was red . . . And crows flew up. There were so many of them that I screamed . . . Father couldn't eat anything for several days after that. He would see a crow and run back to the cottage shaking all over . . . Like in a fever . . .

In the park in Slutsk two partisan families were hanged. It was freezing cold, and the hanged people were so frozen that, when the wind swung them, they tinkled. Tinkled like frozen trees in the forest . . . That tinkling . . .

When we were liberated, father went to the front. He went with the army. He was already gone when my mother made me the first dress I had during the war. Mama made it out of foot-cloths. They were white, and she dyed them with ink. There wasn't enough ink for one of the sleeves. But I wanted to show the dress to my friends. So I stood sideways in the gate, to show the good sleeve and hide the bad one. I thought I looked so dressed up, so beautiful!

At school there was a girl, Anya, who sat in front of me. Her father and mother had been killed, and she lived with her grandmother. They were refugees from near Smolensk. The school bought her a coat, felt boots, and a pair of shiny galoshes. The teacher brought them and put them on her desk. We all sat silently, because no one had such boots or such a coat. We envied her. One of the boys nudged Anya and said, "Some people are lucky!" She fell on the desk and cried. She sobbed through four lessons.

My father returned from the front, everybody came to look at him. And also at us, because our papa came back to us.

That girl was the first to come . . .

"I'M YOUR MAMA . . ."

Tamara Parkhimovich

SEVEN YEARS OLD. NOW A SECRETARY-TYPIST.

All through the war I thought about my mama. I lost my mama in the first days . . .

We were sleeping, and our Pioneer camp was bombed. We ran out of the tents, ran around crying: "Mama! Mama!" The teacher shook me by the shoulders to calm me down, and I shouted, "Mama! Where's my mama?" Finally she pressed me to her: "I'm your mama."

I had a skirt, a white blouse, and a red kerchief hanging on my bedstead. I put them on, and we went on foot to Minsk. On the way many children were met by their parents, but my mama wasn't there. Suddenly they said, "The Germans are in the city . . ." We all turned back. Somebody said he had seen my mother—dead.

Here there's a gap in my memory . . .

How we reached Penza I don't remember, how they brought me to the orphanage I don't remember. Blank pages in my memory . . . All I remember is that there were many of us, and we slept two to a bed. If one cried, the other also began to cry: "Mama! Where's my mama?" I was little, one nanny wanted to adopt me. But I kept thinking about mama . . .

I was coming from the dining room, the children all cried, "Your mama is here!" It rang in my ears: "Your ma-a-a-ama . . . Your ma-a-a-ama . . ." I had dreams about mama every night. My real mama. And suddenly she came in reality, but I thought it was a dream. I

see—mama! And I don't believe it. They spent several days persuad-
ing me, but I was afraid to get close to mama. What if it's a dream? A
dream! Mama cried, and I shouted, "Don't come near me! My mama
was killed!" I was afraid . . . I was afraid to believe my happiness . . .

Even now I . . . All my life I've cried in the happiest moments of
my life. Drowning in tears. All my life . . . My husband . . . We've
lived in love for many years. When he proposed to me: "I love you.
Let's get married"—I burst into tears. He was frightened: "Did I
upset you?" "No! No! I'm happy!" But I can never be completely
happy. Totally happy. It somehow doesn't come out. I'm afraid of
happiness. It always seems that it's just about to end. This "just about"
always lives in me. That childhood fear . . .

"WE ASK: CAN WE LICK IT? . . ."

Vera Tashkina

TEN YEARS OLD. NOW AN UNSKILLED WORKER.

Before the war I cried a lot . . .

My father died. Mama was left with seven children on her hands. It was a poor life. Hard. But later, during the war, that peaceful life seemed happy.

Grown-ups wept, but we weren't afraid. We often played "war," and the word was very familiar to us. I wondered why mama wept all night. Went around with red eyes. Only later did I understand . . .

We ate . . . water . . . Dinnertime came, mama put on the table a pot of hot water. We poured it into bowls. It's evening. Suppertime. A pot of hot water on the table. Colorless hot water, there was nothing to put in for color in winter. Not even grass.

My brother was so hungry he ate a corner of the stove. He gnawed away at it every day until we noticed there was a little dent in it. Then mama took our last things, went to the market, and exchanged them for potatoes or corn. She would cook some cornmeal, divide it among us, and we would look at the pot and ask, "Can we lick it?" We took turns licking it. And after us our cat also licked it, she was hungry, too. I don't know whether there was anything left there for her. We didn't leave even a drop. There wasn't even any smell left. We licked up the smell.

We kept waiting for our troops . . .

When our planes started bombing, I didn't run to hide, but dashed out to look at our bombs. I found a piece of shrapnel . . .

"Where on earth have you been?" Frightened mama met me at home. "What're you hiding there?"

"I'm not hiding anything. I brought a piece of shrapnel."

"You'll be killed, that'll teach you."

"Why, mama? It's shrapnel from one of our bombs. How could it kill me?"

I kept it for a long time . . .

". . . AN EXTRA HALF-SPOON OF SUGAR"

Emma Levina

THIRTEEN YEARS OLD. NOW A PRINTER.

That day I was a month shy of fourteen years old . . .

"No! We won't go anywhere. What an idea—war! Before we get out of town, it'll be over. We won't go! We wo-o-on't!" So said my father, a party member since 1905. He had been in czarist prisons more than once, had taken part in the October Revolution.

But even so we had to leave. We gave the plants on windowsills a good watering (we had many of them), locked the windows and doors, only leaving a vent open so that the cat could go out when he wanted. We took the most necessary things. Papa persuaded everybody that we'd be back in a few days. Yet Minsk was burning.

Only my second sister didn't go with us, she was three years older than me. For a long time we didn't know anything about her. We worried. We were already in evacuation . . . In Ukraine . . . We received a letter from my sister from the front, then another and another. Later came a letter of appreciation from the commanders of the unit where she served as a medical assistant. My mother showed this letter to everybody! She was proud. In honor of the event the chairman of the kolkhoz issued us two pounds of forage flour. My mother treated everybody to tasty flatcakes.

We did all kinds of village work, though we were all true-blue city people. We worked well. My oldest sister, who had been a judge before the war, now learned to drive a tractor. But soon the bombing of Kharkov began, and we went farther on.

On our way we learned that we were being taken to Kazakhstan. Some ten families traveled in the same car with us. In one family the daughter was pregnant. The train was bombed, the planes came all of a sudden, no one had time to get out of the car. Then we heard a cry: the pregnant woman's foot was blown off. This horror is still lodged in my memory. The woman went into labor . . . And her own father began to assist in the delivery. All that in front of everybody. Noise. Blood, dirt. A baby being born . . .

We left Kharkov in the summer, and we reached our final destination in winter. We came to the Kazakh steppes. For a long time I couldn't get used to not being bombed and shelled. We had one more enemy—lice! Huge, middle-sized, small. Black! Gray! All sorts. But all equally merciless, leaving us no peace day or night. No, not so! When the train moved, they didn't bite as badly. They behaved more or less quietly. But as soon as we were in a house . . . my God, what they did . . . My God! My whole back and arms were bitten and covered with ulcers. It got better when I took my blouse off, but I had nothing else to put on. In any case I had to burn this blouse, it was so infested, and I covered myself with a newspaper, and wore this newspaper in the guise of a blouse. The mistress of the house we stayed in washed me with such hot water that, if I were to wash with such water now, my skin would peel off. But then . . . It was such happiness—warm water. Hot!

Our mother was an excellent housewife, an excellent cook. Only she could prepare a gopher so that it became good to eat, though gopher meat isn't considered edible. A gopher on the table . . . It stinks for a mile around, an unspeakably disgusting smell. But there's no other meat, and we have nothing else. So we eat these gophers . . .

A very nice, kind woman lived next to us. She saw our sufferings and said to mama, "Let your daughter help me in the house." I was very weak. She went to the field, and left me with her grandson, showed me where everything was, so that I could feed him and eat myself. I went to the table, looked at the food, but was afraid to take it. It seemed to me that if I took something, it would all disappear, that it was a dream. Not only did I not eat, I was even afraid to touch it with my finger—for fear it would cease to exist. I preferred to look at it, to look at it for a long time. I came from the side, or from the back. Afraid to close my eyes. I didn't put anything in my mouth during the whole day. This woman had a cow, sheep, chickens. And she left me butter, eggs . . .

She came home in the evening and asked, "Did you eat?"

"Yes . . ."

"Go home then. And take this to your mama." And she gave me some bread. "And come back tomorrow."

I went home, and this woman came running after me. I got frightened: what if something's missing? But she kissed me and wept.

"Why didn't you eat anything, silly fool? Why is everything just where it was?" And she caressed me and stroked my head.

Winters in Kazakhstan are severe. We had nothing to burn in the stove. We were saved by cow dung. You get up early in the morning and wait till the cows come out, and you put the bucket under them. You run from one cow to another. I wasn't alone, all the evacuated people were there. You fill the bucket, dump it out by your house, and hurry back. Afterward it's all mixed with straw, dried, and the result is those black cakes. *Kiziak*s. We used them for heating.

Papa died. His heart probably broke from pity for us. He'd had a bad heart for a long time.

I was accepted to a technical school. They issued me a uniform: a coat, shoes, and—bread coupons. I used to have cropped hair, but now it grew back and I could braid it. They gave me a Komsomol card. Took a picture for a newspaper. I carried the card in my hands, not in my pocket. Such a treasure . . . I was afraid to put it in my pocket—what if I should lose it? My heart pounded: *tock-tock-tock*. How happy papa would have been if he could have seen me.

Now I think: "What a terrible time, but what extraordinary people." I am amazed at how we were then! How we believed! I don't want to forget it . . . I long ago lost my faith in Stalin, in communist ideas. I would like to forget that part of my life, but I keep those feelings in my heart. That loftiness. I don't want to forget those feelings. They're precious . . .

That evening at home mama made real tea, with tea leaves. Of course, it was such a feast! And I—as the cause of it—received an extra half-spoon of sugar . . .

"DEAR HOUSE, DON'T BURN
DEAR HOUSE, DON'T BURN! . . ."

Nina Rachitskaya

SEVEN YEARS OLD. NOW A WORKER.

Sometimes it's very vivid . . . Everything comes back.

How the Germans arrived on motorcycles . . . Each had a bucket, and their buckets clanked. We hid . . . I had two little brothers—four and two years old. We hid under the bed and stayed there the whole day.

I was very surprised that the young fascist officer who moved in with us wore glasses. My idea was that only teachers wore glasses. He and his orderly lived in one half of the house, and we in the other. My youngest brother caught a cold and had a bad cough. He had a high fever, was all burning, and wept during the night. In the morning, the officer came to our half and told mama that if the *kinder* cries and keeps him from sleeping at night, he'll go *puf-puf,* and he pointed to his pistol. At night, as soon as my brother began to cough or cry, mother grabbed him with his blanket, ran outside, and rocked him there till he fell asleep or calmed down. *Puf-puf* . . .

They took everything from us, we were starving. They wouldn't let us into the kitchen, and they cooked only for themselves. My little brothers smelled the food and crawled to the kitchen to this smell. They cooked pea soup every day, and it had a very strong smell. Five minutes later we heard my brother's cry, a terrible shriek. They splashed boiling water on him in the kitchen because he asked to eat.

He was so hungry that he said to mama, "Let's cook my duckling." This duckling was his favorite toy, he had never let anyone touch it. He slept with it.

Our children's conversations . . .

We sat and debated: if we catch a mouse (there were many of them during the war, both in the house and in the fields), could we eat it? Can we eat chickadees? Magpies? Why doesn't mama make a soup out of fat beetles?

We wouldn't let potatoes grow, we felt around in the ground with our hands to see if they were big or still small. And somehow everything grew so slowly: the corn, the sunflowers . . .

On the last day . . . Before their retreat the Germans set fire to our house. Mama stood looking at the fire, and there weren't any tears on her face. The three of us ran around crying, "Dear house, don't burn! Dear house, don't burn!" We had no time to take anything out, I only snatched my primer. I saved it through the whole war, I cherished it. I slept with it, it was always under my pillow. I wanted to study very much. When in 1944 I started first grade, my primer was the only one for thirteen pupils. For the whole class.

I remember the first after-war concert at school. How they sang, danced . . . My palms hurt, I clapped so much. I was happy until some boy came onstage and began to read a poem. He read loudly, the poem was long, but I heard one word—*war*. I looked around: everybody sat calmly. But I was scared—the war had just ended, and there's war again? I couldn't hear this word. I tore from my seat and ran home. I came and found mama cooking something in the kitchen, meaning there wasn't any war. I went back to school. To the concert. Applauded again.

Our papa didn't come back from the war. Mama received a notice that he was missing in action. Mama would go to work, and the three of us together wept that papa wasn't with us. We turned the house over looking for the notice about papa. We thought it wasn't written that papa had been killed, it said he was missing. We would tear this notice up, and news would come about where our papa was. But we didn't find the notice. When mama came home from work, she couldn't understand why the house was in such disorder. She asked me, "What have you been doing here?" My younger brother answered for me: "Looking for papa . . ."

Before the war I liked it when papa told us fairy tales. He knew many fairy tales and told them well. After the war I no longer wanted to read fairy tales . . .

"SHE CAME IN A WHITE SMOCK, LIKE MAMA . . ."

Sasha Suetin

FOUR YEARS OLD. NOW A LOCKSMITH.

I remember only mama . . .

First picture . . .

Mama always wore a white smock . . . Father was an officer, mama worked in a hospital. My older brother told me that afterward. All I remember is mama's white smock. Not even her face, only the white smock . . . And also the white cap, which always stood on a little table. Precisely stood, not lay, because it was stiffly starched.

Second picture . . .

Mama didn't come home . . . I was used to papa often not coming home, but mama always came home. My brother and I stayed alone in the apartment for several days without going anywhere: what if mama suddenly shows up? Some strange people knock, dress us, and take us somewhere.

I cry, "Mama! Where's my mama?"

"Don't cry, mama will find us," my brother, who is three years older, comforts me.

We wind up in some sort of long house or barn, on a bunk. We're hungry all the time, and I suck on my shirt buttons, they're like the fruit drops father used to bring from his business trips. I'm waiting for mama.

Third picture . . .

Some man shoves me and my brother into the corner of the bunk, covers us with a blanket, throws some rags over us. I begin to cry, he strokes my head. I calm down.

This happens every day. Once I get tired of sitting under the blanket for so long. I begin to cry, first softly, then loudly. Someone pulls the rags, then the blanket off me and my brother. I open my eyes—next to us stands a woman in a white smock.

"Mama!" I crawl to her.

She also caresses me. First my head . . . then my arm . . . Then she takes something out of a metal box. But I pay no attention to that, I only see the white smock and white hat.

Suddenly!—a sharp pain in my arm. There's a needle under my skin. Before I finish shouting, I faint. I come to my senses. The man who had been hiding us sits over me. Next to me lies my brother.

"Don't be frightened," says the man. "He's not dead, he's asleep."

"That wasn't mama?"

"No . . ."

"She came in a white smock, like mama . . ." I repeat again and again.

"I've made a toy for you." The man hands me a rag ball.

I take the toy and stop crying.

I don't remember anything after that: who saved us in the German concentration camp and how? They took blood from the children for the wounded German soldiers. All the children died. How did my brother and I wind up in an orphanage? And how, at the end of the war, did we receive notice that our parents were dead? Something happened to my memory. I don't remember the faces, I don't remember the words . . .

The war was over. I went to first grade. Other children would read a poem two or three times and memorize it. And I would read it ten times and not memorize it. But for some reason the teachers didn't give me bad grades. The others got bad grades, but I didn't.

That's my story . . .

"AUNTIE, TAKE ME ON YOUR KNEES . . ."

Marina Karyanova
FOUR YEARS OLD. NOW WORKS IN CINEMA.

I don't like to remember . . . I don't. In a word—I don't like it . . .

If everybody was asked, "What is childhood?" they would each say something of their own. For me childhood is mama and papa and candies. All my childhood I wanted mama and papa and candies. During the war I not only didn't taste any candies—I didn't even see any. I ate my first candy a few years after the war . . . About three years after . . . I was already a big girl. Ten years old.

I could never understand how anybody could not want chocolate candy. How? It's impossible.

I never found my mama and papa. I don't even know my real last name. They picked me up in Moscow at the Severny train station.

"What's your name?" they asked me in the orphanage.

"Marinochka."

"And your last name?"

"I don't remember my last name . . ."

They wrote down Marina Severnaya.

I wanted to eat all the time. But still more I wanted someone to hug me, to caress me. There was little tenderness then, there was war all around, everybody was in grief. I go down the street . . . Ahead of me a woman walks with her children. She'd take one in her arms, carry him, put him down, take another. They sat on a bench, and she took the youngest on her knees. I kept standing there. Kept looking. I went up to her: "Auntie, take me on your knees." She was surprised.

I asked her again, "Auntie, please . . ."

"... AND BEGAN TO ROCK
HER LIKE A DOLL"

Dima Sufrankov

FIVE YEARS OLD. NOW A MECHANICAL ENGINEER.

Till then I had only been afraid of mice. But all at once there were so many fears! A thousand fears . . .

My child's conscience wasn't so much struck by the word *war* as frightened by the word *airplanes*. "Airplanes!"—and our mother grabs us all off the stove. We were afraid to get off the stove, afraid to leave the cottage, so while she takes one off, the other climbs back. There were five of us. And also our beloved cat.

The planes strafed us . . .

Mama tied the younger ones to her with towels, and we older ones ran by ourselves. When you're little . . . you live in a different world, you don't see what's high up, you live close to the ground. There the planes are still more frightening, the bombs are still more frightening. I remember being envious of the bugs: they were so small that they always could hide somewhere, crawl into the ground . . . I imagined that when I died I'd become some animal, run away to the forest.

The planes strafed us . . .

My cousin, she was ten years old, carried our little three-year-old brother. She ran, ran, and her strength failed her, she fell down. They lay in the snow all night, and he froze to death, but she survived. We dug a hole to bury him, but she wouldn't let us: "Mishenka, don't die! Why are you dying?"

We escaped from the Germans and lived in a swamp . . . on little islands . . . We built *kuren*s and lived in them. A *kuren* is a little hut: bare logs and a hole in the top. For smoke. Underneath is the ground. Water. We lived in them winter and summer. Slept on pine branches. Once mama and I went back from the forest to the village to take something from our cottage. The Germans were there. Whoever they found, they herded into the school. They made us kneel and aimed machine guns at us. We children were the same height as the machine guns. We heard shooting in the forest. The Germans shouted, "Partisans! Partisans!" and ran to their trucks. They left quickly. We went back to the forest.

After the war I was afraid of metal. A piece of shrapnel lies there, and I'm afraid it will explode again. Our neighbors' girl—she was three years and two months old . . . I remember it . . . Her mama kept saying over her coffin, "Three years and two months . . . Three years and two months . . ." She had found a "pineapple." And started rocking it like a doll. Wrapped it in some rags and rocked it . . . The grenade was small, like a toy, but very heavy. Her mother came running, but it was too late . . .

For two years after the war children were buried in our village of Old Golovchitsy in the Petrikovsky district. Military metal lay about everywhere. Exploded black tanks, armored troop carriers. Pieces of mines, bombs . . . We had no toys . . . Later on it was all collected and sent to factories somewhere. Mama explained that this metal would be used to make tractors. Machinery, sewing machines. Whenever I saw a new tractor, I didn't go near it, I expected it to explode. And to turn black like a tank . . .

I knew what metal it was made of . . .

"THEY HAD ALREADY BOUGHT ME A PRIMER . . ."

Lilia Melnikova
SEVEN YEARS OLD. NOW A TEACHER.

I was supposed to start first grade . . .

They had already bought me a primer and a school bag. I was the oldest. My sister Raya was five years old, and our Tomochka—three. We lived in Rossony, our father worked as the director of a tree farm, but a year before the war he died. We lived with mama.

The day the war reached us, all three of us were in the kindergarten, the littlest one too. And so all the children were picked up, but we were left, nobody came for us. We were frightened. Mama was the last to come running. She worked at the tree farm, they had to burn or bury some papers. And that had detained her.

Mama said that we would be evacuated, that they had given us a cart. We had to take the most necessary things. I remember there was a big wicker hamper in the corridor. We put this hamper on the cart. My little sister took her doll. Mama wanted to leave the doll . . . It was a big doll . . . My sister cried, "I won't leave her!" We rode out of Rossony, and our cart tipped over, the hamper opened, and shoes poured out of it. It turned out that we had taken nothing with us: no food, no changes of clothes. Mama had lost her head and confused the hampers. She had taken the one in which she kept shoes to be repaired.

Before we had time to pick up these shoes, the planes came flying and began to bomb us, to strafe us with machine guns. Our doll was all bullet-riddled, but my sister was perfectly unharmed, without a scratch. She wept: "I still won't leave her."

We went back and began to live under the Germans. Mama would go to sell our father's clothes. I remember the first time when she traded his two-piece suit for some peas. We ate pea soup for a month. We finished the soup. We had a big old quilted blanket. Mama cut it up to make warm boots, and if anyone wanted them, they paid her as they could. Sometimes we ate mash, sometimes we had one egg for all of us . . . But often we had nothing. Mama just hugged us and caressed us . . .

Mama didn't tell us that she was helping the partisans, but I figured it out. She often went off somewhere and didn't say where. Whenever she went to trade something, we knew about it, but then she would just go off—and that was that. I was proud of mama and said to my sisters, "Soon our troops will come. Uncle Vanya (papa's brother) will come." He fought with the partisans.

That day mama poured milk into a bottle, kissed us, and left, and locked the door with a key. The three of us got under the table covered with a big tablecloth, where it was warm, and played "Mothers-and-Daughters." Suddenly we heard the rattle of motorcycles, then a terrible knocking on the door and a man's voice calling my mother's name distortedly. Incorrectly. I had a bad feeling. There was a ladder standing outside our window on the side of the kitchen garden. We climbed down it on the sly. Quickly. I grabbed one sister's hand, put the other one on my shoulders—we call that "eeny-meeny"—and walked outside.

There were many people gathered there. And children. Those who came to get mama didn't know us and didn't find us. They broke down the door . . . I saw mama appear on the road, so small, so thin. The Germans saw her, ran up the hill, seized her, twisted her arms, and began to beat her. We ran and shouted, all three of us, shouted with all our might: "Mama! Mama!" They shoved her into the motorcycle sidecar, she just called out to a neighbor: "Fenia, dear, look after my children." The neighbors led us away from the road, but they were afraid to take us: what if the Germans came to get us? So we went to cry in a ditch. We couldn't go home, we'd already heard that in another village the parents were taken away and the children were burned, locked up in the house and burned. We were afraid to go to our own house . . . This lasted probably for three days. We sat in the chicken coop, then we'd go to the kitchen garden. We wanted to eat, but we didn't touch anything in the kitchen garden, because mama scolded us for pulling out carrots before they were grown and picking off the peas. We didn't take anything, and we said to each other that mama would be upset that without her we destroyed everything in the kitchen garden. Of course that's what she would think. She wouldn't know that we hadn't touched anything. That we were obedient. The adults sent us with their children—some boiled a turnip, some a potato, some a beet . . .

Then Aunt Arina took us in. She had one boy left, she had lost the other two when she went away with the refugees. We kept remembering mama, and Aunt Arina took us to the prison commandant to ask for a meeting. The commandant said that we couldn't talk to mama, that he would only allow us to pass by her window.

We went past the window and I saw mama . . . We were led very quickly, and I was the only one who saw mama, my sisters didn't have time. Mama's face was red, I realized she had been badly beaten. She also saw us and only cried out, "Children! My girls!" And she didn't look out the window anymore. Afterward we were told that she had seen us and fainted . . .

Several days later we learned that mama had been shot. My sister Raya and I understood that our mama was no more, but the youngest, Tomochka, kept saying that once mama came back she would tell her how we mistreated her and didn't carry her in our arms. When we were given food, I gave her the best pieces. I remembered mama doing that . . .

After mama was shot . . . The next day a car drove up to our house . . . They began to take our things . . . The neighbors called out to us, "Go, ask for your felt boots, your warm coats! It will be winter soon, and you only have summer clothes." The three of us stood there, little Tomochka sat on my shoulders, and I said, "Mister, give her her felt boots." The policeman was just then carrying them in his hands. Before I finished, he kicked me with his foot, and my sister fell off . . . And she hit her head against the stone. In the morning we saw a big abscess there, and it began to grow. Aunt Arina had a thick kerchief, she wrapped it around her head, but the abscess still showed. At night I would put my arms around her head, and her head was very, very big. I was afraid she would die.

The partisans learned about it all and took us to stay with them. They comforted us the best they could, and loved us very much. We even forgot for a while that we had no papa and mama. Someone had a torn shirt; they twisted the sleeve, drew eyes, a nose—and made a doll for us. They taught us to read, they even made up verses about me not liking to wash with cold water. What facilities were there in the forest? In winter we washed with snow . . .

> Lilia sits in the tub,
> And Lilia frets,
> "Help me, help me,
> The water is so wet."

When it became dangerous, they took us back to Aunt Arina. The commander—and the unit commander was the legendary Pyotr Mironovich Masherov—asked, "What do you need? Is there anything you want?" And we needed many things, first of all some shirts. They made dresses for us from the same fabric army shirts were made of. Green dresses with patch pockets. They made felt boots for the three of us, winter coats, and knitted us mittens. I remember that they brought us to Aunt Arina on a cart and gave us sacks of flour and grain. Even pieces of leather, so that she could make shoes for us.

When there was a search at Aunt Arina's, she passed us off as her children. They kept asking why we were blond and her son was dark-haired. They knew something . . . They put us in a truck with Aunt Arina and her boy, and brought us to the Igritsky concentration camp. It was winter, everybody slept on the floor, on boards, with some straw. We lay like this: me, then little Toma, next to her Raya, then Aunt Arina and her son. I wound up at the edge. The people next to me changed often. I would touch a cold hand at night and know that the man was dead. In the morning I would look—he's as if alive, only cold. Once I was frightened . . . I saw that rats had eaten the lips and cheeks of a dead man. The rats were fat and insolent. I was afraid of them most of all . . . While we were with the partisans, the abscess on my little sister's head went away, but in the concentration camp it appeared again. Aunt Arina used to hide this abscess all the time, because she knew that if they saw the girl was sick, they would shoot her. She wrapped my sister's head with a thick kerchief. At night I heard her pray: "Lord, you took their mother, preserve the children." I also prayed . . . I asked, "At least let little Tomochka survive, she's so young, she shouldn't die."

We were taken somewhere from the concentration camp . . . We rode in cattle cars. On the floor were dried cow flops. I remember that we only reached Latvia, and there local people took us. Tomochka was the first to be taken. Aunt Arina carried her in her arms, handed her to an old Latvian man, and knelt before him: "Only save her. Save her." He said, "If I reach my home with her, she'll live. I have a mile and a half to walk. Across the river, then through the cemetery . . ." We all wound up with different people. Aunt Arina was also taken from us . . .

We heard . . . They told us—Victory. I went to the people who had taken my sister Raya: "We have no mama . . . Let's go and take our Toma. And we must find Aunt Arina."

We discussed it and went to look for Aunt Arina. That we found her was a miracle. We found her because she was a very good seamstress. We stopped at some house to have a drink of water. They asked us where we were going. We replied that we were looking for Aunt Arina. The hostess's daughter said at once, "Let's go, I'll show you where she lives." Aunt Arina just gasped when she saw us. We were skinny as sticks. It was the end of June, the most difficult time: the old harvest was eaten, and the new one wasn't ripe yet. We ate the still green ears: we'd rub a bit in our hands and swallow it, even without chewing, we were so hungry.

Not far from our parts was the town of Kraslava. Aunt Arina said we had to go there and get to the orphanage. She was already very sick, and she asked that we be taken there. We were brought there early in the morning, the gates were still closed, they deposited us by the window of the orphanage and left. The sun rose in the morning . . . Children ran out of the house, all wearing red shoes, trunks without tops, towels in their hands. They ran to the river, laughing. And we watched . . . We didn't believe that there could be a life like that. The children noticed us—we were sitting there raggedy, dirty—and shouted, "New ones have come!" They called the teachers. No one asked us for any papers. They brought some bread and cans of food right away. We didn't eat, we were afraid that this happiness would suddenly end. This impossible happiness . . . They reassured us: "Sit here for now, girls, we'll go to heat the bath house. We'll wash you and show you where you'll live."

In the evening the director came, saw us, and said that they were overcrowded and that we had to be taken to the Minsk children's center and from there sent to some orphanage. When we heard that again we had to go somewhere, we began to cry and begged them to let us stay. The director said, "Don't cry, children. I can't bear the sight of your tears." She called somewhere, and we were allowed to stay in that orphanage. It was a beautiful, wonderful orphanage; the teachers there were such as probably don't exist now. With such hearts! How could they have kept such hearts after the war?

They loved us very much. Taught us how to behave with each other. There was this incident. They told us that if you treat someone to candies, don't take them out of the bag, but offer the whole bag. And the person it's offered to should take one candy, not the whole bag. One boy was absent when we had this conversation. The sister of one girl came and brought a box of candies. The girl offered the box to that boy, and he took the whole box from her. We laughed. He was embarrassed and asked, "What should I have done?" They told him that he was supposed to take one candy. Then he realized: "I see now—we should always share. Otherwise it's good for me, but bad for everybody else." Yes, we were taught to act so that it's good for everybody, not for some one person. It was easy to teach us, because we had been through a lot.

The older girls made book bags for everybody, they even made them out of old skirts. On holidays the director of the orphanage always rolled out raw dough into a pancake huge as a sheet. Each of us cut off a piece and made a dumpling of whatever shape we wanted: small, big, round, triangular . . .

When there were many of us together, we rarely remembered our papas and mamas. But when we were sick in a special ward, and lay there with nothing to do, they were all we talked about, and about how we wound up in the orphanage. One boy told me that all his family were burned up while he was riding a horse to the neighboring village. He said he was very sorry for his mama, very sorry for his papa, but most of all he was sorry for little Nadenka. Little Nadenka lay in white swaddling clothes, and they burned her. Or else, when we gathered in a small circle in the clearing, we told each other about home. About how we had lived before the war.

A little girl was brought to the orphanage. They asked her, "What's your last name?"

"Marya Ivanovna."

"What's your first name?"

"Marya Ivanovna."

"What was your mother's name?"

"Marya Ivanovna."

Her only response was "Marya Ivanovna." Our teacher was Marya Ivanovna, and this girl was Marya Ivanovna.

For the New Year she recited a poem by Marshak: "I had a pretty little chicken."* And the children nicknamed her "Chicken." Children are children, we were all tired of calling her Marya Ivanovna. Then one of our boys went to see his friend at a vocational school that had taken us under its patronage, and they argued about something, and he called the other boy "Chicken." The boy was hurt. "Why did you call me 'Chicken'? Do I look like a chicken?" And our boy said that there was a girl in our orphanage who resembled him very much. She had the same nose, the same eyes, and we called her "Chicken," and he told him why.

It turned out that the girl was that boy's sister. When they met, they remembered that they had ridden in a cart . . . Their grandmother had heated something for them in a can, and then she had been killed during a bombing . . . And an old neighbor, the grandmother's friend, called to her when she was already dead: "Marya Ivanovna, get up, you have two grandchildren . . . How could you die, Marya Ivanovna? Why did you die, Marya Ivanovna?" It turned out that the girl remembered it all, but she wasn't sure that she did and that it had all happened to her. She only had two words in her ears: *Marya Ivanovna.*

We were all very glad that she had found her brother, because we all had somebody, and she didn't have anybody. I, for instance, had two sisters, someone else had a brother, or cousins. Those who didn't have anybody would decide: you be my brother, or you be my sister. And then they would protect and take care of each other. In our orphanage there were eleven Tamaras . . . Their last names were: Tamara Unknown, Tamara Strange, Tamara Nameless, Tamara Big, and Tamara Small . . .

What else do I remember? I remember that they scolded us very little in this orphanage, no, they didn't scold us at all. We used to go

---

* Samuil Marshak (1887–1964) was a poet, writer, and translator most famous for his books for children. However, the poem "Chicken" was in fact written by his friend and fellow children's poet Kornei Chukovsky (1882–1969).

sleigh riding in winter with children who had families, and I saw mothers scold and even spank their children, if they put felt boots on their bare feet. When we did that nobody scolded us. I deliberately put my boots on that way so as to be scolded. I wanted so much to be scolded.

I was a good student, and they told me I should help a boy with his math. A village boy. We went to school together—the orphanage children and local village children. I had to go to his family. To his house. I was frightened. I thought, "What kind of things do they have there, how do they stand in the house, how should I behave myself?" Home was something inaccessible to us, the most desirable.

I knocked on the door and my heart skipped a beat . . .

". . . NEITHER SUITORS NOR SOLDIERS . . ."

Vera Novikova

THIRTEEN YEARS OLD. NOW A TRAMWAY DISPATCHER.

It was so long ago . . . But it's still frightening . . .

I remember such a sunny day, the wind ruffles the spiderwebs. Our village is burning, our house is burning. We come out of the forest. The little children cry, "A bonfire! A bonfire! Beautiful!" And all the others weep. Mama weeps and crosses herself.

The house burned down . . . We rummaged in the ashes, but didn't find anything. Only charred forks. The stove stayed as it had stood. There was food in it—potato pancakes. Mama took the frying pan out with her hands: "Eat, children." It was impossible to eat those pancakes, they smelled so much of smoke, but we ate them, because we had nothing else but grass. All we had left was the grass and the ground.

It was so long ago . . . But it's still frightening . . .

My cousin was hanged . . . Her husband was the commander of a partisan unit, and she was pregnant. Someone denounced her to the Germans, and they came. They chased everybody out to the square. Ordered that no one should cry. Next to the village council grew a tall tree. They drove the horse up to it. My cousin stood on the sledge . . . She had a long braid . . . They put the noose around her neck, she took the braid out of it. The horse pulled the sledge away, and she hung there spinning . . . The women shouted . . . They shouted without tears, just with voices. We weren't allowed to cry.

We could shout, but not cry—not be sorry. They came up and killed those who cried. There were adolescent boys, sixteen or seventeen years old. They were shot. They had cried.

So young . . . As yet neither suitors nor soldiers . . .

Why have I told you this? It's more frightening for me now than then. That's why I don't recall it . . .

"IF ONLY ONE SON COULD BE LEFT . . ."

Sasha Kavrus

TEN YEARS OLD. NOW DOCTOR OF PHILOLOGY.

I was at school . . .

We went outside and began to play as usual. Just then fascist planes came flying and dropped bombs on our village. We had already heard stories about the battles in Spain, about the fate of Spanish children. Now the bombs were dropping on us. Old women fell to the ground and prayed . . . So . . . I've remembered all my life the voice of Levitan* announcing the beginning of the war. Stalin's speech I don't remember. People stood for whole days by the kolkhoz loudspeaker waiting for something, and I stood next to my father.

The first to burst into our village of Brusy, in the Myadelsky district, was a punitive squad. They opened fire, shot all the cats and dogs, and then began interrogations, trying to find out where the activists lived. Before the war the village council was in our cottage, but no one pointed to my father. So . . . they didn't betray him . . . During the night I had a dream. I had been shot, I lie there and think, but for some reason I don't die . . .

I remember an episode of the Germans chasing chickens. They'd catch one, hold it up, and whirl it around until only the head was left in their hand. They laughed. But it seemed to me that our chickens

---

* Yuri Levitan (1914–1983), the principal Soviet radio announcer during WWII and after, was known as "the voice of the war."

cried out . . . like people . . . in human voices . . . So did the cats and the dogs when they were being shot . . . I had never seen any sort of death before. Neither human nor any other sort. Once I saw dead nestlings in the forest, that was all. I hadn't seen any more death . . .

Our village was set on fire in 1943 . . . That day we were digging potatoes. Our neighbor Vassily—he had been in WWI and knew a little German—said, "I'll go and ask the Germans not to burn the village. There are children here." He went and got burned up himself. They burned the school. All the books. They burned our vegetable patches. Our gardens.

Where were we to go? Father took us to the partisans in the Kozinsky forests. On the way we met people from another village, which had also been burned. They said the Germans were very close by. We got into some sort of a hole: me, my brother Volodya, mama with our little sister, and father. Father took a grenade, and we decided that if the Germans noticed us, he'd pull the pin. We already said goodbye to each other. My brother and I made nooses to hang ourselves and put them around our necks. Mama kissed us all. I heard her say to father, "If only one son could be left . . ." Then father said, "Let them run for it. They're young, maybe they'll save themselves." But I felt so sorry for mama that I didn't go. So . . . I didn't go . . .

We heard dogs barking, we heard foreign words of command, we heard shooting. Our forest was all windfall, fir trees uprooted, you couldn't see anything ten paces away. It was all close, then we heard the voices from farther and farther off. When it became quiet, mama couldn't get up, her legs were paralyzed. Papa carried her on his back.

Several days later we met some partisans who knew father. By then we could barely walk, we were so hungry. Our feet hurt. We were walking and one partisan asked me, "What would you like to find under a pine tree: candy? cookies? a piece of bread?" "A handful of bullets," I replied. The partisans remembered it long after. I hated the Germans so much for everything . . . And for mama . . .

We walked past a burned-down village . . . The rye hadn't been harvested, there were potatoes growing. Apples lying on the ground.

Pears . . . But no people. Cats and dogs running around. Solitary. So . . . No people. Not a single human being. Hungry cats . . .

I remember after the war we had one primer in the village, and the first book I found and read was a collection of arithmetic problems.

I read it like poetry. Yes, so . . .

"HE WIPED HIS TEARS WITH HIS SLEEVE . . ."

Oleg Boldyrev

EIGHT YEARS OLD. NOW AN ARTISAN.

A good question . . . What's better—to remember or to forget? Maybe it's better to keep quiet? For many years I tried to forget . . .

We spent a month getting to Tashkent. A month! It was way in the rear. My father was sent there as an expert. Factories and mills were being relocated there. The whole country was moving to the rear. Deep inside. A good thing our country is big.

There I learned that my older brother had been killed at Stalingrad. He had been eager to get to the front, but I hadn't even been taken to work at the factory yet, because I was young. "You've still got half a year before you turn ten." My mother shook her head. "Forget these childish thoughts." Father also frowned: "A factory isn't a kindergarten, you have to work twelve hours a day. And what work!"

The factory made mines, shells, bombs. Adolescents were accepted to do polishing . . . The unfinished molded metal parts were polished by hand . . . The method was simple—a stream of sand heated to 300 degrees Fahrenheit was directed through a hose under high pressure. The sand bounced off the metal, burned your lungs, hit your face, your eyes. It was rare that anyone could stand it longer than a week. It called for strong character.

But in 1943 . . . I turned ten and father took me with him anyhow.

To his workshop number three. To the section where fuses for bombs were welded.

Three of us worked together: me, Oleg, and Vaniushka, who were only two years older than me. We assembled the fuse, and Yakov Mironovich Sapozhnikov (his last name is stamped in my memory), an expert at his work, welded it. After that you had to get on a box in order to reach the vise, clamp the sleeve of the fuse, and calibrate the inner thread with a tap. We quickly got the knack of it . . . The rest was simpler still: you insert a plug and put it in a box. Once the box was full, we brought it to where it would be loaded. It was a bit heavy, up to a hundred pounds, but two of us could manage it. We didn't distract Yakov Mironovich: his was the finest work. The most responsible—the welding!

The most unpleasant thing was the fire of the electric welding. You tried not to look at the blue sparks, yet in twelve hours you got enough of those flashes. Your eyes feel as if they're filled with sand. You rub them, but it doesn't help. Whether from that or from the monotonous humming of the electric generator that supplied the current for the welding, or simply from fatigue, we sometimes wanted terribly to sleep. Especially during the night. To sleep! To sleep!

Whenever Yakov Mironovich saw the least possibility for us to have a break, he ordered, "Off you go to the electrode room!"

He didn't need to tell us twice: there was no cozier or warmer corner in the whole factory than where the electrodes were dried by hot air. We climbed onto a warm wooden shelf and instantly fell asleep. A quarter of an hour later Yakov Mironovich would come to wake us up.

Once I woke up before he began to rouse us. I saw Yakov Mironovich looking at us. Drawing out the minutes. And wiping his tears with his sleeve.

"HE HUNG ON THE
STRING LIKE A BABY . . ."

Liuba Alexandrovich

ELEVEN YEARS OLD. NOW A WORKER.

I don't want to . . . I don't even want to repeat this word *war* . . .

The war reached us quickly. On July 9, after a few weeks, I remember, a battle was already going on for our regional center of Senno. There were many refugees, so many that there weren't enough houses to put them all in. For instance, we had six families with children in our house. It was the same in all of them.

First came people and then an evacuation of livestock began. I remember it very well, because it was frightening. Frightening pictures. The nearest station to us was Bogdan, it still exists, between Orsha and Lepiel. Livestock were evacuated in that direction not only from our village but from the entire Vitebsk region. It was a hot summer, the livestock were driven in big herds: cows, sheep, pigs, calves. Horses were driven separately. The people who drove them were so tired they no longer cared . . . The cows weren't milked. They would go into a yard and stand there by the porch until somebody milked them. They were milked onto the road, onto the ground . . . The pigs suffered especially badly. They're unable to stand heat and long walking. They walked and fell down. The heat made their bodies swell, and it was so scary that in the evening I was afraid to go outside. Dead horses . . . sheep . . . cows . . . lay everywhere. There was no time to bury them, and they swelled more each day . . . They swelled and puffed up . . .

Peasants know what it takes to raise one cow, how much work. How much time. They wept watching the livestock perish. It wasn't like a tree that falls down silently; there was noise, whinnying, bleating. Moaning.

I remember my grandfather's words: "And these innocent ones, why must they perish? They can't even say anything." My grandfather was a bookish man, he always read in the evenings.

Before the war my older sister worked in the regional party committee, and she stayed behind for the underground work. She brought home many books from the committee library, portraits, red banners. We buried them in the garden under the apple trees. Also her party card. We did it during the night, and I had the feeling that the red . . . the red color . . . would be seen from under the ground.

For some reason I don't remember how the Germans came . . . I remember that they had been there, had been there for a long time, and then they drove us all together, the whole village. They put machine guns in front of us: Where are the partisans? Who do they come to? Everybody was silent. Then they counted off every third person and brought them out to be shot. They shot six people: two men, two women, and two adolescents. And drove away.

Overnight fresh snow fell . . . It was the New Year . . . The dead people lay under this fresh snow. There was no one to bury them, no one to make the coffins. The men were hiding in the forest. Old women burned wood to heat up the ground at least a little and dig the graves. They spent a long time beating their shovels against the frozen ground . . .

Soon the Germans came back . . . Several days later . . . They gathered all the children, there were thirteen of us, and put us at the head of their column—they were afraid of partisan mines. We walked ahead of them, and they drove behind. If, for instance, they had to stop and take water from a well, they sent us first. We walked for ten miles like that. The boys weren't much afraid, but the girls walked

and cried. They followed us in trucks . . . Impossible to run away . . .
I remember we walked barefoot, and it was just the beginning of
spring. The first days . . .

I want to forget . . . I want to forget this . . .

The Germans went from cottage to cottage . . . They gathered
those whose children had joined the partisans . . . They cut their heads
off in the middle of the village . . . We were ordered to watch. In one
cottage they didn't find anybody, so they caught the cat and hanged
him. He hung on the string like a baby . . .

I want to forget it all . . .

"YOU'LL BE MY CHILDREN NOW . . ."

Nina Shunto
SIX YEARS OLD. NOW A COOK.

Aie-aie-aie! My heart begins to ache at once . . .

Before the war we lived only with papa . . . Mama was dead. When papa went to the front, we were left with our aunt. Our aunt lived in the village of Zadory, in the Lepiel district. Soon after papa brought us to her, she ran into a branch with her eye and lost the eye. An infection set in and she died. Our only aunt. I was left alone with my brother, who was little. He and I went to look for the partisans, because for some reason we decided that our papa was there. We spent nights wherever we happened to be. I remember hiding in a haystack during a thunderstorm. We pulled some hay away, made a hole and hid in it. There were many children like us. They all looked for their parents. Even if they knew their parents were dead, they still told us that they were also looking for papa and mama. Or some other relations.

We walked . . . walked . . . In some village . . . a window was open. Probably potato pies had been baked there a little earlier. When we came closer, my brother smelled these pies and fainted. I went into the cottage, I wanted to ask for a piece for my brother, because otherwise he wouldn't have gotten up. And I couldn't carry him, I wasn't strong enough. I didn't find anyone in the cottage, but I couldn't help myself and broke off a piece of the pie. We sat and waited for the owners, so that they wouldn't think we were thieves. The owner came, she lived alone. She didn't let us go, she said: "You'll be my children now . . ." As soon as she said it, my brother and I fell asleep right there at the table. We felt so good. We had a home now.

Soon this village was burned down. All the people in it, too. And our new auntie. We stayed alive because early in the morning we went to pick berries . . . We sat on a hillock and looked at the fire . . . We already understood . . . We didn't know where to go. How would we find another auntie? We had just come to love this one. We even said to each other that we would call our new auntie "mama." She was so nice, she always kissed us before we went to sleep.

We were picked up by the partisans. From the partisan unit we were sent away from the front on a plane . . .

What do I have left from the war? I don't understand what strangers are, because my brother and I grew up among strangers. Strangers saved us. But what kind of strangers are they? All people are one's own. I live with that feeling, though I'm often disappointed. Peacetime life is different . . .

"WE KISSED THEIR HANDS . . ."

David Goldberg
FOURTEEN YEARS OLD. NOW A MUSICIAN.

We were preparing for a celebration . . .

That day we were supposed to solemnly open our Pioneer camp "Talka." We invited some border patrol soldiers, and in the morning went to the forest to get some flowers. We published a festive issue of the camp newspaper, decorated the entrance arch. The place was wonderful, the weather fine. We were on vacation! We were so happy that even the noise of the airplanes we heard all morning didn't alarm us.

Suddenly we were asked to line up, and they informed us that in the morning, while we were asleep, Hitler had attacked our country. In my mind war was connected with the events of Khalkhyn Gol,* it was something distant and brief. There was no doubt about our army being invincible and indestructible, our tanks and airplanes were the best. All this we had heard at school. And at home. The boys were confident, but many girls cried a lot and were frightened. The older children were charged with going around the units and calming everybody, especially the little ones. In the evening the boys who were already fourteen or fifteen years old were handed small caliber rifles. Great! In fact, we became very proud. Held our heads high. There were four rifles in the camp. We took turns standing guard three at a

---

* In 1939 Soviet forces fought a series of battles against the Japanese on the border of Mongolia. The conflict was named for the river Khalkhyn Gol, which flowed through the battlefield.

time and protecting the camp. I even liked it. I went to the forest with this rifle to see if I was afraid or not. I didn't want to turn out to be a coward.

For several days we waited for them to come for us. No one came, and we ourselves went to the Pukhovichi station. We stayed there for a long time. The stationmaster said there wouldn't be any trains from Minsk, that there was no connection. Suddenly one of the children came running and shouted that there was a very heavy train pulling in. We got onto the tracks . . . First we waved our hands, then we took off our red neckerchiefs. We waved our red neckerchiefs to stop the train. The engineer saw us and started showing desperately with his hands that he couldn't stop the train—that he wouldn't be able to start it afterward. "Throw the children onto the flatcars if you can!" he shouted. Some people sitting on the flatcars also shouted to us, "Save the children! Save the children!"

The train slowed down a little. Wounded men reached down from the flatcars to pick up the little children. All the children were put onto this train. It was the last train from Minsk . . .

We rode for a long time. The train moved slowly, we could see very well . . . Dead people lay on the embankment, arranged neatly like railway ties. This has stayed in my memory . . . They bombed us, and we shrieked, and the shrapnel whizzed. At the stations some women fed us—they knew from somewhere that a train with children was coming—and we kissed their hands. A nursing baby turned up among us. His mother had been killed in the shelling. And a woman at the station saw him and took off her kerchief to use as a diaper . . .

That's it! Enough! I'm too agitated. I shouldn't get agitated, I have a bad heart. I'll tell you in case you don't know: those who were children during the war often died before their fathers who fought at the front. Before the former soldiers. Before . . .

I've already buried so many of my friends . . .

"I LOOKED AT THEM WITH
A LITTLE GIRL'S EYES . . ."

Zina Gurskaya

SEVEN YEARS OLD. NOW A POLISHER.

I looked at them with a little girl's eyes. A little village girl. With wide open eyes . . .

I saw my first German closely . . . A tall man, blue eyes. I was so surprised: "Such a handsome one, and yet he kills." It was probably my strongest impression. My first impression of the war . . .

We lived—mama, two little sisters, a little brother, and a hen. We had just one hen left, she lived with us in the cottage, she slept with us. Hid from the bombs with us. She got used to following us like a dog. No matter how hungry we were, we spared the hen. We starved so much that during the winter mama boiled an old leather coat and all the whips, and they smelled of meat to us. My little brother was a nursling. We cooked an egg in boiling water and gave him the water instead of milk. Then he would stop crying and dying.

Around us there was killing, killing, killing . . . People, horses, dogs . . . during the war all our horses were killed. All the dogs. True, the cats survived.

During the day the Germans would come: "Mother, give us eggs. Mother, give us lard." There was shooting. During the night the partisans would come . . . The partisans had a hard time surviving in the forest, especially in winter. They knocked on the window during the night. Sometimes they took things peaceably, sometimes by force . . .

They led away our cow . . . Mama wept. And the partisans wept . . . I can't tell about it. I can't, my dear. No, no!

Mama and grandma plowed like this: first mama put the yoke on her neck and grandma walked behind the plow. Then they changed places and the other became the horse. I wanted to grow up quickly. I was sorry for mama and grandma.

After the war there was one dog for the whole village (a stray one who stayed) and one hen, ours. We didn't eat eggs. We collected them to hatch some chicks.

I went to school . . . I tore off a piece of old wallpaper—that was my notebook. Instead of an eraser—a cork from a bottle. We had beets in the fall, and we were glad because we could grate some beets and have ink. The gratings stand for a day or two and turn black. We had something to write with.

I also remember that mama and I liked to embroider in satin stitch, and always wanted to have gay little flowers. I didn't like black threads.

I still don't like the color black . . .

"OUR MAMA DIDN'T SMILE . . ."

Kima Murzich

TWELVE YEARS OLD. NOW A RADIO TECHNICIAN.

Our family . . .

We were three sisters—Rema, Maya, and Kima. Rema stood for Electrification and Peace, Maya for May 1, Kima for Communist Youth International. Our father gave us these names. He was a Communist. He joined the party when he was young. He brought us up this way. There were many books at home, also portraits of Lenin and Stalin. In the first days of the war we buried them in the shed. The only one I kept for myself was *The Children of Captain Grant* by Jules Verne. My favorite book. I read and reread it all through the war.

Mama went to the villages near Minsk and exchanged shawls for food. She had a pair of nice shoes. She even took her only dress made of crepe de chine. Maya and I sat and waited for mama: will she come back or not? We tried to distract each other from these thoughts, we remembered how we used to run to the lake before the war, to swim, to lie in the sun, how we danced in school amateur performances. How long the alley was that led to our school. The smell of the cherry preserves mama cooked in the yard on stones . . . They were so far away now, all these good things. We talked about Rema, our older sister. All through the war we thought she was dead. She left for her work at the factory on June 23 and never came back . . .

When the war was over, mama sent requests everywhere, searching for Rema. There was an address bureau, there was always a crowd of people there, people were all looking for each other. I kept going there carrying mama's letters. But there was no letter for us. On her days off mama used to sit by the window waiting for the mail woman to come. But she always went past.

Once mama came back from work. A neighbor called on us. "Dance!" she said to mama—and she held something behind her back. Mama realized that it was a letter. She didn't dance, she sat down on a bench and couldn't get up. Or speak.

Our sister was found. She had been evacuated. Mama began to smile. All through the war, until we found our sister, our mama hadn't smiled . . .

"I COULDN'T GET USED TO MY NAME . . ."

Lena Kravchenko

SEVEN YEARS OLD. NOW AN ACCOUNTANT.

Of course I knew nothing about death . . . No one had time to explain it, but I just saw it . . .

When the machine guns rattle away from an airplane, it feels as if all the bullets are aimed at you. In your direction. I begged, "Mama, dear, lie on me . . ." She would lie on me, and then I didn't see or hear anything.

Most frightening was to lose mama . . . I saw a dead young woman with a baby nursing at her breast. She must have been killed a minute before. The baby didn't even cry. And I was sitting right there . . .

As long as I don't lose mama . . . Mama holds my hand all the time and strokes my head: "Everything will be all right. Everything will be all right."

We rode in some truck, and all the children wore buckets on their heads. I didn't obey mama . . .

Then I remember—we're being driven in a column . . . They're taking my mama away from me . . . I seize her hands, I clutch at her marquisette dress. She wasn't dressed for war. It was her fancy dress. Her best. I won't let go . . . I cry . . . The fascist shoves me aside first with his submachine gun, and then, when I'm on the ground—with his boot. Some woman picks me up. Now she and I are for some reason riding on a train. Where? She calls me "Anechka" . . . But I think I had a different name . . . I seem to remember that it was different, but what it was I forgot. From fear. From fear that they'd taken my mama from me . . . Where are we going? I seem to understand from the conversation of the adults that we're being taken to Germany. I remember my thoughts: why do the Germans need such a little girl? What am I going to do there? When it grew dark, the women took me to the door of the car and just pushed me out: "Run for it! Maybe you'll save yourself."

I landed in some ditch and fell asleep there. It was cold, and I dreamed that mama was wrapping me in something warm and saying gentle words. I've had that dream all my life . . .

Twenty-five years after the war I found just one of my aunts. She told me my real name, and for a long time I couldn't get used to it.

I didn't respond to it . . .

"HIS ARMY SHIRT WAS WET . . ."

Valia Matiushkova

FIVE YEARS OLD. NOW AN ENGINEER.

You'll be surprised! But I would like to recall something funny. Merry. I like to laugh, I don't want to cry. O-o-oh . . . I'm already crying . . .

Papa is taking me to mama in the maternity hospital and says that we'll soon buy ourselves a boy. I try to imagine what sort of little brother I'll have. I ask papa, "What's he like?" Papa says, "Small."

Suddenly papa and I are somewhere high up, and there's smoke coming through the window. Papa carries me in his arms, and I ask him to go back for my little purse. I fuss. Papa says nothing and firmly presses me to himself, so firmly that I have a hard time breathing. Soon there is no papa; I'm walking down the street with some woman. We walk along the barbed wire. There are prisoners of war behind it. It's hot, they ask for a drink of water. All I have is two pieces of candy in my pocket. I throw them over the wire. Where did I get them, these candies? I no longer remember. Someone throws bread . . . Cucumbers . . . The guard shoots, we run away . . .

It's astonishing, but I remember it all . . . In detail . . .

Then I remember myself in a children's center, also surrounded by barbed wire. We were guarded by German soldiers and German shepherds. There were some children who couldn't walk yet, they crawled. When they were hungry they licked the floor . . . Ate dirt . . . They died quickly. The food was bad. They gave us bread that made our tongues swell so much that we couldn't even speak. All we thought about was food. You finish breakfast and think—what will there be for lunch? You finish lunch—what's for supper? We crawled under the barbed wire and escaped to town. There was one goal—the garbage dumps. It was an inexpressible joy when you found a herring skin or potato peels. We ate them raw.

I remember being caught at the dump by some man. I was frightened. "I won't do it anymore, mister."

He asked, "Whose child are you?"

"Nobody's. I'm from a children's center."

He took me to his place and gave me something to eat. They only had potatoes in his house. They boiled them, and I ate a whole pot of potatoes.

From the center they transferred us to an orphanage. The orphanage was across the street from a medical institute, which housed a German hospital. I remember low windows, heavy shutters, which were closed at night. They fed us well there, and my health improved. The cleaning woman there loved me very much. She pitied everybody, but especially me. When they came to take our blood, everybody hid: "The doctors are coming . . ."—and she put me in some corner. She kept saying that I resembled her daughter. Other children hid under the beds. They got pulled out. Lured by something. By a piece of bread, or else they'd show some toy. I remember a red ball . . .

The "doctors" would go away, and I'd go back to the room . . . I remember a little boy lying there, his arm hanging from the bed, bleeding. And other children crying . . . Every two or three weeks new children came. Some were taken somewhere, they were already pale and weak, and others were brought. Fattened up.

German doctors thought that the blood of children under five years old contributed to the speedy recovery of the wounded. That it had a rejuvenating effect. I found this out later . . . of course, later . . .

And then . . . I wanted to get a pretty toy. A red ball.

When the Germans began to flee from Minsk . . . to retreat . . . that woman who tried to save me led us outside the gate: "Those of you who have somebody, search for them. Those who don't, go to any village, people there will save you."

And I went. I lived with some grandmother . . . I don't remember her name or the name of the village. I do remember that her daughter had been arrested, and we were left just the two of us—the old one and the little one. We had a piece of bread for a week.

I was the last to find out that our troops were in the village. I was sick. When I heard about it, I got up and ran to school. I saw a soldier and clung to him. I remember that his army shirt was wet.

He had been embraced, and kissed, and wept over so much.

"AS IF SHE HAD SAVED HIS OWN DAUGHTER . . ."

Genia Zavoiner

SEVEN YEARS OLD. NOW A RADIO TECHNICIAN.

What have I preserved most in my memory? From those days . . .

How they took my father away . . . He was in a quilted jacket, and I don't remember his face, it has vanished completely from my memory. I remember his hands . . . They bound them with ropes. Papa's hands . . . But no matter how I try, I can't remember the faces of those who came for him either. There were several of them . . .

Mama didn't cry. She stood at the window all day.

Father was taken away, and we were moved to the ghetto and began to live behind barbed wire. Our house stood by the road, and every day sticks came flying into our courtyard. I saw a fascist by our gate. When a group of people was being led out to be shot, he beat those people with sticks. The sticks would break, and he'd throw them over his shoulder. Into our courtyard. I wanted to have a better look at him, not just his back, and once I did see him: he was small, with a bald spot. He grunted and puffed. My child's imagination was struck because he was so ordinary . . .

We found our grandmother killed in her apartment . . . We buried her ourselves . . . Our cheerful and wise grandmother, who loved German music. German literature.

Mama went to exchange things for food, and a pogrom began in the ghetto. Usually we hid in the cellar, but this time we went up to the attic. It was totally broken down on one side and that saved us. The Germans came into the house and poked the ceiling with their bayonets. They didn't climb to the attic, because it was all broken down. But they threw grenades into the cellar.

The pogrom lasted for three days, and we sat for three days in the attic. Mama wasn't with us. We thought only about her. When the pogrom was over, we stood at the gate waiting to see if she was alive or not. Suddenly our former neighbor came around the corner; he passed by without stopping, but we heard: "Your mama is alive." When mama came back, the three of us stood and looked at her. No one cried, we had no tears, but some sense of peace came over us. We didn't even feel hungry.

Mama and I stood by the barbed wire, and there was a beautiful woman passing by. She stopped next to us on the other side and said to mama, "I'm so sorry for you." Mama replied, "If you're sorry, take my daughter to live with you." "All right"—and the woman began to think. The rest they said to each other in whispers.

The next day mama brought me to the gate of the ghetto.

"Genechka, take your doll carriage and go to Aunt Marussia" (our neighbor).

I remember what I was wearing then: a blue top and a sweater with white pompoms. My best fancy clothes.

Mama pushed me out the gate of the ghetto, and I pressed myself to her. She pushed me, and her face was flooded with tears. I remember how I went . . . I remember the gate, the sentry booth . . .

I went with my doll carriage where mama told me to go. They put a warm jacket on me there and sat me in a wagon. I wept all the way and kept saying, "Wherever you are, mama, I'm there, too. Wherever you are . . ."

They brought me to a farmstead and sat me on a long bench. There were four children in the family I came to. And they took me as well. I want everybody to know the name of the woman who saved me: Olympia Pozharitskaya, from the village of Genevichi, in the Volozhinsk district. As long as I lived in this family, fear lived in

it. They could have been shot at any moment . . . the whole family . . . including the four children. For harboring a Jewish child from
the ghetto. I was their death . . . What great hearts they had to have!
Superhumanly human hearts . . . Whenever the Germans appeared,
they would send me off somewhere at once. The forest was nearby,
the forest saved us. That woman pitied me very much, she had the
same pity for her own children and for me. When she gave something, she gave it to us all; when she kissed, she kissed us all. And she
petted us all in the same way. I called her "mamusya." Somewhere I
had a mama, and here I had mamusya . . .

When tanks came to the farmstead, I was herding cows. I saw the
tanks and hid. I couldn't believe they were our tanks, but when I
made out the red stars on them, I came out to the road. An officer
jumped off the first tank, picked me up and raised me very, very high.
Then the owner of the farm came running. She was so happy, so
beautiful, she wanted so much to share something good, to tell that
she, too, had done something for this victory. And she told how they
had saved me. A Jewish girl . . . This officer pressed me to him, and I
was so thin, I vanished under his arms. And he embraced that woman,
he embraced her with such a look as if she had saved his own daughter. He said that all his family had been killed, and that when the war
was over, he would come back and take me to Moscow. But I wouldn't
agree for anything, although I didn't know whether my mama was
alive or not.

Other people came running, they also embraced me. And they all
admitted that they knew who had been hidden at the farmstead.

Then mama came to get me. She came into the yard and knelt
down before that woman and her children . . .

"THEY CARRIED ME TO THE UNIT IN THEIR ARMS . . . I WAS ALL ONE BRUISE FROM HEAD TO FOOT . . ."

Volodia Ampilogov

TEN YEARS OLD. NOW A LOCKSMITH.

I'm ten years old, exactly ten years old . . . And it's war. That bastardly war!

I was playing hide-and-seek in the yard with the boys. A big truck drove into the yard, German soldiers leaped out of it, began to catch us and throw us into the back under the canvas. They brought us to the railway station. The truck backed up to the freight car, and they threw us in like sacks. Onto the straw.

The car was so full that at first we could only stand. There were no adults, only children and adolescents. For two days and two nights we were driven with the doors shut, we didn't see anything, and only heard the wheels knocking against the rails. During the day some light came through the cracks, but during the night we were so frightened we all cried: we were being taken somewhere far away, and our parents didn't know where we were. On the third day the door opened, and a soldier threw in several loaves of bread. Those who were close managed to snatch some, and swallowed the bread instantly. I was at the far end from the door and didn't see the bread, I only thought I smelled bread for a moment when I heard the shout: "Bread!" Just the smell of it.

I don't remember how many days we were on the road . . . But we couldn't breathe anymore, because there was no toilet in this car. So for number one and number two . . . The train was bombarded . . . the roof was blown off our car. I wasn't alone, I was with my buddy Grishka; he was ten like me, and before the war we had been in the same class. From the first moments of the bombing, we held on to each other, so as not to get lost. When the roof was blown off, we decided to climb out of the car through the top and escape. Escape! It was clear by then that we were being taken to the west. To Germany.

It was dark in the forest, and we kept turning to look—our train was burning, it was all a big bonfire. High flames. We walked all night. By morning we came upon some village, but there was no village. Instead of the houses . . . it was the first time I saw it: only black stoves stood there. There was low fog . . . We walked as if in a cemetery . . . among black monuments . . . We looked for something to eat, but the stoves stood empty and cold . . . We walked on and on . . . Grisha suddenly fell down and died; his heart stopped. I sat over him all night waiting for morning. In the morning I dug a hole in the sand with my hands and buried Grisha. I wanted to remember the spot, but how could I remember it if everything around was unfamiliar?

I walk along feeling dizzy from hunger. Suddenly I hear, "Stop! Where are you going, boy?" I asked, "Who are you?" "We're Russians," they say, "partisans." From them I learned that I was in the Vitebsk region, and so I wound up in the Alexeevsky partisan brigade . . .

When I got a little stronger, I started asking to fight. They joked in response and sent me to help in the kitchen. But then a chance came . . . Such a chance . . . Scouts had been sent three times to a railway station and had never come back. After the third time, our commander lined us all up and said, "I can't send anybody for a fourth time. Only volunteers will go . . ."

I stood in the second row and when I heard, "Are there any volunteers?" I raised my hand like at school. I had a long jacket on, the sleeves hung to the ground. I raised my hand, but it wasn't seen, because of the hanging sleeves, and I couldn't get out of them.

The commander ordered, "Volunteers, step forward."

I stepped forward.

"Dear boy . . ." the commander said to me. "Dear boy . . ."

They gave me a little bag and an old hat with one ear flap torn off.

As soon as I came out on the high road, I had the feeling that I was being watched. I looked around—no one was there. Then I noticed three thick bushy pines. I cautiously took a better look at them and saw German snipers sitting in them. They would "skim off" anyone who came out of the forest. But when a boy appeared at the edge carrying a little bag, they didn't touch him.

I returned to the unit and reported to the commander that German snipers were sitting in the pine trees. During the night we took them without a single shot and brought them to the unit alive. That was my first scout mission . . .

At the end of 1943 . . . SS soldiers caught me in the village of Old Chelnyshki, Beshenkovichi district . . . They beat me with ramrods. With their feet in iron-shod boots. Hard as stone . . . After torturing me, they dragged me outside and poured water on me. It was winter, and I was covered by a bloody crust of ice. I couldn't figure what the hammering was I heard above me. They were building a gallows. I saw it when they picked me up and put me on a block of wood. The last thing I remember? The smell of fresh wood . . . A living smell . . .

The noose tightened, but they had time to tear it off . . . There were partisans in ambush. When I regained consciousness, I recognized our doctor. "Two more seconds—and that's it, I wouldn't have been able to save you," he said. "You're lucky to be alive, dear boy."

They carried me to the unit in their arms. I was all one bruise from head to foot. I hurt so badly that I wondered: will I ever grow up?

"AND WHY AM I SO SMALL? . . ."

Sasha Streltsov
FOUR YEARS OLD. NOW A PILOT.

My father had never seen me . . .

I was born without him. He had two wars: he came back from the Finnish War, and the Patriotic War began.* He left home for the second time.

Of my mama I have kept the memory of how we walked in the forest, and she taught me: "Don't hurry. Listen to how the leaves fall. How the forest sounds . . ." And we sat on the road and she drew little birds for me in the sand with a twig.

I also remember that I wanted to be tall and I asked mama, "Is papa tall?"

Mama replied, "Very tall and handsome. But he never shows it off."

"And why am I so small?"

I was still growing up . . . We didn't have any photographs of my father left, but I needed a confirmation that I was like him.

"You're like him. Very much like him," mama reassured me.

In 1945 we learned that my father had been killed. Mama loved him so much that she went mad . . . She didn't recognize anybody, not even me. And as far back as I can remember, I always had only my grandmother with me. Grandmother's name was Shura, and so as not

---

* The Soviet name for WWII was the Great Patriotic War (or Great Fatherland War).

to get confused, we decided I would be Shurik, and she Grandma Sasha.*

Grandma Sasha didn't tell me any fairy tales, she spent the time from morning to late at night doing laundry, plowing, cooking, bleaching. Tending the cow. On holidays she liked to recall how I was born. Here I am telling you, and there's my grandmother's voice in my ears: "It was a warm day. Uncle Ignat's cow calved, and thieves broke into old Yakimshchuk's garden. And you came into the world . . ."

Planes kept flying over our cottage . . . Our planes. In the second grade I firmly decided to become a pilot.

My grandmother went to the recruiting office. They asked for my documents. She didn't have any, but she had my father's death notice with her. She came home and said, "We'll dig potatoes, and you'll go to the Suvorov School in Minsk."†

Before sending me on my way, she borrowed flour from somebody and baked little pies. The military commissar put me in a truck and said, "You're honored on account of your father."

It was the first time in my life that I rode in a truck.

After a few months my grandmother came to visit me at school and brought me an apple as a treat. She asked me to eat it.

But I didn't want to part with her gift so soon . . .

---

* Shura, Sasha, and Shurik are all diminutives of the names Alexander and Alexandra.

† Suvorov Schools, founded in the Soviet Union in 1943 and still operating, are boarding schools for boys fourteen to eighteen years old, with an emphasis on military training. They give preference to boys from military families, particularly war orphans. The name comes from Alexander Suvorov (1730–1800), the last generalissimo of the Russian army, who was reputed never to have lost a battle.

"THEY WERE DRAWN BY
THE HUMAN SCENT . . ."

Nadia Savitskaya

TWELVE YEARS OLD. NOW A WORKER.

We were waiting for my brother to come home from the army. He wrote in a letter that he would come in June . . .

We thought my brother would return and we'd build him a house. Father had already transported some beams by horses, and in the evenings we all sat on these beams, and I remember mama telling father that they would put up a big house. They'd have many grandchildren.

The war began, and my brother didn't come home from the army. We were five sisters and one brother, and he was the oldest. All through the war mama wept, and all through the war we waited for our brother. I remember that: we waited for him every day.

Whenever we heard that our prisoners of war were being driven somewhere, we'd quickly go there. Mama would bake a dozen potatoes, tie them up in a bundle, and we would go. Once we had nothing to bring, and there was ripe rye in the field. We broke off some ears, rubbed them to get the grains out. And we ran into a German patrol that guarded the field. They poured our grains out and indicated to us that we should line up to be shot. We began to howl, and our mama kissed their boots. They were on horseback, high up, and she clutched at their feet, kissed them, and begged, "Dear sirs! Have pity . . . Dear sirs, these are my children. You see, all girls." They didn't shoot us and rode off.

As soon as they rode off, I began to laugh. I laughed and laughed, ten minutes went by and I still laughed. Twenty minutes . . . I fell down laughing. Mama scolded me—it didn't help; mama begged me—it didn't help. I laughed all the while we walked. I came home and laughed. I buried my face in the pillows and couldn't calm down—I laughed. And I laughed like that the whole day. They thought that I . . . Well, you know . . . They were all frightened . . . They were afraid I'd lost my mind. Turned lunatic.

It has stayed with me to this day: whenever I'm frightened, I start laughing loudly. Very loudly.

In 1945 . . . We were liberated, and then we received a letter that my brother had been killed. Mama wept and wept, and went blind. We lived outside the village in German bunkers, because our village had all burned down, our old cottage had burned down and the beams for the new house. Nothing of ours was left. We found some army helmets in the forest and cooked in them. German helmets were big as cauldrons. We found food in the forest. It was scary going for berries and mushrooms. There were lots of German shepherds left; they attacked people and killed little children. They were used to human flesh and human blood. To its fresh scent . . . When we went to the forest, we gathered in a big group. Some twenty of us . . . Our mothers taught us that we should shout as we walked in the forest, so that the dogs would get scared. While you were picking a basket of berries, you'd shout so much that you'd lose your voice. Get hoarse. Your throat would be all swollen. The dogs were big as wolves.

They were drawn by the human scent . . .

"WHY DID THEY SHOOT HER IN THE FACE? MY MAMA WAS SO BEAUTIFUL . . ."

Volodia Korshuk

SEVEN YEARS OLD. NOW A PROFESSOR,
A DOCTOR IN HISTORY.

We lived in Brest. Right on the border . . .

In the evening all three of us were at the movies: mama, papa, and I. It rarely happened that we went anywhere together, because my father was always busy. He was the director of the regional department of education, and was always on business trips.

The last evening without war . . . The last night . . .

When mama roused me in the morning, everything around rumbled, banged, boomed. It was very early. I remember that outside the windows it was still dark. My parents bustled about, packing suitcases; for some reason they couldn't find anything.

We had our own house, a big garden. My father went somewhere. Mama and I looked out the window: there were some military people in the garden speaking broken Russian and dressed in our uniforms. Mama said they were saboteurs. I couldn't quite figure out how it was possible that in our garden, where a samovar was still standing on a little table from the evening before, there were suddenly saboteurs! And where were our frontier guards?

We left the city on foot. Before my eyes a stone house ahead of us fell to pieces and a telephone flew out of a window. In the middle of the street stood a bed; on it lay a dead little girl under a blanket. As if the bed had been taken out and put there: everything was intact, only the blanket was slightly singed. Just outside the city were rye fields. Planes fired at us with machine guns, and everybody moved, not along the road, but over those fields.

We entered the forest, and it became less frightening. From the forest I saw big trucks. It was the Germans coming, and they were laughing loudly. I heard unfamiliar speech. There was a lot of *r-r-r* in it . . .

My parents kept asking each other: where are our soldiers? our army? I pictured to myself that at any moment Budenny would come galloping on his warhorse, and the Germans would flee in terror. There was nothing to equal our cavalry—so my father had convinced me recently.

We walked for a long time. At night we stopped at farms. They fed us, kept us warm. Many of them knew my father, and my father knew many of them. We stopped at one farm, I still remember the name of the teacher who lived there—Pauk ["Spider"]. They had two houses—a new and an old one side by side. They offered to let us stay; they would give us one of the houses. But my father declined. The owner drove us to the high road. Mama tried to give him money, but he shook his head and said that he could not take money for friendship at a difficult moment. I remembered that.

So we reached the town of Uzda, my father's native area. We lived at my grandfather's in the village of Mrochki.

I saw partisans in our house for the first time that winter, and ever since, my picture of them has been of people in white camouflage smocks. Soon my father left with them for the forest, and mama and I stayed with my grandfather.

Mama was sewing something . . . No . . . She was sitting at the big table and doing embroidery on a tambour, and I was sitting on the stove. The Germans came into the cottage with the village headman, and the headman pointed at mama: "Here she is." They told mama to get ready. Then I became very frightened. Mama was taken outside, she called me to say goodbye, but I huddled under a bench and they couldn't pull me out from there.

They took mama and two other women whose husbands were with the partisans, and drove somewhere. No one knew where. In which direction. The next day they were found not far outside the village. They lay in the snow . . . It had snowed all night . . . What I remember, from when my mama was brought home, was that for some reason they had shot her in the face. She had several black bullet holes in her cheek. I kept asking my grandfather, "Why did they shoot her in the face? My mama was so beautiful . . ." Mama was buried . . . My grandfather, my grandmother, and I followed the coffin. People were afraid. They came to take leave of her during the night . . . All night our door stayed open, but during the day we were by ourselves. I couldn't understand why they had killed my mama, if she hadn't done anything bad. She was sitting and embroidering . . .

One night my father came and said he was taking me with him. I was happy. At first my partisan life was not much different from my life with grandfather. Father would go on a mission and leave me with someone in a village. I remember a woman I was staying with had her dead husband brought to her on a sledge. She beat her head against the table on which the coffin stood and repeated the one word, *fiends*.

Father was absent for a very long time. I waited for him and thought, "I have no mama, grandpa and grandma are somewhere far away, what will I, a little boy, do, if they bring me my dead father on a sledge?" It seemed like an eternity before my father returned. While I was waiting, I promised myself to address him only formally from then on. I wanted to emphasize how I loved him, how I missed him, and that he was my only one. At first my father probably didn't notice how I addressed him, but then he asked, "Why do you address me formally?" I confessed to him what I had promised myself and why. But he explained to me, "You, too, are my only one, so we should address each other informally. We're the closest to each other in the world." I also asked him that we never part from each other. "You're already an adult, you're a man," my father persuaded me.

I remember my father's gentleness. We were under fire . . . We lay on the cold April ground, there was no grass yet . . . Father found a deep depression and told me, "You lie underneath and I'll lie on top. If they kill me, you'll stay alive." Everybody in the unit pitied me. I remember an older partisan came up, took my hat off, and caressed my head for a long time, saying to my father that he had a boy like that running around somewhere. And when we walked through a swamp, up to our waists in water, father tried to carry me on his back, but quickly became tired. Then the partisans started taking turns carrying me. I'll never forget that. I won't forget how they found a little sorrel and gave it all to me. And went to sleep hungry.

. . . In the orphanage of Gomel, where I was transported by plane with several other partisan children as soon as the town was liberated, someone handed me money sent by my father, a big red paper note. I went with the boys to the market and spent all the money on candy. It was a lot of candy, enough for everybody. The teacher asked, "What did you do with the money your father sent you?" I confessed that I bought candy. "That's all?" she asked, surprised.

Minsk was liberated . . . A man came and said he would take me to my father. It was hard to get on the train. The man got in and people handed me to him through the window.

I met with my father and asked him again that he and I should never part, because it is bad to be alone. I remember he met me not alone, but with a new mama. She pressed my head to herself, and I missed my mother's caress so much and so enjoyed her touch that I fell asleep in the car at once. On her shoulder.

I was ten when I went to first grade. I was big, and I knew how to read, and after six months they transferred me to second grade. I knew how to read, but not how to write. I was called to the blackboard and had to write a word with the letter *Ю* in it. I stood there terrified, thinking that I didn't know how to write the letter *Ю*. But I knew how to shoot. I was a good shot.

One day I didn't find my father's pistol in the closet. I turned everything in it upside down—the pistol wasn't there.

"How come? What are you going to do now?" I asked my father when he came home from work.

"I'll teach children," he said.

I was puzzled . . . I thought the only work was war . . .

"YOU ASKED ME TO FINISH YOU OFF . . ."

Vasya Baikachev

**TWELVE YEARS OLD. NOW A TEACHER
OF MANUAL EDUCATION.**

I've often remembered it . . . Those were the last days of my childhood . . .

During the winter vacation our whole school took part in a military game. Before that we studied drilling, made wooden rifles, sewed camouflage coats, clothes for medical orderlies. Our chiefs from the military unit came flying to us in biplanes. We were completely thrilled.

In June German planes were already flying over us dropping scouts. They were young fellows in gray checkered jackets and caps. Together with some adults we caught several of them and handed them over to the village council. We were proud of having taken part in a military operation, it reminded us of our winter game. But soon others appeared. They did not wear checkered jackets and caps, but green uniforms with the sleeves rolled up, boots with wide tops and iron-shod heels. They had calfskin packs on their backs, long gas-mask canisters at their sides, and held submachine guns at the ready. Well-fed, hefty. They sang and shouted, "*Zwei Monat—Moskva kaput.*" My father explained, "*Zwei Monat*" means two months. Only two months? Only? This war was not at all like the one we had played at just recently and which I had liked.

In the first few days the Germans didn't stop in our village of Malevichi, they drove on to the Zhlobin station. My father worked there. But he no longer went to the station, he waited for our troops to come any day and drive the Germans back to the border. We believed father and also waited for our soldiers. We expected them any day. And they . . . our soldiers . . . lay all around: on the roads, in the forest, in the ditches, in the fields . . . in the kitchen gardens . . . in the peat pits . . . They lay dead. They lay with their rifles. With their grenades. It was warm, and they grew bigger from the warmth, and there seemed to be more and more of them every day. A whole army. No one buried them . . .

Father hitched up the horse and we went to the field. We began to collect the dead men. We dug holes . . . Put them in rows of ten to twelve men . . . My school bag was filling with papers. I remember from the addresses that they were natives of the city of Ulyanovsk, in the Kuibyshev region.

Several days later I found my father and my best friend, fourteen-year-old Vasya Shevtsov, killed outside the village. My grandfather and I came to that spot . . . Bombing began . . . We buried Vasya, but had no time to bury father. After the bombing we found nothing left of him. Not a trace. We put a cross at the cemetery—that's all. Just a cross. We buried father's best Sunday suit under it . . .

A week later we could no longer collect the soldiers . . . We couldn't lift them . . . There was water sloshing under the army shirts . . . We collected their rifles. Their army cards.

Grandfather was killed in the bombing . . .

How were we to go on living? Without father? Without grandfather? Mama wept and wept. What to do with the weapons we gathered and buried in a safe place? Who to give them to? There was nobody to ask. Mama wept.

In winter I got in touch with some underground fighters. They were happy to have my gift. They sent the weapons to the partisans . . .

Time passed, I don't remember how much . . . Maybe four months. I remember that that day I gathered last year's frozen potatoes in a field. I came home wet, hungry, but I brought a full bucket. I had just taken my wet bast shoes off, when there was knocking on the door of the cellar we lived in. Somebody asked, "Is Baikachev here?" When I appeared in the cellar door, I was ordered to come out. I hurriedly put on a *budenovka* instead of a winter hat, for which I got a whipping at once.

By the cellar stood three horses, with Germans and *polizei***** mounted on them. One of the *polizei* dismounted, put a strap around my neck, and tied me to the saddle. Mother began to beg: "Let me feed him." She went back to the cellar to get a flatbread of defrosted potatoes, and they whipped up the horses and set off at a trot. They dragged me like that for three miles to the village of Vesely.

At the first interrogation the fascist officer asked simple questions: last name, first name, date of birth . . . Who are your father and mother? The interpreter was a young *polizei*. At the end of the interrogation he said, "Now you'll go and clean the torture room. Take a good look at the bench there . . ." They gave me a bucket of water, a broom, a rag, and took me there . . .

There I saw a terrible picture: in the middle of the room stood a wide bench with three leather straps nailed to it. Three straps to tie a man by the neck, the waist, and the legs. In the corner stood thick birch rods and a bucket of water. The water was red. On the floor were pools of blood . . . of urine . . . of excrement . . .

I kept bringing more and more water. The rag I used was red anyway.

In the morning the officer summoned me.

"Where are the weapons? Who are you connected with in the underground? What were your assignments?" The questions poured out one after the other.

I denied everything, saying that I knew nothing, that I was young and gathered frozen potatoes in the field, not weapons.

---

* Russians who served as police under the German occupation were given the German name of *polizei,* which in Russian became both singular and plural.

"Take him to the cellar," the officer ordered the soldier.

They took me down into a cellar with cold water. Before that they showed me a partisan who had just been taken out of there. He couldn't stand the torture and drowned . . . Now he lay in the street . . .

The water came up to my neck . . . I felt my heart beat and the blood in my veins pulsate and heat the water around my body. My fear was to lose consciousness. To inhale the water. To drown.

The next interrogation: the barrel of a pistol was shoved against my ear, fired—a dry floorboard cracked. They shot at the floor! The blow of a stick at my neck vertebra, I fall down . . . Someone big and heavy stands over me. He smells of sausage and cheap vodka. I feel nauseous, but I have nothing to throw up. I hear: "Now you're going to lick up what you did on the floor . . . With your tongue, understand . . . Understand, you red whelp?!"

Back in the cell I didn't sleep, but lost consciousness from pain. Now it seemed to me that I was at a school lineup and my teacher Liubov Ivanovna Lashkevich was saying, "In the fall you'll enter the fifth grade, and now, children, goodbye. You'll all grow up over the summer. Vasya Baikachev is now the smallest, and he'll become the biggest." Liubov Ivanovna smiled . . .

And then my father and I are walking in the fields, looking for our dead soldiers. Father is somewhere ahead of me, and I find a man under a pine tree . . . Not a man, but what's left of him. He has no arms, no legs . . . He's still alive and he begs, "Finish me off, sonny . . ."

The old man who lies next to me in the cell wakes me up.

"Don't shout, sonny."

"What did I shout?"

"You asked me to finish you off . . ."

Decades have passed, and I'm still wondering: am I alive?!

"AND I DIDN'T EVEN
HAVE A SCARF ON . . ."

Nadia Gorbacheva

SEVEN YEARS OLD. NOW WORKS IN TELEVISION.

I'm interested in the inexplicable in the war . . . I still think a lot about it . . .

I don't remember how my father left for the front . . .

We weren't told. They wanted to spare us. In the morning he took me and my sister to kindergarten. Everything was the same as ever. In the evening we asked, of course, why father wasn't there, but mama reassured us: "He'll come back soon. In a few days."

I remember the road . . . Trucks drove, in them cows mooed, pigs oinked, in one truck a boy held a cactus in his hands and was tossed from one side of the truck to the other . . . My sister and I found it funny the way he ran back and forth . . . We were children . . . We saw the fields, we saw the butterflies. We liked the ride. Mama protected us, we sat under mama's "wings." Somewhere deep in our minds was the awareness of a calamity, but mama was with us and everything would be good in the place we were going to. She shielded us from the bombs, from the frightened adult conversations, from everything bad. If we could have read mama's face, we would have read everything on it. But I don't remember it, I remember a big dragonfly that landed on my sister's shoulder, and I shouted, "A plane!" and all the adults for some reason jumped off the wagon and threw their heads back.

We arrived at our grandfather's in the village of Gorodets, in the Sennensky region. He had a big family, and we lived in the summer kitchen. People started calling us "summer folk," and it stayed with us till the end of the war. I don't remember us playing; at least in the first year of the war we didn't play any summer games. Our little brother was growing up. We had him on our hands, because mama dug, planted, sewed. She would leave us by ourselves, and we had to wash the spoons and the dishes, the floors, to stoke the stove, to gather brushwood for the next day, to bring water: we carried half a bucket because we couldn't carry a full one. In the evening mama assigned us our responsibilities: you for the kitchen, you for your brother. And we each answered for our duties.

We were hungry, yet we acquired a cat and then a dog. They were members of the family; we shared everything with them. Sometimes there wasn't enough for the cat and the dog, so each of us tried to secretly stash away a little piece for them. And when the cat was killed by shrapnel, it was such a loss that it seemed impossible to survive. We wept for two days. We carried her in tears to be buried. Set up a cross, planted flowers, watered them.

Even now, when I remember all the tears we shed, I can't bring myself to have a cat. When my daughter was little, she asked us to buy a dog, but I couldn't.

Then something happened to us. We stopped being afraid of death.

Big German trucks drove in. We were all summoned from the cottages. They lined us up and counted: "*Ein, zwei, drei* . . ." Mama was the ninth, and the tenth person was shot. Our neighbor . . . Mama was holding our brother in her arms, and she dropped him.

I remember smells . . . Now, when I see movies about the fascists, I sense the soldiers' smell. Leather, good broadcloth, sweat . . .

That day my sister was responsible for our brother, and I weeded the kitchen garden. When I bent down among the potatoes, I couldn't be seen. You know how it is in childhood—everything seems big and tall. When I noticed the plane, it was already circling over me. I saw the pilot quite distinctly. His young face. A brief submachine gun volley—*bang-bang*! The plane circles for a second round . . . He wasn't seeking to kill me, he was having fun. I already understood it then, with my child's mind. And I didn't even have a scarf on to cover my head . . .

So, what is it? How to explain it? I wonder: is that pilot still alive? And what does he remember?

The moment when it was decided whether you die from a bullet or from fear would pass, and an in-between time would come: one disaster would blow over, and the next wasn't known yet. Then we laughed a lot. We began to tease one another, to joke: who hid where, how we ran, how the bullet flew by and missed. I remember that well. Even we children would gather and poke fun at one another: who was scared, who wasn't. We laughed and cried at the same time.

I remember the war in order to figure it out . . . Otherwise why do it?

We had two chickens. When we said, "Quiet—Germans!" they were quiet. They sat very quietly with us under the bed and wouldn't cluck even once. However many trained chickens I saw later in the circus, I wasn't surprised. On top of that, ours diligently laid eggs in a box under the bed—two eggs a day. We felt so rich!

Still we did set up some sort of a Christmas tree. It was mama, of course, who remembered that we were children. We cut bright pictures out of books, made paper balls—one side white, the other black, made garlands out of old threads. On that day we especially smiled to each other, and instead of presents (we didn't have any), we left little notes under the tree.

In my notes I wrote to mama: "Mama dear, I love you very much. Very, very much!" We gave each other presents of words.

Years have passed . . . I've read so many books. But I don't know much more about the war than when I was a child.

"NO ONE TO PLAY OUTSIDE WITH . . ."

Valya Nikitenko

FOUR YEARS OLD. NOW AN ENGINEER.

Everything gets stamped in a child's memory like in a photo album. As separate snapshots . . .

Mama begs, "Run, let's run! Stomp, stomp!" Her hands are full. I fuss: "My little legs hurt."

My three-year-old brother pushes me: "Let's lun" (he can't pronounce *r*), "the Gelmans will catch us!" We "lun" together in silence.

I hide my head and my doll from the bombs. My doll already has no arms or legs. I weep and ask mama to bandage her . . .

Someone brought mama a leaflet. I already know what that is. It's a big letter from Moscow, a nice letter. Mama talks with grandma, and I understand that our uncle is with the partisans. Among our neighbors there was a family of *polizei*. You know how children are: they go out and each one boasts of his papa. Their boy says, "My papa has a submachine gun . . ."

I, too, want to boast: "And we got a leaflet from our uncle . . ."

The *polizei*'s mother heard it and came to mama to warn her: it would be death to our family if her son heard my words or one of the children told him.

Mama called me in from outside and begged: "Darling daughter, you won't talk about it anymore?"

"I will, too!"

"You shouldn't talk about it."

"So he can, and I can't?"

Then she pulled a switch from the broom, but she was sorry to whip me. She stood me in the corner.

"If you talk about it, your mama will be killed."

"Uncle will come from the forest in a plane and save you."

I fell asleep there in the corner . . .

Our house is burning. Someone carries me out of it, sleepy. My coat and shoes get burned up. I wear mama's blazer; it reaches to the ground.

We live in a dugout. I climb out of the dugout and smell millet kasha with lard. To this day nothing seems tastier to me than millet kasha with lard. Somebody shouts, "Our troops have come!" In Aunt Vasilisa's kitchen garden—that's what mama calls her, but the children call her "Granny Vasya"—stands a soldiers' field kitchen. They give us kasha in mess tins, I remember precisely that it was mess tins. How we ate it I don't know, there were no spoons . . .

They held out a jug of milk to me, and I had already forgotten about milk during the war. They poured the milk into a cup, I dropped it and it broke. I cried. Everybody thought I was crying because of the broken cup, but I was crying because I spilled the milk. It was so tasty, and I was afraid they wouldn't give me more.

After the war, sicknesses began. Everybody got sick, all the children. There was more sickness than during the war. Incomprehensible, isn't it?

An epidemic of diphtheria . . . Children died. I escaped from a locked-up house to bury twin brothers who were our neighbors and my friends. I stood by their little coffins in mama's blazer and barefoot. Mama pulled me away from there by my hand. She and grandma were afraid that I, too, was infected with diphtheria. No, it was just a cough.

There were no children left in the village at all. No one to play outside with . . .

"I'LL OPEN THE WINDOW AT NIGHT . . . AND GIVE THE PAGES TO THE WIND . . ."

Zoya Mazharova

TWELVE YEARS OLD. NOW A POSTAL WORKER.

I saw an angel . . .

He appeared . . . Came to me in a dream when we were transported to Germany. In a boxcar. Nothing could be seen there, not a spot of sky. But he came . . .

You're not afraid of me? Of my words? I hear voices, then I see an angel . . . Once I start talking about it, not everybody wants to listen for very long. People rarely invite me to visit. To a festive table. Not even the neighbors. I keep talking, talking . . . Maybe I've grown old? I can't stop . . .

I'll begin from the beginning . . . The first year of the war I lived with papa and mama. I reaped and plowed, mowed and threshed. We gave it all to the Germans: grain, potatoes, peas. They came in the fall on horseback to collect—what's it called? I've forgotten the word— *quitrent.* Our *polizei* also came with them. We all knew them, they were from the next village. That's how we lived. We were used to it, one might say. Hitler was already near Moscow, we were told. Near Stalingrad.

During the night the partisans used to come . . . They told us otherwise: Stalin won't give up Moscow for anything. And he won't give up Stalingrad.

And we plowed and reaped. On Sundays and holidays in the evenings we had dances. We danced in the street. We had an accordion.

I remember it happened on Palm Sunday . . . We broke off pussy willow branches,* went to church. Gathered in the street. Waiting for the accordionist. Then a whole lot of Germans arrived. In big covered trucks, with German shepherds. They surrounded us and ordered us to get into the trucks. They pushed us with their rifle butts. Some of us wept, some shouted . . . Before our parents came running, we were already in the trucks. Under the tarpaulins. There was a railway station nearby. They brought us there. Empty boxcars were already standing there waiting. A *polizei* pulled me into a boxcar. I tried to break loose. He wound my braid around his hand.

"Don't shout, fool. The Führer is delivering you from Stalin."

"What do we care about that foreign place?" They had already agitated us before then about going to Germany. Promised us a beautiful life.

"You'll help the German people to defeat Bolshevism."

"I want to go to mama."

"You'll live in a house under a tile roof and eat chocolate candy."

"To mama . . ."

O-o-oh! If people had known their fate, they wouldn't have survived till morning.

They loaded us and the train left. We rode for a long time, but I don't know how long. In my car everybody was from the Vitebsk region. From different villages. They were all young and some, like me, were children. They asked me, "How did you get caught?"

"At a dance."

I kept fainting from hunger and fear. I lie there. I close my eyes. And then for the first time . . . there . . . I saw an angel . . . The angel was small, and his wings were small. Like a bird's. I see that he wants

---

* For lack of palm fronds, Russians traditionally carry pussy willow branches in the services of Palm Sunday.

to save me. "How can he save me," I thought, "if he's so small?" That was the first time I saw him . . .

Thirst . . . We all suffered from thirst, we wanted to drink all the time. Everything inside was so dry that my tongue came out and I couldn't push it back in. During the day we rode with our tongues hanging out. With open mouths. During the night it was a little easier.

I'll remember it all my life . . . I'll never forget it . . .

We had buckets in the corner, where we did our number one during the ride. And one girl . . . She crawled to these buckets, put her arms around one of them, bent over it and began to drink. She drank in big gulps . . . Then she began to vomit . . . She would vomit and again crawl to the bucket . . . Again she would vomit . . .

O-o-oh! If people had known their fate beforehand . . .

I remember the town of Magdeburg . . . Our heads were shaved there and our bodies smeared with some white solution. As a prophylactic. My body burned from this solution, from this liquid, as if it was on fire. The skin peeled off. God spare us! I didn't want to live . . . I no longer felt sorry for anybody: neither for myself, nor for mama and papa. You raise your eyes—they're standing around. With their dogs. German shepherds have frightening eyes. Dogs never look you straight in the eye, they always look away, but these did. They looked us straight in the eye. I didn't want to live . . . I was there with a girl I had known, and she had been taken with her mama, I don't know how. Maybe her mama jumped into the truck with her . . . I don't know . . .

I'll remember it all my life . . . I'll never forget it . . .

This girl stood there and cried, because when they rounded us up for the prophylactic, she lost her mama. Her mama was young . . . a beautiful mama . . . We were always in the dark during the ride, no one opened the doors for us, they were freight cars, without windows. So during the ride she didn't see her mama. For a whole month. She stood there crying and some old woman, her head also shaven, reached out to her, wanted to caress her. She ran away from that woman until she called out: "Daughter dear . . ." Only by the voice did she realize she was her mama.

O-o-oh! If . . . If we had known . . .

We were hungry all the time. I don't remember where I was, where they took me. The names of the places . . . from hunger we lived as if asleep . . .

I remember carrying some boxes in a cartridge and gunpowder factory. Everything there smelled of matches. The smell of smoke . . . There was no smoke, but it smelled of smoke . . .

I remember milking cows at some German farmer's. Splitting wood . . . Twelve hours a day . . .

We were fed potato peels, turnips, and were given tea with saccharine. My workmate, a Ukrainian girl, took my tea from me. She was older . . . stronger . . . She said, "I've got to survive . . . My mama's alone at home."

In the fields she sang beautiful Ukrainian songs. Very beautiful.

I . . . in one evening . . . I can't tell everything in one evening. I won't have time. My heart won't stand it.

Where was it? I don't remember . . . But this was already in the camp . . . I evidently wound up in Buchenwald . . .

We unloaded the trucks of dead people there and stacked them up in layers: a layer of dead people, a layer of tarred railway ties. One layer, another layer . . . and so from morning to night we prepared bonfires. Bonfires of . . . well, obviously . . . of corpses . . . There were some living people among the dead, and they wanted to tell us something. A few words. But we weren't allowed to stay next to them . . .

O-o-oh! Human life . . . I don't know if it's easy for a tree to live, or for all the living creatures that man has tamed. Cattle, birds . . . But about human beings I know everything . . .

I wanted to die, I wasn't sorry for anybody anymore . . . I was getting ready—was at the point of looking for a knife. My angel came flying to me . . . It was more than once . . . I don't remember what his words of comfort were, but they were tender words. He reasoned with me for a long time . . . When I told other people about my angel, they thought I had lost my mind. I had no one around me that I knew, there were only strangers. No one wanted to get acquainted with anyone else, because tomorrow one or the other would die. Why get acquainted? But at some point I came to love a little girl . . . Mashenka . . . She was blond and gentle. She and I were friends for a month. In a camp a month is a whole lifetime, an eternity. She came to me first.

"Have you got a pencil?"

"No."

"And a piece of paper?"

"No again. What do you need it for?"

"I know I'll die soon, and I want to write a letter to my mother."

We weren't allowed to have any pencils or paper in the camp. But we found some for her. Everybody liked her—so blond and gentle. Such a gentle voice.

"How are you going to send the letter?" I asked.

"I'll open the window during the night . . . And give the pages to the wind . . ."

She was probably eight years old, maybe ten. How can you tell by the bones? There were walking skeletons there, not people . . . Soon she fell ill, couldn't get up and go to work. I begged her . . . On the first day I even dragged her as far as the door. She clung to the door, but couldn't walk. She lay for two days, and on the third they came and took her away on a stretcher. There was only one way out of the camp—through the chimney . . . Straight to heaven . . .

I'll remember it all my life . . . I'll never forget it . . .

At night she and I talked.

"Does an angel come to you?" I wanted to tell her about my angel.

"No. Mama comes to me. She always wears a white blouse. I remember this blouse she had with cornflowers embroidered on it."

In the fall . . . I survived till the fall. By what miracle, I don't know . . . In the morning we were driven to work in the field. We harvested carrots, cut cabbages—I liked this work. It had been long since I went to the fields or saw anything green. In the camp you didn't see the sky, you didn't see the ground, because of the smoke. The chimney was tall, black. Smoke came out of it day and night . . . I saw a yellow flower in the field. I'd already forgotten how flowers grow. I caressed this flower . . . The other women also caressed it. We knew that ashes from our crematorium were brought here, and we all had our dead. A sister, or a mother . . . I had Mashenka . . .

If I'd known I would survive, I would have asked her mama's address. But I didn't think I would . . .

How did I survive, after dying a hundred times? I don't know . . . It was my angel who saved me. He persuaded me. He appears even now. He likes nights when the moon shines brightly through the window. White light . . .

Aren't you afraid to be with me? To listen to me? . . .

O-o-oh . . .

"DIG HERE . . ."

Volodia Barsuk

TWELVE YEARS OLD. NOW CHAIRMAN OF THE COUNCIL OF THE SPARTAKUS ATHLETIC SOCIETY OF THE BELORUSSIAN REPUBLIC.

We joined the partisans at once . . .

Our whole family: papa, mama, my brother, and me. My brother was older. They gave him a rifle. I envied him, and he taught me to shoot.

Once my brother didn't come back from a mission . . . For a long time mama refused to believe he was dead. Our unit received information that a partisan group surrounded by the Germans had blown themselves up with an antitank mine so as not to be taken alive. Mama suspected that our Alexander was there. He hadn't been sent with that group, but he could have met them. She went to the unit commander and said, "I sense that my son is lying with them. Allow me to go there."

She was given several fighters, and we went. And here is a mother's heart for you! The fighters began to dig in one place, but my mama pointed to another: "Dig here . . ." They began to dig and found my brother. He was no longer recognizable, he was all black. Mama recognized him by a scar from appendicitis and by the comb in his pocket.

I always remember my mama . . .

I remember how I smoked for the first time. She saw it and called my father: "Look what our Vovka is doing!"

"What is he doing?"

"Smoking."

Father came up to me, looked.

"Let him smoke. We'll sort it out after the war."

During the war we recalled all the time how we lived before the war. We lived all together, several related families in one big house. We lived cheerfully and amiably. On payday Aunt Lena bought a lot of pastry and cheeses, gathered all the children, and treated them. She was killed, along with her husband and her son. All my uncles were killed . . .

The war ended . . . I remember my mama and me walking down the street. She was carrying some potatoes she had been given at the factory where she worked. A German prisoner came to us from the ruins of a building.

"*Mutter, bitte, Kartoffel . . .*"

Mama said, "I won't give you anything. Maybe you killed my son."

The German was taken aback and said nothing. Mama went on . . . Then she turned back, took out a few potatoes, and gave them to him.

"Here, eat . . ."

Now I was taken aback . . . What is it? During the winter we took rides several times on frozen German corpses. They could be found outside town long after the war. We used them as sleds . . . You could kick the dead man with your foot. We jumped on them. We went on hating them.

Mama taught me . . . That was my first postwar lesson in love . . .

"GRANDPA WAS BURIED UNDER THE WINDOW . . ."

Varya Vyrko

EIGHT YEARS OLD. NOW A WEAVER.

I remember winter, cold winter. In winter our grandfather was killed.

They killed him in our courtyard. By the gate.

We buried him under our window . . .

We weren't allowed to bury him in the cemetery, because he had hit a German. *Polizei* stood by our gate and didn't let anyone come to us. Neither relatives nor neighbors. Mama and grandma themselves knocked together a coffin out of some boxes. They themselves washed grandpa, though relatives are not supposed to wash the body. It should be done by strangers. That's our custom. I remember this being discussed at home . . . They lifted the coffin. Carried it to the gate . . . The *polizei* shouted, "Turn back! Or else we'll shoot you all! Bury him in your kitchen garden like a dog."

And so for three days . . . They go to the gate, and are sent back. Driven back . . .

On the third day grandma began to pick at the ground under the window . . . It was minus forty outside, grandma remembered all her life that it was minus forty. It's very difficult to bury a man when it's so cold. I was seven then, no, probably, already eight, and I helped her. Mama pulled me out of the hole, in tears.

There . . . in the place where grandpa was buried, an apple tree grew. It stands there instead of a cross. It's already old . . .

"... AND THEY TAMPED IT DOWN WITH THE SHOVELS, SO IT LOOKED PRETTY."

Leonid Shakinko

TWELVE YEARS OLD. NOW AN ARTIST.

How they shot us . . .

They drove us all to the brigadier's cottage . . . The whole village . . . A warm day, warm grass. Some stood, and some sat. The women wore white kerchiefs, the children were barefoot. People always gathered together at this place on festive occasions. Sang songs. The first day of harvest, the last day of harvest. Then, too, some stood, and some sat. Village meetings were held.

Now . . . no one wept . . . no one spoke . . . Even then it struck me. I had read that people usually cry or shout in the face of death—I don't remember a single tear . . . Recalling it now, I'm beginning to think—maybe in those moments I became deaf and didn't hear anything? Why were there no tears?

The children huddled in a separate little flock, though no one separated us from the grown-ups. For some reason our mothers didn't keep us next to them. Why? To this day I don't know. Usually we boys weren't very friendly with the girls. The normal thing was: if it's a girl, she's got to be hit, or her braids pulled. Here everybody clung to each other. You understand, even the yard dogs didn't bark.

Several steps away from us a machine gun was set up. Next to it two SS soldiers sat, began talking calmly about something, joking, and even laughing.

I remember precisely these details . . .

A young officer came up. And an interpreter translated, "Mister officer orders that you give the names of those who have connections with the partisans. If you keep silent, we'll shoot you all."

People went on standing or sitting where they stood or sat.

"In three minutes you'll be shot," the interpreter said and stuck up three fingers.

Now I was looking at his hand all the time.

"Two minutes—and you'll be shot . . ."

People pressed closer to each other, they said things to each other, not in words, but by the movements of hands, of eyes. I, for instance, clearly imagined that we would be shot and that would be the end of us.

"One last minute—and you're kaput . . ."

I saw a soldier release the lock, load the cartridge belt, and take the machine gun in his hands. Some were two yards away, some ten . . .

They counted off fourteen of those who stood nearest. Gave them shovels and ordered them to dig a hole. And we were driven closer, to watch them dig . . . They dug very quickly. Dust flew. I remember that the hole was big, deep, a full human height deep. Such holes are dug for a house, for a foundation.

They shot three people at a time. They stood them at the edge of the hole and fired point-blank. The rest of us watched. I don't remember parents saying farewell to their children or children to their parents. One mother raised the skirt of her dress and covered her daughter's eyes. But even the little children didn't cry . . .

They shot fourteen people and began to fill up the hole. Again we stood and watched them cover the hole with earth, trample it with boots. And they patted it down with the shovels, so it looked pretty. Neat. You understand, they even rounded the corners, so it looked clean. One older German wiped his forehead with his handkerchief, as if he was working in a field. A little dog ran up to him . . . No one knew where it came from. Whose dog it was. He petted it . . .

Twenty days later we were allowed to dig up the dead. To have the family take and bury them. Then the women did cry, the whole village wailed. Lamented.

Many times I've stretched a canvas. I wanted to paint that . . . But something else came out: trees, grass . . .

"I'LL BUY MYSELF A DRESS WITH A LITTLE BOW . . ."

Polia Pashkevich

FOUR YEARS OLD. NOW A DRESSMAKER.

I was four years old . . . I never thought about war . . .

But this is how I pictured war: a big black forest, and there's some sort of war in it. Something scary. Why in the forest? Because in fairy tales the most scary things happened in the forest.

More and more troops kept passing through our Belynichi, and I didn't understand then that this was a retreat. We were being abandoned. I remember many military men in the house. They held me in their arms. Pitied me. Wanted to give me a treat, but didn't have anything. In the morning, when they went away, there were many cartridges left on the windowsills and everywhere. And torn-off red badges. Decorations. I played with them . . . I didn't understand what these toys were . . .

And here is something my aunt told me . . . When the Germans entered our town, they had a list of the Communists. My father was on it and the teacher who lived across the street from us. They had a son who was my friend, we called him Igrushka, "Toy." His name was probably Igor, so I think now. Because I have the memory of this name or nickname, Igrushka. Our fathers were taken away together . . .

In front of my eyes . . . mama was shot down in the street. When she fell, her overcoat opened, it became red, and the snow around mama became red . . .

Then we were kept for a long time in some shed. It was very frightening, we wept, we shouted. I had a sister and a brother, two and a half, and one year old. I was four, I was the oldest. We were little, but we already knew that, when there was shelling, it wasn't planes dropping bombs, but artillery. We could tell by the sound whether or not it was one of our planes coming, and whether the bomb would fall near us or far off. It was frightening, very frightening, but you covered your head, and then it wasn't. The main thing was not to see anything.

Later we went somewhere on a sledge, all three of us, and in a village women took us to their cottages one by one. No one took my little brother for a long time, and he cried, "What about me?" My sister and I were afraid they would separate us and we'd no longer be together. We had always lived together.

Once I was almost eaten by a German shepherd. I was sitting by the window. The Germans came down the street with two big German shepherds. One of them dashed at my window and broke the glass. Someone snatched me from the windowsill, but I was so frightened that from that day on I began to stutter. Even now I'm afraid of big dogs.

. . . After the war we were sent to an orphanage that stood near the road. There were many German prisoners. They walked down the road for days. We threw dirt and stones at them. The convoy soldiers chased us away and scolded us.

In the orphanage all the children waited for their parents to come and take them home. An unknown man or woman would appear; we'd all run to them and shout, "My papa . . . My mama . . ."

"No, it's my papa!"

"They came to take me!"

"No, it's me they'll take!"

We envied very much those who were found by their parents. They wouldn't let us come near their mamas and papas: "Don't touch her, she's my mama" or "Don't touch him, he's my papa." They wouldn't let go of them for a moment, afraid someone would take them away. Or for fear they would suddenly go off somewhere again.

Children from the orphanage and ordinary children went to school together. At that time everybody lived poorly, but a child would come from home and have a slice of bread in his bag or a potato, while we had nothing. We were all dressed the same way when we were little, but once we grew up, we would get upset. When you're twelve or thirteen, you want a pretty dress, pretty shoes, but we all wore ankle-high laced shoes. Both boys and girls. A girl wanted a bright ribbon in her braids, colored pencils. A book bag. We wanted candy, but we had it only for the New Year—fruit drops. Whenever we had a lot of black bread, we sucked it like candy—we thought it was very tasty.

We had one young teacher, the rest were elderly women, so we all loved her very much. We adored her. Lessons wouldn't begin until she came to school. We sat by the window and waited: "She's co-o-oming! She's co-o-oming . . ." She came into the classroom, and each one of us wanted to touch her, each of us thought, "My mama is like that . . ."

My dream: I'll grow up, start working, and buy myself many dresses—a red one, a green one, a polka-dot one, with a little bow. The little bow was a must! In the seventh grade they asked me what I wanted to study, and I had long since decided: dress-making.

I sew dresses.

"HOW DID HE DIE, IF THERE WAS NO SHOOTING TODAY? . . ."

Eduard Voroshilov

ELEVEN YEARS OLD. NOW WORKS IN TELEVISION.

I only told mama about the war . . . My mama . . . Only someone close . . .

In the village where our partisan unit was stationed, an old man died. I was living in his cottage. When we were burying him, a boy of about seven stopped by and asked, "Why is the grandpa lying on the table?"[*]

"Grandpa died," they answered.

The boy was terribly surprised.

"How did he die, if there was no shooting today?"

The boy was seven years old, but he'd been hearing for two years already that people die only when there's shooting.

I remembered that . . .

I began my story with a partisan unit, which I did not get to at once. Only by the end of the second year of the war. I didn't tell you how, a week before the war, mama and I went to Minsk, and she took me to a Pioneer camp near town . . .

In the camp we sang songs: "If There Is War Tomorrow," "Three Tankers," "Over Hill and Dale." This last one my father liked very

---

[*] It is traditional in Russian funerary practice to lay out the body of the dead person on a table until the coffin is brought.

much. He often hummed it . . . Just then the movie *The Children of Captain Grant* was released, and I liked a song from that movie: "Hey, merry wind, sing us a song . . ." I sang this song running out to do morning exercise.

That day there was no morning exercise, there were planes roaring over us . . . I looked up and saw black dots coming down from the planes. We knew nothing about bombs yet. Next to the Pioneer camp was a railroad, and I walked along it to Minsk. My calculation was simple: there was a railroad station near the medical institute where mama worked at the time. If I follow the rails I'll come to mama. I took with me a boy who lived not far from the station. He was much younger than me and cried a lot. He also walked slowly, while I liked to walk. My father and I walked everywhere in the suburbs of my native Leningrad. Of course I was annoyed . . . Still we did make it to the Minsk train station, reached the Western Bridge. There another bombing began, and I lost him.

Mama was not in the institute. Not far from there lived Professor Golub, with whom mama worked, and I found his apartment. But it was empty . . . Many years later I learned what had happened: as soon as the bombing of the city began, mama hitched a ride in a car and went to Ratomka by the high road. She arrived and saw the devastated camp . . .

Everybody was leaving the city and going somewhere. I decided that Leningrad was farther away than Moscow, and although my papa lived in Leningrad, he was at the front, but I had aunts in Moscow, and they surely wouldn't go away anywhere. They wouldn't because they lived in Moscow . . . In our capital . . . On the road I kept near a woman with a little girl. I didn't know the woman, but she realized that I was alone and had nothing and that I was hungry. She called me: "Come to us, we'll eat together."

I remember that I ate onion with lard then for the first time in my life. I winced to begin with, but then I ate it. Whenever the bombing began, I always watched for where this woman with her girl was. In the evening we chose a ditch and settled for a rest. We were constantly bombed. The woman looked around and cried out . . . I also got up and looked in the direction she had just looked in, and saw a low-flying plane and little fires flashing next to the propeller on the wings. And, in the wake of these fires, little spurts of dust rising along the road. Quite instinctively I tumbled to the bottom of the ditch. The machine-gun burst rattled over my head, and the plane flew farther on. I got up and saw that woman lying on the side of the ditch with a bloody spot instead of a face. Then I got frightened, jumped out of the ditch, and ran. The question of what happened to that little girl has tormented me ever since, even now. I never met her again . . .

I reached some village . . . German wounded lay outside under the trees. So I saw Germans for the first time . . .

The villagers had been driven out of their houses, forced to carry water, the German medical orderlies heated it on a bonfire in big buckets. In the morning they put the wounded men in trucks and also one or two boys in each truck. They gave us flasks of water and showed how we should help: one needs to have a handkerchief wetted and placed on his head, another to have his lips wetted. A wounded man begs: "*Wasser . . . Wasser . . .*" You put the flask to his lips, and you shake all over. Even now I can't determine the feeling I experienced then. Squeamishness? No. Hatred? No again. It was everything together. And pity, too . . . Hatred is a feeling that gets formed in a man, it's not an innate thing. At school we were taught to be kind, to love. I'll skip ahead again . . . When I was first hit by a German, I didn't feel pain, it was something else. How can it be that he hit me? By what right? It was a shock.

I went back to Minsk.

And I made friends with Kim. We got acquainted in the street. To my question, "Who do you live with?" he replied, "Nobody."

I learned that he, too, had gotten lost, and I suggested, "Let's live together."

"Yes, let's." He was glad because he had no place to live. But I lived in the abandoned apartment of Professor Golub.

Once Kim and I saw a fellow a bit older than us walking down the street carrying a stand for shining shoes. We listened to his advice: what kind of box we needed, how to make shoe polish. To make shoe polish we needed soot, and the city was full of it, far more than we needed. It had to be mixed with some oil. In short, we prepared some sort of stinking mixture, but it was black. And if it was neatly spread it even shone.

Once a German came up to me and put his foot on the box. His boots were dirty, with old, caked dirt. We had already had to deal with such footwear, and I had a special scraper to scrape the dirt off first and then apply the polish. I took the scraper, passed it over just twice, but he didn't like it. He kicked the box, and then me in the face . . .

I had never been hit in my life. I don't count boys' fights, there was plenty of that in Leningrad schools. But no adult had ever hit me before.

Kim saw my face and shouted, "Don't you dare look at him like that! Don't! He'll kill you . . ."

Just then we encountered people in the streets who had yellow stars sewn on their jackets and coats. We had heard about the ghetto . . . This word was always uttered in a whisper . . . Kim was a Jewish boy, but he shaved his head, and we decided to pass him off as a Tatar. When his hair began to grow in, his curly black hair, who would believe that he was a Tatar? I suffered over my friend. During the night I would wake up, see his curly head and couldn't go back to sleep: something had to be devised so that Kim wouldn't be taken to the ghetto.

We found a hair clipper, and I shaved Kim again. It was already getting cold, and it was useless to polish shoes in winter. We had a new plan. The German authorities set up a hotel in the city for arriving officers. They used to come with big backpacks, suitcases, and the hotel wasn't near. By some miracle we got hold of a big sled, and we waited at the station for the arriving trains. The train would arrive, we would load the sled with two or three persons' luggage, and pull it across the whole city. For that we were given bread or cigarettes, and cigarettes could be exchanged for anything at the market, any food.

Kim was taken one night when the train came very late. We were freezing cold, but couldn't leave the station because the curfew was already in effect. We were chased out of the building and waited in the street. At last the train arrived, we loaded the sled and set out. We pulled, the belts cut into our bodies, and the Germans urged us on: "*Schnell! Schnell!*" We couldn't go quickly, and they began to beat us.

We brought the things into the hotel and waited for them to pay us. One man ordered, "Get out!" and he pushed Kim. Kim's hat fell off. Then they shouted "*Jude!*" They seized him . . .

A few days later I found out that Kim was in the ghetto. I went there . . . I spent whole days circling around it . . . I saw him several times through the wire. I brought him bread, potatoes, carrots. The sentry turns his back, goes to the corner, and I toss in a potato. Kim comes, picks it up . . .

I lived several miles away from the ghetto, but during the night such shouting came from there that the whole city heard it. I would wake up with the thought: is Kim alive? How can I save him? After the next pogrom, I came to the appointed place, and they made signs to me: "Kim isn't there!"

I felt miserable . . . But I still had hope . . .

One morning someone knocked on my door. I jumped out of bed . . . My first thought was: Kim! No, it wasn't him. The boy from downstairs woke me up. He said, "Come outside with me, there are dead people lying there. Let's look for my father." We went outside. The curfew was over, but there were almost no people. The street was covered with light snow and, covered with this snow, at a distance of fifteen to twenty yards from each other, lay our captive soldiers. They had been driven through the city during the night, and those who lagged behind had been shot in the back of the head. They all lay face down.

The boy was unable to touch the dead men, he was afraid that his father was somewhere among them. It was then that I caught myself thinking that for some reason I had no fear of death. Mentally I was already used to it. I turned them over and he looked at each face. We went along the whole street that way . . .

Since then . . . there have been no tears in me . . . Not even when maybe there should have been. I don't know how to cry. I cried only once during the whole war. When our partisan nurse Natasha was killed . . . She loved poetry, and I loved poetry. She loved roses, and I loved roses, and in summer I used to bring her bouquets of wild roses.

Once she asked me, "How many grades did you finish before the war?"

"Four . . ."

"When the war is over, will you go to a Suvorov School?"

Before the war I liked my father's military uniform, I also wanted to bear arms. But I told her, no, I wouldn't be an officer.

Dead, she lay on pine branches by a tent, and I sat over her and cried. Cried for the first time at the sight of a dead human being.

. . . I met my mama . . . When we met, she only looked at me, didn't even caress me, and repeated, "You? Can it be you?"

Many days passed before we could tell each other about the war . . .

"BECAUSE WE'RE GIRLS, AND HE'S A BOY . . ."

Rimma Pozniakova (Kaminskaya)

SIX YEARS OLD. NOW A WORKER.

I was in kindergarten . . . Playing with dolls . . .

They call me: "Your papa's come to take you. It's war!" I don't want to go anywhere. I want to play. I cry.

What is this war? How is it that I'm killed? How is it that papa's killed? There was another unfamiliar word—*refugees*. Mama hung little bags on our necks with our birth certificates and notes with our address. In case she was killed, strangers would know who we were.

We walked for a very long time. We lost papa. Were frightened. Mama said that papa was taken to the concentration camp, but that we would go to papa. And what was a concentration camp? We gathered food, but what kind of food? Baked apples. Our house burned down, our garden burned down, there were baked apples hanging on the apple trees. We gathered them and ate them.

The concentration camp was in Drozdy, near Komsomol Lake. Now it's in Minsk, but then it was the countryside. I remember the black barbed wire. People's faces were also all black, all looking the same. We didn't recognize father, but he recognized us. He wanted to caress me, but for some reason I was afraid to get near the barbed wire and tugged at mama to go home.

When and how father came home I don't remember. I know that he worked at a mill, and mama sent us to him to carry lunch—me and my little sister Toma. Tomochka was still a tiny thing. I was bigger, I already wore a little bra—there were these little girls' bras before the war. Mama gave us a bundle with food and put some leaflets inside my bra. The leaflets were small, a page from a school notebook, written by hand. Mama led us to the gate, wept, and instructed us, "Don't go near anybody except your father." Then she stood waiting for us to return, till she saw us come back alive.

I don't remember being afraid . . . Mama said we had to go, and we went. Mama said this was the main thing. We were afraid not to obey mama, not to do what she asked us to do. She was our beloved mama. We couldn't even imagine not obeying her.

When it was cold we all climbed on the stove. We had a big sheepskin coat, and we all got under this coat. To heat the stove we had to go to the train station and steal coal. We had to crawl on our knees so that the watchman didn't notice. We crawled and helped ourselves along with our elbows. We would bring back a bucket of coal, and we looked like chimneysweeps: knees and elbows and nose and forehead all black.

At night we slept together, nobody wanted to sleep alone. There were four of us: myself, my two sisters, and four-year-old Boris, whom mama adopted. Only later did we find out that Boris was the son of the underground fighter Lelia Revinskaya, mama's friend. At the time mama told us that there was this little boy who was often left at home by himself, was frightened and had nothing to eat. She wanted us to accept him and come to love him. She realized that it wasn't easy. Children are capable of not loving. She did a smart thing: she didn't bring Boris, but sent us to get him. "Go and bring this boy and be friends with him." We went and brought him.

Boris had many books with pretty pictures. He took them all with him, we helped him carry them. We would sit on the stove, and he would tell us fairy tales. We liked him so much that he became as dear to us as could be, maybe because he knew so many fairy tales. We told everybody in the yard, "Don't bully him."

We were all blond, and Boris was dark-haired. His mama had a thick black braid, and when she came to us, she gave me a present of a little mirror. I put it away and decided to look at it in the mornings and then I'd have a braid like hers.

We run around in the yard, and the children shout, "Whose child is Boris?"

"Boris is ours."

"Why are you all blond and he's dark-haired?"

"Because we're girls, and he's a boy." That's what mama told us to answer.

Boris was in fact ours, because his mama had been killed and his papa had been killed, and he could have been thrown into the ghetto. Somehow we already knew that much. Our mama was afraid he'd be recognized and taken. We'd go somewhere and we'd all call our mama "mama," but Boris called her "aunt." She kept begging him, "Say 'mama,'" and she'd give him some bread.

He'd take the bread, step back: "Thank you, Aunt."

And his tears poured down . . .

"YOU'RE NO BROTHER OF MINE
IF YOU PLAY WITH GERMAN BOYS . . ."

Vasya Sigalev-Kniazev

SIX YEARS OLD. NOW AN ATHLETIC COACH.

It was early dawn . . .

Shooting began. Father leaped out of bed, ran to the door, opened it, and cried out. We thought he was frightened, but he fell, he had been hit by an exploding bullet.

Mama found some rags. She didn't turn the light on, because there was still shooting. Father moaned, tossed from side to side. A faint light came through the window, fell on his face . . .

"Lie down on the floor," mama said.

And suddenly she burst into sobs. We rushed to her with a cry. I slipped in my father's blood and fell. I smelled blood and also some other heavy smell—father's intestines had exploded . . .

I remember a big, long coffin, yet my father wasn't tall. "Why does he need such a big coffin?" I wondered. Then I decided that father had been badly wounded, and it would be less painful for him this way. That's how I explained it to the neighbors' boy.

Sometime later, also in the morning, some Germans came and took mama and me. They put us on the square in front of the factory where my father had worked before the war (in the village of Smolovka, Vitebsk region). We stood there with two more partisan families. There were more children than adults. Everybody knew that mama had a big family, five brothers and five sisters, all of them with the partisans.

They started beating mama. The whole village watched her being beaten, and we did, too. Some woman kept bending my head down toward the ground. "Lower your eyes, lower your eyes." I kept wiggling out of her hands. I watched . . .

Beyond the village was a woody hill. They left the children and led the adults there. I clung to mama, she kept pushing me away and cried out, "Farewell, children!" I remember her dress rising in the wind as she fell into the trench . . .

Our troops came, and I saw an officer with epaulettes. I liked it so much that I made epaulettes for myself out of birch bark and drew the insignia with coal. I fixed them on the peasant coat my aunt had made for me, and went as I was—in my best shoes—to report to Captain Ivankin (my aunt told me his name) that Vanya Sigalev wanted to fight the Germans together with him. First there was joking, laughing, then they asked my aunt about my parents. When they discovered that I was an orphan, the soldiers sewed little tarpaulin boots for me overnight, shortened an army coat, made a smaller hat, smaller epaulettes. Someone even fabricated an officer's shoulder strap. Thus I became a son of the special demining unit No. 203. They enlisted me as a liaison. I tried to do my best, but I couldn't read or write. When mama was still alive, my uncle had told me, "Go to the railway bridge and count how many Germans are there . . ." How could I count? He poured a handful of grain into my pocket, and I put the grains one by one from the right pocket to the left. And my uncle counted them afterward.

"War is war, but you've still got to learn to read and write," said the party organizer Shaposhnikov.

The soldiers got hold of some paper, he made a notebook out of it, and wrote the alphabet and the multiplication table in it. I memorized it and recited it for him. He would bring an empty shell box, draw lines on it, and say, "Write."

In Germany there were already three of us boys—Volodia Pochivadlov, Vitia Barinov, and me. Volodia was fourteen years old, Vitia seven, and by then I was nine. We were great friends, like brothers, because we had no one else.

But when I saw Vitia Barinov play "war" with German boys and give one of them his forage cap with a little star, I shouted that he was no longer a brother to me. He would never again be a brother to me! I grabbed my trophy pistol and ordered him to go to our unit's bivouac. And there I put him under arrest in some closet. He was a private and I was a junior sergeant, so I conducted myself like a superior in rank.

Someone told Captain Ivankin about it. He summoned me. "Where is Private Vitia Barinov?"

"Private Barinov is in the guardhouse," I reported.

The captain spent a long time explaining to me that all children are good, that they're not to blame for anything, that Russian and German children will be friends once the war is over.

The war ended. I was awarded three medals: "For the Taking of Königsberg," "For the Taking of Berlin," and "For Victory over Germany." Our unit returned to Zhitkovichi, and there we demined the fields. I learned by chance that my older brother was alive and living in Vileika.

With a recommendation for a Suvorov School, I escaped to Vileika. I found my brother there, and soon a sister came to join us. So we already had a family. We set up house in some attic. But it was hard with provisions until I put on my uniform, pinned my three medals to it, and went to the town council.

I came. Found a door with a sign plate: CHAIRMAN. Knocked. Went in and reported according to regulations: "Junior Sergeant Sigalev comes to petition for state provisions."

The chairman smiled and rose to meet me.

"Where do you live?" he asked.

"In an attic." And I gave him the address.

In the evening they brought us a sack of cabbage, two days later a sack of potatoes.

Once the chairman met me in the street and gave me an address: "Come in the evening, someone will be expecting you."

I was met by a woman. She was his wife. Her name was Nina Maximovna, his Alexei Mikhailovich. They gave me something to eat, I washed myself. My army things were now too small for me, so they gave me a couple of shirts.

I started coming to see them, first occasionally, then more often, then every day. A military patrol would meet me and ask, "Whose medals have you pinned on, lad? Where's your father?"

"I have no father . . ."

I had to carry my papers with me.

When Alexei Mikhailovich asked me, "Would you like to be our son?" I answered, "I'd like it very much."

They adopted me, gave me their last name—Kniazev.

For a long time I couldn't call them "papa" and "mama." Nina Maximovna loved me straight off, pitied me. If there was something sweet, it was always for me. She wanted to caress me. To be nice to me. But I didn't like sweets, because I had never eaten them. Our life before the war was poor, and in the army I got used to everything soldiers get. And I wasn't a gentle boy, because I had lived among men and hadn't seen any special gentleness for a long time. I didn't even know any gentle words.

Once I woke up during the night and heard Nina Maximovna weeping behind the partition. She had probably wept before, but she did it when I didn't see or hear it. She wept and complained, "He'll never be our own, he won't be able to forget his parents . . . His blood . . . There's so little of the child in him, and he isn't gentle." I went up to her quietly and put my arm around her neck: "Don't cry, mama." She stopped crying, and I saw her glistening eyes. It was the first time I had called her "mama." After a while I called my father "papa." Only one thing remained: I couldn't stop addressing them rather formally.

They didn't try to make me into a pampered boy, and I'm grateful to them for that. I had clear duties: to tidy up the house, to shake out the doormats, to bring firewood from the shed, to light the stove after school. Without them I wouldn't have been able to get a higher education. They instilled it in me that one must study, and after the war one must study well. Only well.

While still in the army, when our unit was stationed in Zhitkovichi, the commander had ordered Volodia Pochivadlov, Vitia Barinov, and me to study. The three of us sat at the same desk in the second grade. We carried weapons, and we didn't recognize any authority. We didn't want to obey civilian teachers: how can they give us orders if they're not in military uniform? The only authorities for us were commanders. A teacher walks in, the whole class rises, we go on sitting.

"Why are you sitting?"

"We're not going to answer you. We only obey our commander."

During the long break we lined up all the students by platoons and taught them to march and sing soldiers' songs.

The director of the school came to the unit and told the political commissar about our behavior. We were put in the guardhouse and demoted. Vovka Pochivadlov, who had been a sergeant major, became a sergeant; I had been a sergeant and became a junior sergeant. Vitka Barinov had been junior sergeant and became corporal. The commander had a long talk with each of us, trying to bring home to us that As and Bs in arithmetic were more important for us then than any medals. Our combat mission was to study well. We wanted to shoot, but they told us we had to study.

Even so we wore our medals to school. I keep a photo of myself wearing medals, sitting at the desk drawing for our Pioneer newspaper.

Whenever I brought an A home from school, I shouted from the porch, "Mama, I got an A!"

And it was so easy for me to say "mama" . . .

"WE EVEN FORGOT THAT WORD . . ."

Anya Gurevich

TWO YEARS OLD. NOW A RADIO ENGINEER.

Either I remember it, or mama told me later . . .

We walk down the street. It's hard for us to walk: mama is sick, my sister and I are small—my sister is three years old, I'm two. How could we be saved?

Mama wrote a note: last name, first name, year of birth. She put the note in my pocket and said, "Go." She showed me the house. There were children running around there . . . She wanted me to be evacuated with the orphanage; she was afraid we'd all be killed. She wanted to save at least one of us. I had to go alone: if mama were to take me there, they would send us both away. They took only children who had been left without parents, but I had mama. My whole fate lay in my going without looking back. Otherwise I would never have left mama, I would have thrown myself on her neck in tears, and no one would have forced me to stay in a strange house. My fate . . .

Mama said, "Go and open that door." So I did. But this orphanage did not have time to evacuate . . .

I remember a big room . . . And my little bed by the wall. And many such little beds. We had to make them ourselves, very carefully. The pillow always had to be in the same place. If we did it differently, the house mistresses scolded us, especially when some men in black suits came. Policemen or Germans—I don't know, I remember black suits. I don't remember that we were beaten, but there was the fear that you could be beaten for something. I don't remember our games . . . mischief . . . We were very active—tidied up, washed—but that was work. No childhood memories . . . laughter . . . fretting . . .

No one ever caressed us, but I didn't weep about mama. No one around me had a mama. We didn't even remember the word. We forgot it.

Here's how they fed us: they gave us a bowl of mash and a piece of bread a day. I didn't like mash and I gave my portion to a girl, and she gave me her piece of bread. We became friends because of it. Nobody paid any attention until one house mistress noticed our exchange. They put me on my knees in the corner. I spent a long time kneeling by myself. In a big empty room . . . To this day whenever I hear the word *mash* I immediately want to weep. When I grew up I couldn't understand why this word provoked such revulsion in me. I forgot about the orphanage . . .

I was already sixteen, no, probably seventeen . . . I met my house mistress from the orphanage. There was a woman sitting on a bus . . . I looked at her and felt drawn to her as if by a magnet, drawn so much that I missed my stop. I didn't know the woman, I didn't remember her, but I was drawn to her. I finally couldn't stand it, burst into tears, and got angry with myself: what's the matter with me? I looked at her as at a painting I had seen once, but had forgotten, and wanted to look at again. And there was something dear, maybe like mama . . . closer than mama, but who she was I didn't know. And this anger, these tears just gushed out of me! I turned away, went to the exit, stood there, and cried.

The woman saw it all, came up to me and said, "Don't cry, Anechka."

I cried still more from those words of hers. "But I don't know you."

"Look better!"

"I swear I don't know you." And I howled.

She led me off the bus.

"Look closely at me, you'll remember everything. I'm Stepanida Ivanovna . . ."

I stood my ground.

"I don't know you. I've never met you."

"Do you remember the orphanage?"

"What orphanage? You must be taking me for someone else."

"No, remember the orphanage . . . I was your house mistress."

"My papa was killed, but I have mama. What orphanage?"

I had forgotten about the orphanage, because I was already living with mama. At home. This woman gently stroked my head, but all the same my tears poured down. Then she said, "Here's my phone number . . . Call me if you want to learn about yourself. I remember you well. You were our littlest girl . . ."

She went away, and I couldn't move from the spot. I should, of course, have run after her, asked all sorts of questions. I didn't run and catch up with her.

Why didn't I? I was a wild thing, simply a wild thing. For me people were something alien, dangerous, I didn't know how to speak with anybody. I sat for hours talking to myself. Was afraid of everything.

Mama found me only in 1946 . . . I was eight years old. She had been taken to Germany together with my sister, where they somehow survived. When they came back, mama searched in all the orphanages in Belarus. She lost all hope of finding me. Yet I was right there . . . in Minsk. But evidently the little note mama had given me got lost, and I was registered under another last name. Mama looked at all the girls called Anya in the Minsk orphanages. She decided that I was her daughter by my eyes, and because I was tall. For a week she kept coming and looking at me: was I her Anechka or not? My first name had stayed with me. When I saw mama, some incomprehensible feelings came over me, I began to cry for no reason. No, those were not memories of something familiar, it was something else . . . People around me said, "Mama. Your mama." And some new world opened for me—mama! A mysterious door was thrown open . . . I knew nothing about people called "mama" and "papa." I was frightened, while others rejoiced. Everybody smiled at me.

Mama invited our prewar neighbor to come with her: "Find my Anechka here."

The neighbor immediately pointed at me.

"Here's your Anka! Don't hesitate, take her. Your eyes, your face . . ."

In the evening the house mistress came up to me: "Tomorrow you'll be picked up, you'll leave."

I was terrified.

In the morning they washed me, dressed me, everybody was nice to me. Our gruff old nanny smiled at me. I realized that this was my last day with them, that they were taking leave of me. Suddenly I didn't even feel like going anywhere. They changed me into everything mama brought—mama's shoes, mama's dress—and that way I was already separated from my orphanage friends . . . I stood among them like a stranger. And they gazed at me as if they were seeing me for the first time.

My greatest impression at home was the radio. There were no radio sets yet, but a black dish hung in the corner, and the sound came from there. I looked at it every moment. I ate and looked at it, went to bed and looked at it. How could people be there, how did they all get inside? Nobody could explain it to me, because I was unsociable. In the orphanage I had been friends with Tomochka. I liked her because she was cheerful, smiled often, and nobody liked me, because I never smiled. I began to smile when I was fifteen or sixteen years old. At school I used to hide my smile. I didn't want people to see me smile, I was embarrassed. I didn't know how to communicate, even with the girls: they would talk about all sorts of things during recess, and I couldn't say anything. I sat and was silent.

Mama took me from the orphanage, and a couple of days later we went to a market together. There I saw a policeman and had hysterics. I shouted, "Mama, Germans!"—and started to run.

Mama rushed after me, people surrounded me, and I was shaking all over: "Germans!"

After that I refused to go out for two days. Mama tried to explain to me that it was a policeman, who protects us and keeps order in the street, but I refused to be persuaded. No way . . . The Germans who came to our orphanage wore black army coats . . . True, when they took blood from us, they led us to a separate room and wore white smocks, but I didn't remember the white smocks. I remembered their black uniforms . . .

At home I couldn't get used to my sister. She should have been someone close, but I was seeing her for the first time in my life, and for some reason she was my sister. Mama was at work all day long. We woke up in the morning and she was already gone. There were two pots of kasha in the oven, we had to serve ourselves. I waited for mama all day long—as something extraordinary, as some sort of happiness. But she came home late, when we were already asleep.

I found a doll somewhere, not really a doll, only a doll's head. I loved it. It was my joy. I carried it around from morning till night. It was my only toy. I dreamed of having a ball. I would come out to the yard, all the children had balls, they carried them in special nets, that's how they were sold. I would ask, and they would let me hold it for a while.

I bought myself a ball when I was eighteen and got my first salary at the clock factory. My dream came true: I brought the ball and hung it up in its net. I was ashamed to go outside with it, because I was grown up, so I sat at home and looked at it.

Many years later I decided to go to Stepanida Ivanovna. I couldn't bring myself to do it, but my husband insisted: "Let's go together. How is it you don't want to find out anything about yourself?"

"It's not that I don't want to. I'm afraid."

I dialed her home number and heard the response: "Stepanida Ivanovna Dediulia has died . . ."

I can't forgive myself . . .

"YOU SHOULD GO TO THE FRONT, BUT YOU FALL IN LOVE WITH MY MAMA . . ."

Yania Chernina

TWELVE YEARS OLD. NOW A TEACHER.

An ordinary day . . . That day began as usual . . .

But while I was riding on the tram, people were already saying, "How awful! How awful!" and I couldn't understand what had happened. I came running home and saw my mama. She was kneading dough, and tears poured from her eyes. I asked, "What's happened?" The first thing she said was, "War! Minsk has been bombed . . ." And we had just come back to Rostov from Minsk, after visiting my aunt.

On the first of September we still went to school, but on the tenth the school was closed. The evacuation of Rostov began. Mama said that we must prepare to leave, but I protested: "What evacuation can there be?" I went to the regional Komsomol Committee and asked to join ahead of time. They refused, because the age for joining Komsomol was fourteen and I was only twelve. I thought that if I became a Komsomol member, I would be able to take part in everything right away, would become an adult at once. Would be able to go to the front.

Mama and I got on the train. We had only one suitcase, and there were two dolls in it, a big one and a little one. I remember mama didn't even resist when I put them in. I'll tell later how these dolls saved us . . .

We reached the Kavkazskaya station. The train was destroyed by bombs. We climbed onto some open flatcar. Where we were going we had no idea. We knew one thing: we were going away from the front line. From the battles. It poured rain. Mama covered me with herself. At the Baladzhary station near Baku we got off wet and black from the engine smoke. And hungry. Before the war we had lived modestly, very modestly. We didn't have nice things that we could take to the market to exchange or sell. Mama only had her passport with her. We sat at the train station and didn't know what to decide. Where to go. A soldier walked by, not even a soldier—a very little soldier, dark, with a sack on his shoulders, and carrying a mess tin. You could see he had just been taken into the army and was going to the front. He stopped near us. I clung to mama. He asked, "Where are you going, woman?"

Mama said, "I don't know. We're being evacuated."

He spoke Russian, but with a heavy accent.

"Don't be afraid of us, go to our *aul,** to my mother. All our men have been taken into the army: my father, me, my two brothers. She's all alone. Help her, and you'll survive together. I'll come back and marry your daughter."

And he told us his address. We had nowhere to write it down, so we memorized it: Musa Musaev, village of Kum, Evlakh station, Kakh district. I've remembered the address all my life, though we didn't go there. We were taken by a single woman who lived in a makeshift plywood hut, which had room only for a bed and a small bedside table. We slept on the floor sideways with our legs under the bed.

We were lucky to meet nice people . . .

I'll never forget how an officer came up to mama. They talked, and he told her that his whole family had been killed in Krasnodar, and that he was going to the front. His comrades shouted, called him to the train, and he stood there and couldn't leave us.

"I see that you're in distress. Allow me to leave you my army certificate. I have no one else left," he said suddenly.

---

* In the Caucasus, an *aul* is a fortified village, usually built against a cliffside or a steep slope.

Mama wept. But I understood it all in my own way. I started yelling at him.

"There's war . . . Your whole family got killed. You should go to the front and take revenge on the fascists, but you fall in love with my mama. Shame on you!"

He and my mother stand there, and they both have tears in their eyes, and I can't understand how my good mama can talk with such a bad man: he doesn't want to go to the front; he talks about love, but there can be love only in peacetime. Why did I decide that he was talking about love? He only mentioned his army certificate . . .

I also want to tell about Tashkent . . . Tashkent was my war. We lived in the dormitory of the factory where mama worked. It was in the center of the city, in the former club. Family people lived in the vestibule and the auditorium, and the "bachelors" lived on the stage—they were called "bachelors," but in fact they were workers whose families had been evacuated elsewhere. Mama and I were placed in a corner of the auditorium.

We were given coupons for thirty pounds of potatoes. Mama worked in the factory from morning till night, and I had to go and get these potatoes. I spent half a day waiting in a line, and then dragged the sack on the ground for four or five blocks, because I couldn't lift it. Children weren't allowed on public transportation, because there was flu going around and they had announced a quarantine. Just then . . . No matter how I begged, they wouldn't allow me on a bus. When I only had to cross the street to get to our dormitory, I ran out of strength, fell on the sack, and burst into sobs. Some strangers helped me: they brought me and the potatoes to the dormitory. I can still feel that weight. Each of those blocks . . . I couldn't abandon those potatoes, they were our salvation. I'd have died before abandoning them. Mama used to come back from work hungry, blue.

We were starving, and mama became as skinny as I was. The thought that I had to help somehow never left me. Once we had nothing to eat at all, and I decided to sell our only flannel blanket and buy some bread with the money. Children weren't allowed to sell things, and I was taken to the children's room at the police station. I sat there until they informed mama at the factory. When her shift was over, mama came to get me, but meanwhile I cried my eyes out from shame and from thinking that mama was hungry and there wasn't a crust of bread at home. Mama had bronchial asthma; during the night she coughed terribly and couldn't breathe. She had to swallow at least a little something to feel better. I always hid a bit of bread for her under the pillow. I would already be asleep, but even so I would remember that I had bread under the pillow, and I wanted terribly to eat it.

In secret from mama I went to get a job at the factory. I was such a little thing, a real starveling, and they didn't want to take me. I stood there and cried. Somebody took pity on me. They sent me to the accounting office to fill out work assignments and calculate salaries. I worked on a special machine, which was a prototype of the present-day calculator. Now it works noiselessly, but then it was like a tractor, and it worked with a lamp on. For twelve hours a day my head was like in the hot sun, and toward the end of the day I was deaf from the noise.

Something terrible happened to me: instead of 280 rubles salary, I calculated 80 for a worker who had six children. Nobody noticed my mistake till payday. I heard someone run down the corridor shouting "I'll kill her! I'll kill her! How am I going to feed my children?"

"Hide," they said to me. "It must be you he's after."

The door opened, I pressed myself to the machine, there was nowhere to hide. A big man ran in with something heavy in his hands.

"Where is she?"

They pointed at me: "There she is . . ."

He even leaned against the wall.

"Pah! There's nobody to kill, my own are like that." And he turned and walked away.

I just collapsed by the machine and burst into tears . . .

Mama worked at the technical control section of the same factory. The factory produced missiles for the *"katiushas,"* in two sizes—

thirty-five and seventeen pounds. The body of the missile was checked for its solidity under pressure. The missile was lifted, fixed to a socket, and submitted to the necessary pounds of pressure. If it passed the test, the missile was removed and put in a box. If it didn't, the thread was stripped, the missile took off with a whine and flew up to the ceiling, and then fell who knows where. There was this whining and the fear when the missiles flew off . . . Everybody hid under the machinery . . .

Mama shuddered and shouted during the night. I'd put my arms around her, and she would quiet down.

Nineteen forty-three was coming to an end . . . Our army was advancing. I realized that I had to study. I went to the director of the factory. He had a high desk in his office, and I couldn't be seen from behind it. I began a prepared speech: "I want to quit my factory job. I have to study."

The director became angry: "We don't allow anyone to quit. It's wartime."

"I make mistakes in orders, because I'm uneducated. I miscalculated a man's salary recently."

"You'll learn. I don't have enough people."

"But after the war educated people will be needed, not ignoramuses."

"Ah, you pipsqueak." The director got up from his desk. "So you know everything!"

At school I went to the sixth grade. During the lessons of literature and history the teachers talked to us, and we sat and knitted socks, mittens, tobacco pouches for the army. We knitted and memorized poetry. Recited Pushkin in chorus.

We were waiting for the war to end. It was such a cherished dream that mama and I were even afraid to talk about it. Mama was at work, and some commissioners passed through asking everybody, "What can you give to the defense fund?" They asked me, too. What did we have? We had nothing except some government bonds that mama had saved. Everybody gave something, how could we not give?! I gave them all the bonds.

I remember that when mama came home from work, she didn't scold me, she just said, "That was all we had, besides your dolls."

I parted with my dolls, too . . . Mama lost our monthly bread coupons, and we were literally perishing. And the saving idea came into my head of trying to trade my two dolls—the big one and the little one—for something. We went to the market with them. An old Uzbeck came up to us: "How much?" We said we had to survive for a month, because we had no coupons. The old Uzbeck gave us a big sack of rice. And we didn't starve to death. Mama swore, "I'll buy you two beautiful dolls as soon as we get back home."

When we got back to Rostov, she couldn't buy me any dolls, we were needy again. She bought them for me the day I graduated from the institute. Two dolls—a big one and a little one . . .

"IN THE LAST MOMENTS THEY SHOUTED THEIR NAMES . . ."

Artur Kuzeev

TEN YEARS OLD. NOW A HOTEL ADMINISTRATOR.

Someone was ringing the bell. Pulling and pulling . . .

Our church had long been closed, I don't even remember when it was closed. It had always been a kolkhoz warehouse. Grain was kept in it. Hearing the long-dead bell, the village was dumbstruck: "Calamity!" Mama . . . everybody rushed outside . . .

That was how the war began . . .

I close my eyes . . . I see . . .

Three Red Army soldiers are being led down the road, their arms tied behind them with barbed wire. They are in their underwear. Two are young, one an older man. They walk with their heads down.

They are shot near the school. On the road.

In the last moments they began to shout their names loudly in hopes that someone would hear and remember them. Inform their relatives.

I watched through a hole in the fence . . . I remember . . .

One was Vanechka Ballai, the other Roman Nikonov. And the one who was older shouted, "Long live Comrade Stalin!"

And right after that trucks began to move down that road. Heavy German trucks. And they lay there . . . Trucks with soldiers and ammunition rode over them. Followed by motorcycles. The Germans rode and rode. By day and by night. For many days.

And I kept repeating . . . I'd wake up at night and repeat: Vanechka Ballai, Roman Nikonov . . . The third man's name I didn't know . . .

"ALL FOUR OF US PULLED THAT SLEDGE . . ."

Zina Prikhodko

FOUR YEARS OLD. NOW A WORKER.

The bombing . . . The earth trembles, our house trembles . . .

Our house was small, with a garden. We hid in the house, closed the blinds. The four of us sit there: my two sisters, our mama, and me. Mama says that she closed the blinds and now it's not scary. And we agree that it's not scary, yet we're afraid. But we don't want to upset mama.

. . . We walked behind the cart, then someone sat us little ones on the bundles. For some reason it seemed to me that if I fell asleep I'd be killed, so I did all I could not to close my eyes, yet they closed on their own. Then my older sister and I decided that we'd take turns: first I'd close my eyes and sleep, then she, and the other one would watch that we weren't killed. But we both fell asleep and woke up from mama's cry: "Don't be afraid! Don't be afraid!" There was shooting ahead. People shouted . . . Mama pushed our heads down. But we wanted to look . . .

The shooting ended. We drove farther on. I saw that people were lying in a ditch beside the road, and I asked mama, "What are those people doing?"

"They're sleeping," mama replied.

"Why are they sleeping in a ditch?"

"Because it's war."

"Does that mean we'll sleep in a ditch, too? I don't want to sleep in a ditch." I began to fuss.

I stopped fussing when I saw that mama had tears in her eyes.

Where we were walking, where we were riding, of course I didn't know. I didn't understand. I remember only the word *Azarichi* and the wire, which mama didn't let us get close to. After the war I learned that we wound up in the Azarichi concentration camp. I even went there afterward, to that place. But what could you see there now? Grass, earth . . . All the usual things. If there's anything left, it's only in our memory . . .

When I talk about it, I bite my hands till they bleed, so as not to cry . . .

They bring mama from somewhere and lay her on the ground. We crawl up to her—I remember that we crawled, we didn't walk. We cry, "Mama! Mama!" I beg, "Mama, don't sleep!" And we're all bloody, because mama is all bloody. I think we didn't understand that it was blood and what blood was, but we did realize that it was something terrible.

Trucks came every day, people got into them and went away. We begged, "Mama, dear, let's go on a truck. Maybe it goes toward where grandma lives?" Why did we remember grandma? Because mama always said that our grandma lived nearby and didn't know where we were. She thought we were in Gomel. Mama didn't want to go on those trucks, she pulled us off each time. And we cried, insisted. One morning she agreed . . . Winter came, we were freezing . . .

I bite my hands so as not to cry. I can't hold back the tears . . .

We rode for a long time and someone told mama, or else she figured it out herself, that we were being taken to be shot. When the truck stopped, we were all told to get off. There was a farmstead there, and mama asked a convoy soldier, "Can we drink some water? My children are asking to drink." He allowed us to go into the cottage. We went in, and the woman gave us a big mug of water. Mama drank with small sips, slowly, and I thought, "I want so much to eat, why does mama want to drink?"

Mama drank up one mug, asked for another. The woman drew some water, gave it to her, and said that many people are taken to the forest every day and no one comes back.

"Do you have a back door that we could leave by?" mama asked.

The woman pointed—there it is. One door led to the street, the other to the yard. We ran out of the cottage and crawled. I think we didn't walk but crawled to our grandmother's house. How we crawled and for how long I don't remember.

Grandma put us on the stove, and mama on the bed. In the morning mama began to die. We sat there frightened and couldn't understand: how can mama die and leave us when papa isn't there? I remember mama calling us over, smiling.

"Children, don't ever quarrel."

Why would we quarrel? About what? We had no toys. A big stone was our doll. We had no candy. There was no mama to complain to.

In the morning grandma wrapped mama in a big white sheet and put her on a sledge. All four of us pulled that sledge . . .

Forgive me . . . I can't . . . I'm crying . . .

"THESE TWO BOYS BECAME LIGHT AS SPARROWS . . ."

Raya Ilyinkovskaya

FOURTEEN YEARS OLD. NOW A TEACHER OF LOGIC.

I'll never forget the smell of the lindens in our hometown, Yelsk.

During the war everything that had been before the war seemed the most beautiful in the world. That's how it stayed with me forever. To this day.

We were evacuated from Yelsk—mama, myself, and my younger brother. We stayed in the village of Gribanovka, near Voronezh, hoping to wait there for the war to end, but a few days after our arrival the Germans approached Voronezh. In our tracks.

We got on a freight car. They told us we'd be taken far to the east. Mama comforted us this way: "There'll be a lot of fruit there." We rode for a long time, because we spent a long time standing on side tracks. We didn't know where or for how long we would stay, so we would run out at the stations at great risk in order to get some water. We had a little woodstove burning all the time, and we cooked a bucket of millet on it for everybody in the car. We ate this kasha all the while we rode.

The train stopped at the Kurgan-Tyube station. Near Andijan . . . I was struck by the unfamiliar nature and struck so strongly that for a time I even forgot about the war. Everything was blooming, ablaze, there was so much sun. I became cheerful again. All the former things came back to me.

We were brought to the Kyzyl Yul kolkhoz. So much time has passed, but I remember all the names. I'm even surprised that I haven't forgotten them. I remember learning them at the time, repeating the unfamiliar words. We began to live in a school athletic hall, eight families together. Local people brought us some blankets and pillows. Uzbek blankets are made from multicolored pieces; the pillows are filled with cotton. I quickly learned to gather armfuls of dry cotton stems—we used them to heat the stove.

We didn't understand at once that the war was here, too. They gave us a little flour, but it wasn't enough, and it didn't last long. We began to starve. The Uzbeks were also starving. Together with the Uzbek boys, we ran after the carts, and were happy if something fell off. The greatest joy for us was oil cake, oil cake from linseed, the one from the cottonseed was very hard, yellow, like from peas.

My brother Vadik was six years old. Mama and I left him at home alone and went to work in the kolkhoz. We hilled up rice, gathered cotton. My hands hurt from being unaccustomed, I couldn't fall asleep at night. One evening mama and I came home, and Vadik came running to meet us with three sparrows hanging on a string from his shoulder, and a sling in his hand. He had already washed his "hunting" trophies in the river and waited for mama to start cooking a soup. He was so proud! Mama and I ate the soup and praised it, but the sparrows were so skinny there wasn't a single gleam of fat in the pot. Only my brother's happy eyes gleamed over it.

He made friends with an Uzbek boy who once came to us with his grandmother. She looked at the boys, wagged her head, and said something to mama. Mama didn't understand, but then the foreman stopped by, who knew Russian. He translated for us: "She's talking with her God, with Allah. And complaining to him that war is the business of men, of warriors. Why should children suffer? How did Allah allow that these two boys became light as the sparrows they shoot with a sling?" The grandmother poured a handful of dry golden apricots on the table—hard and sweet as sugar! They could be sucked, nibbled in small bites, and then the stone could be cracked and the crunchy kernel eaten.

Her grandson looked at these apricots, and his eyes were also hungry. They were burning! Mama became confused, but the grandmother patted her hand and hugged her grandson. "He always has a bowl of *katek,* because he lives at home with his grandmother," the foreman translated. *Katek* is sour goat's milk. All the while we were in evacuation, my brother and I thought it was the tastiest thing in the world.

The grandmother and the boy left, and the three of us went on sitting at the table. No one ventured to be the first to reach out and take a dry golden apricot . . .

"I WAS EMBARRASSED TO BE WEARING GIRLS' SHOES . . ."

Marlen Robeichikov

ELEVEN YEARS OLD. NOW SECTION HEAD
IN A TOWN COUNCIL.

I saw the war from a tree . . .

The grown-ups forbade us to do it, but we climbed the trees anyway and watched the dogfights from tall firs. We wept when our planes burned, but there was no fear, as if we were watching a movie. On the second or third day there was a general roll call, and the director announced that our Pioneer camp was being evacuated. We already knew that Minsk was being bombarded and burning, and that we wouldn't be taken home, but somewhere farther away from the war.

I want to tell you how we prepared for the road . . . We were told to take suitcases and put in only the most necessary things: T-shirts, shirts, socks, handkerchiefs. We packed them, and each of us put his Pioneer neckerchief on top. In our childish imagination we pictured meeting the Germans, who would open our suitcases and there would be our Pioneer neckerchief. This would be our revenge for everything . . .

Our train was speedier than the war. It got ahead of it . . . When we stopped at stations, people there didn't know about the war, hadn't seen it. And we children told the adults about the war: how Minsk was burning, how our camp was bombed, how our planes burned.

But the farther we moved away from home, the more we expected our parents to come and take us, and we didn't suspect that many of us no longer had any parents. This thought couldn't even occur to us. We talked about the war, but we were still children of peace.

From the train we were transferred to a steamboat, *The Paris Commune,* and taken down the Volga. By then we had been traveling for two weeks, and we had not undressed even once. On the steamboat I took off my sneakers for the first time. They allowed us to. I had rubber-soled lace-up sneakers. When I took them off, they really stank! I tried to wash them and then threw them out. I came to Khvalynsk barefoot.

So many of us had arrived that two Belorussian orphanages were created, one for schoolchildren, the other for preschoolers. How do I know about it? Because those who had to be separated from a brother or a sister cried very much, especially the younger ones, who were afraid to lose the older ones. When we were left without our parents in the Pioneer camp, it was interesting, like a game, but now we all became frightened. We had been raised at home, were used to having parents, parental care. My mother always woke me up in the morning and kissed me goodnight. Near us was an orphanage for "real" orphans. We were very different from them. They were used to living without parents, but we had to get used to it.

I remember the food in 1943: a spoonful of scalded milk and a piece of bread a day, boiled beets, in summer a soup made from watermelon rinds. We saw a film, *March–April*. There was a story in it about our scouts cooking kasha from birch bark. Our girls also learned to cook birch-bark soup.

In the fall we stocked up on firewood ourselves. Each one had a norm—three cubic feet. The forest was in the hills. We had to fell the trees, trim them, then cut them into three-foot lengths and stack them up. The norm was supposed to be for an adult, but we also had girls working with us. We boys had a bigger share of the work. At home we never had to use a saw, because we were all city boys, but here we had to saw very thick logs. Split them.

We were hungry day and night, while working and while sleeping. We were always hungry, especially in winter. We used to run over from the orphanage to an army unit, and often were lucky to get a ladle of soup there. But there were many of us, they couldn't feed us all. If you came first, you got something; if you were late, you got nothing. I had a friend, Mishka Cherkasov. We were sitting once and he said, "I'd go fifteen miles now if I knew I'd get a bowl of kasha." It was minus twenty outside, but he got dressed and ran to the army unit. He asked the soldiers for something to eat. They said they had a little soup—go, boy, fetch your tin. He went out and saw children from the other orphanage coming, so if he ran to get a tin, there'd be nothing left.

He went back and said to the soldiers, "Pour it here!" And he took his hat off and held it out to them instead of a tin. He looked so resolute that the soldier just poured a whole ladle for him. With a heroic air, Misha went past the orphans who were left with nothing and came running back to his orphanage. His ears were frostbitten, but he brought us the soup, which was no longer soup, but a hatful of ice. We turned this ice out onto a plate, and while the girls rubbed Misha's ears, we ate it as it was, without waiting for it to thaw. There was so much joy on his face over bringing it for everybody that he didn't even start eating first!

The tastiest food for us was oil cake. We distinguished it by varieties according to taste, and one variety was called "halva." We conducted "Operation Cake." Several of us got onto a moving truck and threw down chunks of cake, and the others picked them up. We came back to the orphanage covered with bruises, but we had eaten. And of course there were the summer and autumn markets! That was a good time for us. We'd try a bit of everything: a piece of apple from one market woman, a piece of tomato from another. To steal something at a market wasn't regarded as shameful, on the contrary—it was heroism! We didn't care what we pilfered, so long as it was something to eat. What it was didn't matter.

There was a boy studying in our class who was the son of the director of an oil factory. We were children, we sat in class and played "naval battle." And he sat behind us eating bread with vegetable oil. The smell filled the whole classroom.

We exchanged whispers, shook our fists at him, meaning just wait till the class is over . . .

We look—our teacher isn't there, she's lying on the floor. She was hungry and also smelled this oil. And fainted. Our girls took her home; she lived with her mother. In the evening we decided that beginning that day each of us would set aside a small piece of bread to give to our teacher. She would never have taken it from us, so we secretly gave it to her mother and asked her not to tell it was from us.

We had our orchard and our kitchen garden. In the orchard we had apple trees, and in the kitchen garden—cabbages, carrots, beets. We guarded them, several of us taking turns on duty. In changing watch, we counted everything: each head of cabbage, each carrot. During the night I thought, "Ah, if only one more carrot would grow overnight! It wouldn't be on the list and could be eaten." If it had been put on the list, God forbid it should disappear. For shame!

We sat at the kitchen garden with food all around us, and held ourselves back. We were terribly hungry. Once I was on duty with an older boy. An idea came to his head.

"Look, there's a cow grazing . . ."

"Well, what of it?"

"Fool! Don't you know there's a decree that if a private cow grazes on government land, it's either taken away or the owner gets fined?"

"But it's grazing in a meadow."

"It's not tied to it."

And he explains his plan to me: we take the cow, bring it to our orchard, and tie it up there. Then we go looking for the owner. And so we did. We brought the cow to our orphanage orchard and tied it up. My partner ran to the village, found the woman who owned the cow: thus and so, your cow is in the government-owned orchard, and you know the decree . . .

I don't think . . . Now I doubt that the woman believed us and was frightened. She actually felt sorry for us, seeing we were hungry. We made this arrangement: we look after her cow, and she gives us several potatoes for it.

One of our girls fell ill and needed a blood transfusion. There wasn't a single child in the whole orphanage who could give blood. Do you understand?

Our dream? To get to the front. Several boys, the most reckless ones, got together and decided to escape. As luck would have it, an army choirmaster came to the orphanage, Captain Gordeev. He chose four musical boys, including me. That was how I wound up at the front.

The whole orphanage came to see us off. I had nothing to wear, and one girl gave me her sailor suit, and another had two pairs of shoes and gave one to me.

Thus equipped I went to the front. Most of all I was embarrassed to be wearing girls' shoes . . .

"I SCREAMED AND SCREAMED . . .
I COULDN'T STOP . . ."

Liuda Andreeva

FIVE YEARS OLD. NOW AN AUDITOR.

The war left me with the impression of a bonfire . . . Burning and burning. Endlessly . . .

We little children would get together, and you know what we talked about? That before the war we had liked sweet rolls and tea with sugar, and that we would never have them again.

Our mamas often wept, they wept every day . . . So we tried to cry less than in peacetime. We fussed less.

I knew that my mama was young and beautiful. Other children's mamas were older, but at the age of five I understood that it was bad for us that mama was young and beautiful. It was dangerous. I figured it out at the age of five . . . I even understood that it was good that I was little. How could a child understand that? Nobody explained anything to me . . .

After so many years . . . I'm afraid to remember it . . . to touch it . . .

A German truck stopped by our house, not on purpose, but something broke down in it. The soldiers came into the house, sent me and grandma into another room, and made mama help them. They boiled water, cooked supper. They spoke so loudly that it seemed to me they weren't talking together and laughing, but yelling at my mama.

It was evening, already dark. Nighttime. Suddenly mama runs

into the room, grabs me, and runs outside. We had no garden, the courtyard was empty, we ran around and didn't know where to hide. We got under the truck. They came out and looked for us with a flashlight. Mama lay on top of me, and I heard her teeth chatter. She turned cold, cold all over.

In the morning, when the Germans left, we went into the house . . . Grandma lay on the bed . . . tied to it with ropes . . . Naked! Grandma . . . My grandma! Horrified . . . Frightened, I began to scream. Mama pushed me outside. I screamed and screamed . . . I couldn't stop . . .

For a long time I was afraid of trucks. As soon as I heard the sound of a truck, I began to tremble. The war ended, we were already going to school . . . I would see a tram coming, and I couldn't help myself, my teeth chattered. From trembling. In our class there were three of us who had lived under the occupation. One boy was afraid of the noise of planes. In spring it was warm, the teacher would open the windows . . . The noise of a plane . . . or of a truck driving . . . This boy's eyes and mine would grow big, the pupils would get dilated, we'd panic. And the children who had been evacuated and came back laughed at us.

They fired the first salute . . . People ran outside, and mama and I hid in a ditch. We sat there until the neighbors came: "Come out—this isn't the war, it's the Victory celebration."

How I wanted children's toys! I wanted a childhood . . . We would take a piece of brick and pretend it was a doll. Or the smallest of us pretended that he was a doll. Today, if I see pieces of colored glass in the sand, I want to pick them up. They look beautiful to me even now.

I grew up . . . And someone said, "You're so beautiful. Like your mama." I wasn't glad, I got scared. I've never liked to hear those words said to me . . .

"WE ALL JOINED HANDS . . ."

Andrei Tolstik

SEVEN YEARS OLD. NOW A DOCTOR OF ECONOMICS.

I was a little boy . . .

I remember my mama . . . She baked the best bread in the village, she had the most beautiful kitchen garden beds. The biggest dahlias blossomed in our front garden and backyard. She embroidered beautiful shirts for us all—my father, my two older brothers, and me. The collars were embroidered. In red, blue, and green cross-stitch . . .

I don't remember who it was who first told me that mama had been shot. Some neighbor woman. I ran home. They said, "She was shot outside the village, not at home." My father was away with the partisans, my older brothers were with the partisans, my cousin was with the partisans. I went to our neighbor, old Karp.

"Mama's been killed. We must bring her here."

We harnessed a cow (we didn't have a horse) and went. Old Karp left me near the forest: "You stay here. I'm old, I'm not afraid to be killed. But you're a kid."

I waited. With all sorts of thoughts in my head. What will I tell father? How am I to tell him that mama was killed? And also a child's thinking—if I see mama dead, she'll never be alive again. But if I don't see her dead, I'll come home and she'll be there.

Mama's chest was shot through with a submachine gun volley. In a row across her blouse . . . And a black one on her temple . . . I wanted them to quickly put a white kerchief on her head so as not to see this black hole. It felt as if it still hurt her.

I didn't get into the cart, I walked beside it . . .

Every day they buried someone in the village . . . I remember four partisans being buried. Three men and a girl. We buried partisans often, but it was the first time I saw a woman buried. They dug a separate little grave for her . . . She lay alone on the grass under an old pear tree . . . Old women sat by her and stroked her hands . . .

"Why did they lay her there separately?" I asked.

"She's a young one . . ." the women replied.

When I was left alone, without family, without relations, I became frightened. What to do? They took me to the village of Zalesye to Aunt Marfa. She had no children of her own, and her husband was fighting at the front. We would hide in the cellar. She used to press my head to hers: "My dear son . . ."

Aunt Marfa came down with typhus. After her I came down with it. The old woman Zenka took me in. She had two sons fighting at the front. I would wake up at night, and she was there dozing next to me on the bed: "My dear son . . ." Everybody fled from the Germans to the forest, but old Zenka stayed with me. Never once did she leave me. "We'll die together, my dear son."

After the typhus I couldn't walk for a long time. If the road was level I could, but if it was slightly uphill my legs gave way. We were already expecting our soldiers. The women went to the forest, gathered some strawberries. There was nothing else to treat them with.

The soldiers came tired. Old Zenka poured some red strawberries into their helmets. They all offered me some. But I sat on the ground and couldn't get up.

Father came back from the partisans. He knew I had been ill, and he brought me a slice of bread and a piece of lard thick as a finger. The lard and the bread smelled of tobacco. Everything smelled of father.

We heard the word *Victory!* while gathering sorrel in the meadow. The children all joined hands and ran to the village like that . . .

"WE DIDN'T EVEN KNOW HOW TO BURY . . .
BUT NOW WE SOMEHOW RECALLED IT . . ."

Mikhail Shinkarev
THIRTEEN YEARS OLD. NOW A RAILROAD WORKER.

Our neighbors had a deaf daughter . . .

Everybody shouted "War! War!" but she would come running to my sister with her doll, sing little songs. Other children no longer even laughed. "Good for her," I thought, "she hasn't heard anything about the war."

My friends and I wrapped our red badges and red neckerchiefs in oilcloth and buried them among the bushes near the river. In the sand. Some conspirators! We came to that place every day.

Everybody was afraid of the Germans, even the children and the dogs. Mama used to put eggs out on the bench near the house. Outside. So as not to have them come into the cottage and ask, *"Jude?"* My sister and I had curly black hair . . .

We were swimming in the river . . . And we saw something black rising from the bottom. Just at that moment! We thought it was a sunken log, but this something was being pushed by the current to the bank, and we made out arms, a head . . . We saw that it was a man. I think no one got scared. No one cried out. We remembered the adults saying that our machine-gun operator had been killed at that spot and fell into the water with his "coffee grinder."

Just a few months of war . . . And we already didn't have any fear at the sight of death. We pulled the man out of the water and buried him. Someone fetched a shovel, and we dug a hole. Put him in and covered him with soil. Stood around silently. One girl even made the sign of the cross. Her grandmother used to help in the church, and the girl knew some prayers.

We did everything by ourselves. Without adults. Before the war we didn't even know how to bury. But now we somehow recalled it.

For two days we kept diving for the machine gun . . .

"HE GATHERED THEM IN A BASKET . . ."

Leonid Sivakov

SIX YEARS OLD. NOW A TOOLMAKER.

The sun was already up . . .

The herdsmen were rounding up the cows. The punitive squad soldiers gave them time to drive the herd beyond the river Greza and started on a round of the cottages. They came with a list, and they shot people according to the list. They read: mother, grandmother, the children so-and-so, of such-and-such age . . . They checked the list. If anyone was missing, they would start searching. They'd find a child under the bed, under the stove . . .

Once they had found everybody, they shot them . . .

Six people gathered in our cottage: grandmother, mama, my older sister, me, and my two younger brothers. Six people . . . Through the window we saw them going to our neighbors, and we ran to the entryway with my youngest brother and shut the door with a hook. Sat on a trunk, huddling around mama.

The hook was weak, the German tore it off at once. He stepped across the threshold and fired a burst. I had no time to make out whether he was young or old. We all fell down, I ended up behind the trunk . . .

I came to for the first time when I felt something dripping on me . . . Drip-drip, like water. I raised my head: it was mama's blood dripping. Mama lay there dead. I crawled under the bed, everything was covered with blood . . . I was all soaked with blood . . .

I heard two men come in. They counted how many people were killed. One says, "There's one missing. We should make a search." They started searching, bent down to look under the bed, and there was a sack of grain mama had hidden there, and I lay behind it. They pulled the sack out and went off pleased. They forgot that one person on the list was missing. They left, and I lost consciousness . . .

The second time I came to was when our cottage began to burn . . .

I felt terribly hot and also nauseous. I could see I was covered with blood, but I didn't realize I was wounded, because I didn't feel any pain. The cottage was filled with smoke . . . I somehow crawled out to the kitchen garden, then to the neighbor's orchard. Only then did I feel that I was wounded in the leg and my arm was broken. The pain just hit me. For some time I again lost all memory . . .

The third time consciousness returned to me was when I heard a woman's terrible scream . . . I crawled toward it . . .

The scream hung in the air. I crawled toward it as if following a thread and wound up by a kolkhoz garage. I didn't see anyone . . . The scream came from somewhere under the ground . . . Then I figured out that someone was screaming in the inspection pit . . .

I couldn't stand up, so I crawled and bent down . . . The pit was full of people . . . These were all refugees from Smolensk who had been living in our school. Some twenty families. They all lay in the pit, and on top a wounded girl kept trying to get up and then fell back. And screamed. I looked around: where was I to crawl to now? The whole village was burning . . . And no living people . . . Only this girl. I fell down to her . . . I don't know how long I lay there.

I felt that the girl was dead. I nudged her and called to her—she didn't respond. I alone was alive, and they were all dead. The sun was warm, there was steam coming from the warm blood. My head spun . . .

I lay there for a long time, sometimes conscious, sometimes not. We had been shot on Friday, and on Saturday grandfather and mama's sister came from another village. They found me in the pit, lay me in a wheelbarrow. The wheelbarrow jolted, I was in pain, but I had no voice. I could only cry . . . I didn't talk for a long time. For seven years . . . I whispered a little, but no one could make out my words. After seven years I began to pronounce one word well, then another . . . I listened to myself . . .

At the place where our cottage had been grandfather gathered bones in a basket . . . The basket wasn't even full . . .

So I've told you . . . Is that all? All that's left of such horror? A few dozen words . . .

"THEY TOOK THE KITTENS OUT OF THE COTTAGE . . ."

Tonia Rudakova

FIVE YEARS OLD. NOW DIRECTOR OF A KINDERGARTEN.

The first year of the war . . . I remember little . . .

The Germans arrived in the morning; it was still gray outside. They lined everybody up on the meadow and ordered all those who had cropped heads to step forward. These were prisoners of war whom people had taken into their homes. They drove them into the woods and shot them.

Before that we used to run around outside the village. We played near the woods. But now we got scared.

I remember mama baking bread. A lot of bread: it lay on the benches, on the table, on towels on the floor, in the entryway. I was surprised.

"Mama, what do we need so much bread for? Those men have been shot. Who are you going to feed?"

She chased me out of the house. "Go play with the children . . ."

I was afraid that mama would be killed and followed her all the time.

During the night the partisans took the bread. Never again did I see so much bread. The Germans picked all the cottages clean, and we were starving. I didn't understand . . . I asked mama, "Heat the oven and bake bread. Lots and lots."

That's all I remember from the first year of the war . . .

I probably grew older, because I remember more from later on. How our village was burned down . . . First they shot us, then they burned us. I came back from the other world . . .

They didn't shoot people outside, but came into the cottages. We all stood by the window.

"Now they're going to shoot Aniska . . ."

"They've finished at Aniska's. They're going to Aunt Anfisa's . . ."

And we stood there, we waited. They were coming to shoot us. Nobody cried, nobody shouted. We stood there. We had a neighbor and her little sons with us. She said, "Let's go outside. They don't shoot people outside."

They came into the front yard: the first one was a soldier, the second an officer. The officer was tall, his boots were tall, his cap was tall. I remember it very well . . .

They started pushing us toward the house. Our neighbor fell on the grass and kissed the officer's boots. "We won't go. We know you'll shoot us there."

They shout, "*Zurük! Zurük!*"—meaning "Go back." In the house mama was sitting on a bench by the table. And I remember that she took a little mug of milk and began to feed our little brother. It was so quiet that we heard him slurping.

I sat in a corner and put a broom in front of me. There was a long tablecloth on the table. Our neighbor's son hid under the table. Under the tablecloth. My brother got under the bed. And the neighbor knelt by the door and pleaded for everybody.

"Dear sir, we have little children. Many little children . . ."

I remember her pleading. For a long time.

The officer went to the table, lifted up the tablecloth, and fired. A cry came from there. He fired again. The neighbor's son cried out . . . He fired five times . . .

He looked at me . . . No matter how I tried to hide behind the broom, I couldn't do it. He had such beautiful brown eyes . . . Just think, I remember that . . . I was so frightened that I asked, "Are you going to kill me, mister?" He didn't say anything. Just then the soldier came out from the other room. I mean . . . he tore down the big curtain dividing the rooms, that's all. He called the officer and showed him—there were little kittens lying on the bed. There was no cat, just the kittens. They picked them up, smiled, started playing with them. They finished playing, and the officer gave them to the soldier to be taken outside. They took the kittens out of the cottage . . .

I remember my dead mama's hair burning . . . And, next to her, our little brother's swaddling clothes . . . My older brother and I crawled over them, me holding on to his pant leg: first to the backyard, then to the kitchen garden. We hid among the potatoes till evening, then we crawled into the bushes. There I burst into tears . . .

How did we manage to stay alive? I don't remember . . . My brother and I and the four kittens stayed alive. Our grandmother, who lived across the river, came and took us all . . .

"REMEMBER:
6 PARK STREET, MARIUPOL . . ."

Sasha Solianin

**FOURTEEN YEARS OLD. NOW A
FIRST-DEGREE WAR INVALID.**

I really didn't want to die . . . I especially didn't want to die at dawn . . .

We are being led out to be shot. We walk quickly. The Germans are in a hurry somewhere, I understood it from their conversation. Before the war I liked German lessons. I even learned several poems of Heine's by heart. There are three of us—two first lieutenants, prisoners of war, and me. A boy . . . I was caught in the forest when I was gathering weapons. Several times I escaped, the third time they got me.

I didn't want to die . . .

I hear a whisper: "Run for it! We'll attack the convoy, and you jump into the bushes."

"I won't . . ."

"Why?"

"I'm staying with you."

I wanted to die with them. Like a soldier.

"We order you: run for it! Live!"

One, Danila Grigorievich Iordanov, was from Mariupol . . . the other, Aleksandr Ivanovich Ilyinsky, from Briansk . . .

"Remember: 6 Park Street, Mariupol . . . You remember?"

". . . Street . . . Briansk . . . You remember?"

Shooting began . . .

I started running . . . I ran . . . It throbbed in my head: *rat-a-tat-tat* . . . remember . . . *rat-a-tat-tat* . . . remember. And out of fear I forgot. I forgot the name of the street and the house number in Briansk.

"I HEARD HIS HEART STOP . . ."

Lena Aronova

TWELVE YEARS OLD. NOW A LAWYER.

Our city suddenly became militarized. Our quiet and green Gomel . . .

My parents decided to send me to Moscow, where my brother was studying at the military academy. Everybody thought that Moscow would never be taken, that it was an impregnable fortress. I didn't want to leave, but my parents insisted, because when we were bombed, I couldn't eat for whole days, they had to force the food on me. I became noticeably thinner. Mama decided that Moscow was calm, that Moscow would be good for me. That I'd get better there. And she and papa would come as soon as the war was over. Very soon.

The train didn't reach Moscow; we were told to get off in Maloyaroslavets. There was a long-distance telephone at the train station, and I kept calling my brother to find out what to do next. I finally reached him and he said, "Sit and wait, I'll come to get you." It was an anxious night; there were a great many people. Suddenly it was announced: in half an hour a train will be leaving for Moscow, get aboard. I collected my luggage, ran to the train, climbed to the upper shelf and fell asleep. When I woke up the train was standing by a small river; women were doing laundry. "Where's Moscow?" I asked in astonishment. They replied that we were being taken to the east . . .

I got out of the car and burst into tears from resentment, from despair. And—oh! Dina, my friend, caught sight of me. We left

Gomel together, our mamas saw us off together, but in Maloyaroslavets we lost each other. Now there were two of us, and I wasn't so
frightened. At the stops people brought food to the train: sandwiches,
canned milk on carts, once they even brought soup.

They dropped us off at the Djarkul station, in the Kustanai region.
For the first time Dina and I rode on a wagon. We reassured each
other, saying that once we arrived we would immediately write
home. I said, "If our houses aren't destroyed, our parents will get our
letters, but if they are—where shall we write to?" My mama was the
head doctor of a children's hospital, and papa was director of a technical school. My papa was a peaceful man, he looked the teacher all
over. When he came home from work for the first time with a pistol
(they had given out pistols), and he put the holster over his suit jacket,
I got scared. I think he was also scared of it. In the evenings he took
it off carefully and put it on the table. We lived in a big house, but
there were no military in it, and I had never seen weapons before. It
seemed to me that the pistol would start shooting by itself, that the
war was already living in our home. When papa took off the pistol,
the war would be over.

Dina and I were city girls, we didn't know how to do anything.
The day after our arrival, we were sent to work in the fields. We spent
the whole day bent over. I got dizzy and fell down. Dina stood over
me and wept, but she didn't know how to help me. We were ashamed:
the local girls fulfilled the norm; we would reach the middle of the
field, and they'd already be far ahead. The most terrible thing was
when I was sent to milk the cow. They handed me a milk pail, but I
had never milked a cow and was afraid to go near it.

Once someone came from the station and brought newspapers.
We read in them that Gomel had been taken, and Dina and I wept a
lot. If Gomel was taken, it meant that our parents were dead, and we
had to go to the orphanage. I didn't want even to hear about an orphanage, I intended to go looking for my brother. But Dina's parents
came to get us. They found us by some miracle. Her father worked as

a head doctor in the town of Saraktash, the Chkalov region. There was a small house on the grounds of the hospital, and we lived in it. We slept on wooden bunks, on mattresses stuffed with straw. I suffered very much because of my long braids, which reached below my knees. I couldn't cut them off without mama's permission. I still hoped that mama was somehow alive and would find me. Mama loved my braids and would scold me if I cut them off.

Once . . . at dawn . . . Such things happen only in fairy tales, and also in war. There was a knocking on the window . . . I got up: my mama was standing there. I fainted . . . Soon mama cut off my braids and rubbed my head with kerosene to get rid of the lice.

Mama already knew that papa's school had been evacuated to Novosibirsk, and we went to join him. There I began going to school. In the morning we studied, and after lunch we went to help in the hospital. There were many wounded who had been sent from the front to the rear. We were taken as paramedics. I was sent to the surgery section, the most difficult one. They gave us old sheets. We tore them to make bandages, rolled them up, put them in containers, and took them to be sterilized. We also laundered old bandages, but lots of bandages came from the front in such condition that we carried them out in baskets and buried them in the backyard. They were all soaked with blood, with pus . . .

I grew up in a doctor's family and dreamed before the war of becoming a doctor. If it was surgery, let it be surgery. Other girls were afraid, but I didn't care, as long as I could help, could feel I was needed. The lessons ended, and we ran quickly to the hospital, so as to come in time, not to be late. I remember fainting several times. When they unbandage the wound, it all gets stuck, the men scream . . . Several times I became nauseous from the smell of the bandages. They smelled very strongly, not with medications but . . . with something . . . unfamiliar, suffocating . . . Death . . . I already knew the smell of death. You come to the ward—the wounded man is still alive, but there's already this smell . . . Many girls left, they couldn't stand it. They sewed mittens for the front; those who knew how—knitted. But I couldn't leave the hospital—how could I if everybody knew that my mama was a doctor?

But I cried very much when the wounded men died. When they were dying they called out, "Doctor! Doctor! Quick!" A doctor comes running, but he can't save him. The wounded in the surgical section were serious ones. I remember one lieutenant . . . He asked me for a hot-water bottle. I gave it to him, he seized my hand . . . I couldn't take it away . . . He pressed it to himself. He held on to me, held on with all his strength. I heard his heart stop. It beat, beat, and then stopped . . .

I learned so much during the war . . . More than during my whole life . . .

"I RAN AWAY TO THE FRONT FOLLOWING MY SISTER, FIRST SERGEANT VERA REDKINA . . ."

Nikolai Redkin

ELEVEN YEARS OLD. NOW A MECHANIC.

The house became quiet . . . Our family grew smaller.

My older brothers were called up to the army at once. My sister Vera kept going to the recruiting office and in March 1942 also left for the front. Only my younger sister and I stayed at home.

In the evacuation we were taken by our relations in the Orel region. I worked in the kolkhoz. There weren't any men left; all the men's tasks lay on the shoulders of those like me. Adolescents. We replaced the men—boys from nine to fourteen. I went to plow for the first time. The women stood next to their horses and urged them on. I stood there waiting for someone to come and teach me, and they went down one furrow and turned to the second one. I was alone. All right, so I drove by myself, off the furrow or along it. In the morning I was in the field, and at night tending the horses with the boys in the pasture. One day like that, two . . . On the third day I plowed and plowed and collapsed.

In 1944 my sister Vera came to us for one day on her way from the hospital after being wounded. In the morning she was taken to the train station in a wagon, and I ran after her on foot. At the station a soldier refused to let me on the train: "Who are you with, boy?"

I wasn't at a loss: "I'm with First Sergeant Vera Redkina."

That's how I made it to the war . . .

"IN THE DIRECTION OF THE SUNRISE . . ."

Valya Kozhanovskaya

TEN YEARS OLD. NOW A WORKER.

A child's memory . . . Only fear or something good stays in a child's memory . . .

Our house stood near an army hospital. The hospital was bombed, and I saw wounded men on crutches fall out of the windows. Our house caught fire . . . Mama ran into the flames: "I'll get some clothes for the children."

Our house burned . . . Our mama burned . . . We rushed after her, but people caught us and held us back: "You won't save your mama, children." We ran where everybody else did. There were dead people lying around . . . The wounded moaned, asked for help. How could we help them? I was eleven, my sister nine. We lost each other . . .

We met again in the orphanage of Ostroshitsk village, near Minsk. Before the war our father took us there to a Pioneer camp. A beautiful place. The Germans turned the Pioneer camp into an orphanage. Everything was both familiar and alien. For several days there was nothing but weeping, nothing but tears: we were left without parents, our house was burned down. The house mistresses were the same, but the rules were German. A year later . . . I think it was a year later . . . they began selecting children to be taken to Germany. They selected not by age but by size, and unfortunately I was tall, like our father, while my sister was short, like our mother. The trucks came. They were surrounded by Germans with submachine guns. I was driven onto a truck. My sister cried, they pushed her, fired under her feet to keep her from coming to me. So we were separated . . .

The train car. Jam-packed . . . A whole car full of children, none older than thirteen. Our first stop was Warsaw. No one gave us anything to eat or drink, only some little old man came with his pockets full of folded pieces of paper on which the prayer "Our Father" was written in Russian. He gave each of us one of these papers.

After Warsaw we rode for two more days. Were brought to what seemed to be a sanitation center. Were all stripped naked, boys and girls together. I wept from shame. The girls wanted to be on one side, the boys on the other, but we were all herded together and they aimed a hose at us . . . With cold water . . . With some strange smell I never met with afterward, and I don't know what disinfectant was in it. They paid no attention whether it was eyes, or mouth, or ears—they performed their sanitary treatment. Then they handed us striped trousers and tops like pajamas, wooden sandals for our feet, and on our chests were pinned metal labels saying *Ost* ("East").

They drove us outside and lined us up as for a roll call. I thought they would take us somewhere, to some camp, but someone whispered behind me, "We're going to be sold." An old German man came over, selected three girls and myself, paid the money and pointed to a wagon with some straw in it: "Get in!"

We were brought to some estate . . . There was a big, tall house with an old park around it. We were housed in a shed. Half of it was occupied by twelve dogs, the other half by us. At once there was work for us in the field—to gather stones, so that plows and seeders didn't break. The stones had to be stacked neatly in one place. In our wooden sandals, our feet got all covered with blisters. We were fed with bad bread and skim milk.

One girl couldn't bear it and died. They drove her body to the forest on a horse drawn cart and put her in the ground just like that. The wooden sandals and striped pajamas were brought back to the estate. I remember her name was Olya.

There was a very old German man there who fed the dogs. He

spoke very poor Russian, but he tried to encourage us saying, *"Kinder, Hitler kaput. Russky kom."* He would go to the chicken coop, steal some eggs in his hat, and hide them in his toolbox—he also did carpentry on the estate. He'd take an ax and pretend to go and do some work, but instead he'd put his toolbox next to us and look around, gesturing to us to make us eat quickly. We sucked the eggs and buried the shells.

Two Serbian boys who also worked on this estate talked to us. They were slaves like us. They told us their secret . . . They confessed that they had a plan. "We must escape, otherwise we'll all die, like Olya. They'll put us in the ground in the forest and bring back the wooden clogs and pajamas." We were afraid, but they persuaded us. It was like this . . . Behind the estate was a swamp. We snuck off there in the morning unnoticed and then ran for it. We ran in the direction of the sunrise, to the east.

In the evening we all collapsed in the bushes and fell asleep. We were exhausted. In the morning we opened our eyes—it was quiet, only toads croaking. We got up, washed with dew, and started on our way. We walked a little and saw a high road ahead of us and on the other side a dense and beautiful forest. Our salvation. One boy crawled over, looked at the road, and called to us, "Let's run!" We ran out onto the road, and a German truck with armed soldiers drove out of the forest to meet us. They surrounded us and started beating and trampling the boys.

They threw them dead into the truck, and put me and another girl next to them. They said that the boys were lucky, and you'll be luckier still, Russian swine. They knew by the labels that we were from the east. We were so frightened that we didn't even cry.

They brought us to a concentration camp. There we saw children sitting on straw with lice crawling on them. The straw was brought from the fields that began right behind the barbed wire with live electric current.

Every morning an iron bar clanged, in came a laughing officer and a beautiful woman, who said to us in Russian, "Whoever wants kasha quickly line up by twos. We'll take you to eat . . ."

The children stumbled, shoved, everybody wanted kasha.

"We only need twenty-five," the woman said as she counted. "Don't quarrel, the rest of you can wait till tomorrow."

At first I believed her, and ran and shoved along with the little children, but then I became afraid: "Why did those who were led away to eat kasha not come back?" I started sitting right by the steel door at the entrance, and even when there were only a few of us left, the woman still didn't notice me. She always stood and counted with her back to me. I can't tell how long it went on. I think . . . I lost memory then . . .

I never saw a single bird or even a beetle in the concentration camp. I dreamed of seeing at least a worm. But they didn't live there . . .

One day we heard noise, shouts, shooting. The iron bar clanged—and our soldiers burst in shouting, "Dear children!" They took us on their shoulders, in their arms, several children at a time, because we weighed nothing by then. They kissed us, embraced us, and wept. They took us outside . . .

We saw the black chimney of the crematorium . . .

They fed us, treated us medically for several weeks. They asked me, "How old are you?"

I replied, "Thirteen . . ."

"And we thought, maybe eight."

When we became stronger, they took us in the direction of the sunrise.

Home . . .

"A WHITE SHIRT SHINES FAR OFF
IN THE DARK . . ."

Efim Friedland

NINE YEARS OLD. NOW DEPUTY DIRECTOR
OF A SILICATE FACTORY.

My childhood ended . . . with the first gunshots. A child still lived inside me, but now alongside someone else . . .

Before the war, I was afraid to be left alone in the apartment, but then the fear went away. I no longer believed in my mother's hobgoblins crouching behind the stove, and she stopped mentioning them. We left Khotimsk on a cart. My mother had bought a basket of apples; she set it beside my sister and me and we ate. The bombing started. My sister was holding two nice apples in her hands, and we began fighting over them. She wouldn't give them up. My mother yelled, "Hide!"—but we were quarreling over the apples. We fought until I asked my sister, "Give me at least one apple, or I'll die without having tasted them." She gave me one, the nicest one. Then the bombing stopped. I didn't eat the lucky apple.

We rode on the cart, and ahead of us went a herd. We knew from our father (before the war, in Khotimsk, he was the director of the stockyard) that they weren't ordinary cows, but a breeding herd, which had been purchased abroad for big money. I remember that my father was unable to explain how much "big money" it was, until he gave the example that each cow was worth a tractor. A tank. If it's a tank, that means it's a lot. We cherished each cow.

Since I grew up in the family of a zootechnician, I liked animals. After the umpteenth bombing, we were left without our cart, and I walked in front of the herd, tied to the bull Vaska. He had a ring in his nose with a rope tied to it, and I tied myself to the end of the rope. For a long time, the cows couldn't get used to the bombings. They were heavy, not suited for these long marches; their hooves cracked, and they got terribly tired. After the shelling, it was hard to round them up, but if the bull went on the road, they all followed him. And the bull obeyed only me.

During the night, my mother would wash my white shirt somewhere . . . At dawn First Lieutenant Turchin, who led the convoy, shouted, "Rise and shine!" I would put on the shirt and set off with the bull. I remember that I always wore a white shirt. It shone in the dark, everybody could see me from far off. I slept next to the bull, under his front legs—it was warmer that way. Vaska never got up first; he waited until I got up. He sensed that a child was next to him, and he could cause him harm. I lay with him and never worried.

We reached Tula on foot. Nearly a thousand miles. We walked for three months, walked barefoot by then, everything we had on was in shreds. There were few herdsmen left. The cows had swollen udders, we had no time to milk them. The udder is sore, the cow stands next to you and looks. I had cramps in my hands from milking fifteen or twenty cows a day. I can still see it: a cow lay on the road with a broken hind leg, milk dripping from her bruised udder. She looked at people. Waited. The soldiers stopped—and took up their rifles to shoot her, so she wouldn't suffer. I asked them to wait . . .

I went over and let the milk out on the ground. The cow gratefully licked my shoulder. "Well." I stood up. "Now shoot." But I ran off so as not to see it . . .

In Tula we learned that the entire breeding herd we had brought would go to the slaughterhouse—there was nowhere else to put them. The Germans were nearing the city. I put on my white shirt and went to say goodbye to Vaska. The bull breathed heavily in my face . . .

. . . May 1945 . . . We were returning home. Our train was approaching Orsha. At that moment I was standing by the window. My mother came over to me. I opened the window. My mother said, "Can you smell our swamps?" I rarely cried, but here I sobbed. During our evacuation, I even dreamed of how we cut the swamp hay, how it was gathered in haystacks, and how it smelled, having dried and cured a bit. Our very own inimitable smell of swamp hay. It seems to me that only we in Belorussia have this pungent smell of swamp hay. It followed me everywhere. I even smelled it in my sleep.

On Victory Day, our neighbor Uncle Kolya ran outside and started firing into the air. The boys surrounded him.

"Uncle Kolya, let me!"

"Uncle Kolya, let me . . ."

He let everybody. And I fired a shot for the first time . . .

"ON THE CLEAN FLOOR THAT I HAD JUST WASHED . . ."

Masha Ivanova

EIGHT YEARS OLD. NOW A TEACHER.

We had a close-knit family. We all loved each other . . .

My father fought in the Civil War. After that he walked with crutches. But he was head of a kolkhoz; his was a model farm. When I learned to read, he showed me clippings from the newspaper *Pravda* about our kolkhoz. As best chairman, he was sent before the war to a congress of "shock kolkhozniks" and to an agricultural exposition in Moscow. He brought me back pretty children's books and a tin of chocolates.

Mama and I loved our papa. I adored him, and he adored us. Mama and me. Maybe I'm embellishing my childhood? But in my memory, everything from before the war is joyful and bright. Because . . . it was childhood. Real childhood . . .

I remember songs. The women return from the fields singing songs. The sun is setting over the horizon, and from behind the hill, drawn-out singing reaches us:

It's time to go home. It's time.
Twilight is upon us . . .

I run to meet the song—there is my mama, I hear her voice. Mama picks me up, I embrace her tightly around the neck, jump back down and run ahead, and the song catches up, filling the entire world around me—and it's so joyful, so good!

After such a happy childhood . . . suddenly . . . all at once—war!

My father went off in the early days . . . He was assigned to work in the underground. He didn't live at home, because everyone here knew him. He came home only at night.

One day I heard him talking with my mother.

"We blew up a German truck on the road near . . ."

I coughed on the stove, my parents were startled.

"Nobody must know about this, dear daughter," they warned me.

I started being afraid of the night. Father comes to us at night, and the fascists find out and take away our papa, whom I love so much.

I always waited for him. I would climb to the farthest corner of our big stove, hugging my grandmother, but I was afraid to fall asleep, and if I did, I kept waking up. A storm howled through the chimney, the damper trembled and clanked. I had one thing in mind: don't oversleep and miss papa.

Suddenly it seemed to me that it wasn't a storm howling, but my mother crying. I had a fever. Typhus.

My father came back late at night. I was the first to hear him, and I called to my grandmother. My father was cold, and I was burning hot. He sat by my side and couldn't leave. Weary, aged, but my own, my very own. There was unexpected knocking at the door. Loud knocking. My father didn't even have time to slip on his coat. *Polizei* broke into the house. They pushed him outside. I went after him, he reached out for me, but they hit his hands with their guns. They beat him on the head. I ran after him barefoot through the snow as far as the river and shouted, "Papa! Dear papa . . ." My grandmother was wailing in the house: "And where is God? Where is He hiding?"

My father was killed . . .

My grandmother couldn't bear such grief. She cried more and more softly, and after two weeks she died at night, on the stove. I was sleeping next to her and held her in my arms, dead. There was no one left in the house; my mother and brother were hiding in a neighbor's house.

After my father's death, my mother, too, became quite different. She never left the house. She only talked about my father, and got tired quickly, though before the war she had been a Stakhanovite, always the very best.* She didn't notice me, though I always tried to catch her attention. To gladden her somehow. But she brightened up only when we remembered papa.

I remember how happy women came running: "A boy from the nearby village has been sent on horseback—the war is over. Our men will come home soon."

My mother collapsed on the clean floor that I had just washed . . .

* A Stakhanovite was a follower of the example of Alexei Stakhanov (1906–1977), a coal miner who in less than six hours dug fourteen times his daily quota of coal. The Stakhanovite movement started in 1935, and the title was highly honored.

"DID GOD WATCH THIS? AND WHAT DID HE THINK? . . ."

Yura Karpovich

EIGHT YEARS OLD. NOW A DRIVER.

I saw what shouldn't be seen . . . What a man shouldn't see. And I was little . . .

I saw a soldier who was running and seemed to stumble. He fell. For a long time he clawed at the ground, he clung to it . . .

I saw how they drove our prisoners of war through our village. In long columns. In torn and burned greatcoats. Where they stayed overnight, the bark was gnawed off the trees. Instead of food, they threw them a dead horse. The men tore it to pieces.

I saw a German train go off the rails and burn up during the night, and in the morning they laid all those who worked for the railroad on the tracks and drove a locomotive over them . . .

I saw how they harnessed people to a carriage. They had yellow stars on their backs. They drove them with whips. They rode along merrily.

I saw how they knocked children from their mother's arms with bayonets. And threw them into the fire. Into a well . . . Our turn, mama's and mine, didn't come . . .

I saw my neighbor's dog crying. He sat in the ashes of our neighbor's house. Alone. He had an old man's eyes . . .

And I was little . . .

I grew up with this . . . I grew up gloomy and mistrustful, I have a difficult character. When someone cries, I don't feel sorry; on the contrary, I feel better, because I myself don't know how to cry. I've been married twice, and twice my wife has left me. No one could stand me for long. It's hard to love me. I know it . . . I know it myself . . .

Many years have passed . . . Now I want to ask: Did God watch this? And what did He think?

"THE WIDE WORLD IS WONDROUS . . ."

Ludmila Nikanorova

TWELVE YEARS OLD. NOW AN ENGINEER.

I wish I could remember . . . Did we talk about war before the war?

Songs played on the radio: "If There Is War Tomorrow" and "Our Armor Is Strong and Our Tanks Are Swift." Children could sleep peacefully . . .

Our family lived in Voronezh. The city of my childhood . . . In the schools, many teachers were part of the old intelligentsia. A high level of musical culture. The children's choir of our school, where I sang, was very popular in the city. I believe everyone loved the theater.

Our house was inhabited by military families. A four-story house with rooms along the corridors; in summer, a sweet-scented acacia bloomed in the yard. We played a lot in the little park in front of the house. There were hiding places there. I was very lucky with my parents. My father was a career soldier. All through my childhood, I had seen military uniforms. My mother had a gentle character, golden hands. I was their only daughter. As expected in such cases, I was persistent, capricious, and shy at the same time. I took lessons of music and ballet dancing at the House of the Red Army. On Sundays—the only day when he wasn't busy—papa loved walking around the city with us. My mother and I had to walk to his left, as my father kept greeting oncoming officers and raising his right hand to his visor.

He also loved to read poetry with me, especially Pushkin:

Study, my son: for learning shortens
The lessons of our swift-passing life.*

That June day . . . In my pretty dress I was going with a friend to
the garden of the House of the Red Army to see a play that was supposed to start at noon. We saw everybody listening to a loudspeaker
fastened to a pole. Bewildered faces.

"You hear—it's war!" my friend said.

I rushed home. Flung the door open. The apartment was quiet,
mama wasn't there, my father was shaving with concentration in
front of the mirror, one cheek covered with lather.

"Papa, it's war!"

Papa turned to me and went on shaving. I saw an unfamiliar ex-
pression in his eyes. I remember that the speaker on the wall was
switched off. That's all he could do to postpone for us the moment of
the terrible news.

Life changed instantly . . . I don't remember my father being at
home at all during those days. Everyday life became different. We
held general meetings of the tenants: how to extinguish a fire if the
house started burning, how to cover the windows for the night—the
city had to be without lights. Provisions disappeared from the counters, ration cards appeared.

And then came that last evening. It wasn't at all like those I see
now in the movies: tears, embraces, jumping onto moving trains. We
didn't have that. Everything was as if my father was leaving on ma-
neuvers. My mother folded his belongings, his collar, his tabs were
already sewn on, she checked his buttons, socks, handkerchiefs. My
father rolled up his greatcoat—I think I was holding it.

The three of us went out to the corridor. It was late. At that hour
all the doors were locked except the front one—to go out to the
courtyard, we had to go up from the first floor to the second, pass

---

* The lines are from the tenth scene of Pushkin's play *Boris Godunov* (1825), spoken by Boris
Godunov to his son Feodor.

through a long corridor and go back down. It was dark outside, and our always thoughtful father said, "There's no need to accompany me any farther."

He embraced us. "Everything will be fine. Don't worry, girls."

And he left.

He sent us several letters from the front: "We'll soon be victorious, then we'll live differently. How is our Ludmilochka behaving?" I can't remember what I did till the first of September. Of course, I upset my mother by staying at my girlfriends' for a long time without permission. Air-raid warnings became, one might say, a usual thing. Everyone quickly got used to them: we didn't go down into the shelter, but stayed at home. Many times I was caught under bombings in the streets downtown. I would just run into a store or into an entryway.

There were many rumors, but they didn't stay in my memory. In my child's mind . . .

My mother was on duty at the hospital. Every day trains arrived with wounded soldiers.

Surprisingly, goods appeared again on the counters, and people bought them. For several days, my mother and I wondered: shouldn't we buy a new piano? We decided not to for the time being, but to wait for my father. It's a major purchase, after all.

Incredible as it seems, we went back to school, as usual, on the first of September. Not a word from my father all through August. We had faith, and waited, though we already knew such words as *encirclement* and *partisans*. At the end of the month, they announced: Be prepared for evacuation at any moment. We were informed of the exact day, I think, the day before. The mothers had a hard time. Anyway, we were convinced that we would leave for a couple of months, sit it out somewhere in Saratov, and come back. One bundle for the bed things, one bundle for the dishes, and a suitcase with our clothes. We were ready.

I remember this picture on the way: our train leaves without a signal, people grab their pans, there's no time to put out the cook fires. We get on the train and go, and there is a chain of fires along the embankment. The train arrived in Alma-Ata, then went back to Chimkent. And so several times—there and back. Finally, with sluggish oxen harnessed to carts, we rode into the *aul*. I saw a *kibitka* for the first time . . . * Like in an eastern fairy tale . . . Everything was so colorful, unusual. I found it interesting.

But when I noticed my mother's first gray hair, I was dumbstruck. I began to grow up very quickly. Mama's hands! I don't know what they couldn't do. How did mama have the presence of mind at the last moment to grab the sewing machine (without the case, putting it with the pillows) and toss it into the car going to the train? That sewing machine was our breadwinner. Mama managed to sew at night. Did she ever sleep?

On the horizon were the snowy spurs of the Tien Shan mountains. In spring the steppe is red with tulips, and in the fall there are grape clusters, melons. But how could we buy them? And the war! We were looking for our dear papa! Over three years, we wrote three dozen requests: to army headquarters, field post office 116, to the defense commissariat, to the Head Office of Red Army Personnel in Buguruslan . . . They all sent the same answer: "Not listed among the wounded or the dead." Since he wasn't listed, we waited and waited, still hoping.

Good news began to come over the radio. Our troops were liberating one city after another. Now Orsha was liberated. That's my mother's birthplace. My grandmother was there, and my mother's sisters. Voronezh was liberated, too . . . But Voronezh without papa was foreign to us. We wrote to my grandmother and went to her place. We traveled all the way on the rear platform, it was impossible to get inside. Five days on the platform . . .

My favorite place in my grandmother's house was by the warm Russian stove. At school we sat with our coats on. Many girls had

---

* In the Russian far east, a *kibitka* is a round tent of lattice work covered with felt, sometimes mounted on wheels. In European Russia, a *kibitka* is a large covered wagon.

coats sewn out of army greatcoats, and the boys simply wore the greatcoats. Early in the morning, I heard from the loudspeaker: victory! I was fifteen years old . . . I put on my father's present from before the war—a worsted cardigan—and my brand-new high-heeled shoes, and went to school. We kept these things, we had bought them in bigger sizes, so there was room to grow, and now I had grown.

In the evening we sat at the table, and on the table was a photo of my papa and a battered volume of Pushkin . . . It was his wedding gift to my mother. I remember how papa and I read poetry together, and when there was something he especially liked, he said, "The wide world is wondrous . . ." He always repeated those words in good moments.

I can't imagine such a beloved papa not alive . . .

"THEY BROUGHT LONG, THIN CANDY . . . IT LOOKED LIKE PENCILS . . ."

Leonida Belaya

THREE YEARS OLD. NOW A CLOTHES PRESSER.

Does a three-year-old child remember anything? I'll tell you . . .

I remember three or four images very clearly.

. . . Behind the house, by the meadow, some men were doing exercises, swimming in the river. Splashing, shouting, laughing, chasing each other, like our village boys. Only mama allowed me to play with the boys, but here she was scared and shouted that I mustn't leave the cottage. When I asked, "Who are those men?" she answered in a frightened voice, "Germans." Other kids ran to the river and brought back long, thin candy . . . They offered me some . . .

During the day, those same men marched along our streets. They shot all the dogs that barked at them.

After that, my mother forbade me to show myself outside during the day. I sat at home all day with my cat.

. . . We're running somewhere . . . The dew is cold. My grandmother's skirt is wet up to the waist, and my whole dress is wet, and so is my head. We hide in the forest. I dry off in my grandmother's jacket, while my dress is drying. One of our neighbors climbs a tree. I hear: "Burning . . . burning . . . burning . . ." Just that one word . . .

. . . We return to the village. In place of our cottages—black cinders. Where our neighbors lived, we find a comb. I recognize that comb. The neighbors' daughter—her name was Anyuta—used to comb my hair with it. My mama can't answer me when I ask where she and her mama are and why they don't come back. My mama clutches her heart. And I remember how Anyuta used to bring long, thin candy from those men who were merrily bathing in the river. Long as pencils . . . Very tasty. We didn't have candy like that . . . She was pretty, she always got a lot of candy. More than anyone. At night we would put our feet in the ashes to get warm and fall asleep. Warm, soft ashes . . .

"THE LITTLE TRUNK WAS JUST HIS SIZE . . ."

Dunya Golubeva
ELEVEN YEARS OLD. NOW A MILKER.

War . . . But we still had to plow . . .

Mama, my sister and brother went to the fields to sow linseed. They drove off, and an hour later, not more, women came running: "Your people have been shot, Dunya. They're lying in the field . . ."

My mother lay on a sack, and the grain was pouring out of it. There were many, many little bullet holes . . .

I remained alone with my little nephew. My sister had recently given birth, but her husband was with the partisans. It was me and this little boy . . .

I didn't know how to milk the cow. She was bellowing in the stable, she sensed that her mistress was gone. The dog howled all night long. So did the cow . . .

The baby clung to me . . . He wanted my breast . . . Milk . . . I remembered how my sister fed him . . . I pulled out my nipple for him, he sucked and sucked and fell asleep. I had no milk, but he got tired and fell asleep. Where did he catch cold? How did he get sick? I was little, what did I know? He coughed and coughed. We had nothing to eat. The *polizei* had already taken away the cow.

And so the little boy died. Moaned and moaned and died. I heard it grow quiet. I lifted the little sheet. He lay there all black, only his little face was white, it remained clean. A white little face, the rest completely black.

Night. Dark windows. Where to go? I'll wait till morning, in the morning I'll call people. I sat and wept, because there was no one in the house, not even that little boy. Day was breaking. I put him in a trunk . . . We had kept our grandfather's trunk, where he stored his tools; a small trunk, like a box. I was afraid that cats or rats would come and gnaw at him. He lay there, so small, smaller than when he was alive. I wrapped him in a clean towel. A linen one. And kissed him.

The little trunk was just his size . . .

"I WAS AFRAID OF THAT DREAM . . ."

Lena Starovoitova

FIVE YEARS OLD. NOW A PLASTERER.

All I have left is a dream . . . One dream . . . Mama put on her green coat, her boots, wrapped my six-month-old sister in a warm blanket, and left. I sat by the window and waited for her to come back. Suddenly I saw a few people being led down the road, and among them my mama and my little sister. Near our house, mama turned her head and looked through the window. I don't know whether she saw me or not. A fascist hit her with the butt of his rifle . . . He hit her so hard that she doubled over . . .

In the evening, my aunt came, my mother's sister . . . She cried a lot, she tore her hair, and called me "little orphan, little orphan." I heard that word for the first time . . .

That night I dreamed that mama was stoking the stove, the fire was burning brightly, and my little sister was crying. Mama called to me . . . But I was somewhere far away and didn't hear. I woke up in fear: mama called to me and I didn't answer. Mama wept in my dream . . . I couldn't forgive myself that she was weeping. I dreamed that dream for a long time . . . Always the same. I wanted . . . and was afraid of that dream . . .

I don't even have a photograph of mama. Only that dream . . . There's nowhere else I can see mama now . . .

"I WANTED TO BE MAMA'S ONLY CHILD . . . SO SHE COULD PAMPER ME . . ."

Maria Puzan

SEVEN YEARS OLD. NOW A WORKER.

Forgive me, but when I remember this . . . I can't . . . I . . . I can't look another person in the eyes . . .

They drove the kolkhoz cows out of the barn and pushed people inside. Our mama, too. I sat in the bushes with my little brother, he was two years old, he didn't cry. And the dog sat there with us.

In the morning we came home, the house was there, but mama wasn't. There was nobody. We were alone. I went to fetch water. I had to stoke the oven, my little brother was asking to eat. Our neighbors were hanging from the well pole. I turned to the other end of the village, there was an artesian well there, with the best water. The tastiest. There were people hanging there, too. I came home with empty buckets. My little brother cried, because he was hungry. "Give me some bread. Give me a crust." One time I bit him so he wouldn't cry.

We lived like that for a few days. Alone in the village. People lay or hung dead. We weren't afraid of the dead, they were all people we knew. Later we met a woman we didn't know. We started crying, "Let us live with you. We're afraid alone." She sat us on her sledge and drove us to her village. She had two boys and the two of us. We lived like that until our soldiers came.

. . . At the orphanage, they gave me an orange dress with pockets.

I loved it so much that I told everyone, "If I die, bury me in this dress." Mama died, papa died, and I would die soon. For a long time I waited to die. I always cried when I heard the word *mama*. Once they scolded me for some reason and stood me in a corner. I ran away from the orphanage. I ran away several times to go and look for mama.

I didn't remember my birthday . . . They told me: Choose your favorite day, any one you want. Well, any one you like. And I liked the May holidays. "But," I thought, "nobody will believe me if I say I was born on the first of May, or on the second, but if I say the third of May, it will seem like the truth." Every three months they gathered the children who had had birthdays; they set a festive table with candy and tea, and gave them presents: girls got fabric for their dresses, boys got shirts. Once an unknown old man came to the orphanage and brought a lot of boiled eggs, gave them out to everybody, and was so happy to do something nice for us. It was right on my birthday . . .

I was already a big girl, but I was bored without toys. When we went to bed and everybody fell asleep, I pulled feathers from my pillow and examined them. It was my favorite game. If I was sick, I lay and dreamed of mama. I wanted to be mama's only child . . . so she could pamper me.

I was a long time growing up . . . Everybody in the orphanage had trouble growing up. I think it's probably from pining. We didn't grow up because we heard so few tender words. We couldn't grow up without mamas . . .

"BUT, LIKE RUBBER BALLS, THEY DIDN'T SINK . . ."

Valya Yurkevich

SEVEN YEARS OLD. NOW RETIRED.

Mama was hoping for a boy . . . And my father wanted a boy. But a girl was born . . .

Yet they all wanted a boy so much . . . So I grew up more like a boy than a girl. My parents dressed me in boys' clothing and cut my hair like a boy's. I liked boys' games: "Cops and Robbers," "War," "Mumblety-peg." I especially liked to play "War." I believed I was brave.

Near Smolensk our train carriage with the evacuated was completely destroyed by bombing. We somehow survived, and we were pulled out from under the rubble. We reached a village, and there a battle had started. We sat in someone's basement. The house collapsed, and we were buried under it. The battle subsided, and we somehow crawled out of the basement, and the first thing I remember is the cars. Passenger cars drove by, and in them sat smiling people wearing shiny black raincoats. I can't express that feeling—there was fear, and some kind of morbid curiosity. They drove through the village and disappeared. We children went to see what was happening outside the village. When we went out to the fields, it was something terrible. The entire rye field was strewn with dead bodies. I guess I didn't have a girlish character, because I wasn't afraid to look at all this, though I was seeing it for the first time. They lay in black soot.

There were so many it was hard to believe these were people lying there. That was my first impression of the war . . . our blackened soldiers . . .

We went back to Vitebsk with my mother. Our house was destroyed, but our grandmother was waiting for us . . . A Jewish family sheltered us, a very sick and very kind old couple. We always worried about them, because all across the city hung announcements saying that Jews had to register at the ghetto; we asked them not to leave the house. One day we were away . . . My sister and I were playing somewhere. My mother was out, and my grandmother . . . When we returned, we found a note saying that the owners had left for the ghetto, because they were afraid for us; we had to live, but they were old. Orders were posted across the city: Russians must hand over the Jews to the ghetto, if they knew where they were hiding. Otherwise they, too, would be shot.

We read the note, and my sister and I ran to the Dvina. There was no bridge at that spot, people were transported to the ghetto by boat. The bank was encircled by Germans. Before our eyes, they loaded the boats with old people, children, towed them to the middle of the river, and overturned them. We searched for our old ones; they weren't there. We saw a family sitting in a boat—a man, his wife, and two children. When the boat was overturned, the adults immediately sank to the bottom, but the children kept resurfacing. The fascists hit them with their paddles, laughing. They hit them here, they would resurface somewhere else; they would catch up with them and hit them again. But, like rubber balls, they didn't sink . . .

There was such silence, or maybe my ears got blocked and it seemed to me that it was quiet, that everything died down. Suddenly, amid this silence, laughter rang out. Such young belly laughter . . . Young Germans were standing nearby, watching it all and laughing. I don't remember how I got home with my sister, how I dragged her back. Children obviously grew up quickly then. She was three years old, but I could see that she understood everything, kept quiet and didn't cry.

I was afraid to walk in the street, and for some reason I felt calmer when I walked through the ruins. One night, Germans broke into the house and began shaking us. Get up. I slept with my sister, mama with my grandmother. They led us all outside, didn't allow us to take anything (and it was the beginning of winter), loaded us into trucks, and drove us to the train.

Alytus was the name of the Lithuanian town where we wound up a few weeks later. At the station they arranged us in ranks and led us away. On the road we met some Lithuanians. They most likely knew where we were being taken. One woman came up to mama and said, "They're taking you to the death camp. Give me your girl, I'll save her. If you survive, you'll find her." My sister was pretty, everyone pitied her. But what mother would give up her child?

At the camp, they immediately took our grandmother from us. They said that the elderly were transferred to another barrack. We waited for our grandmother to give us a sign of life, but she disappeared. Later it somehow became known that, in the first days, all the old people had been taken to the gas chamber. After my grandmother, one morning they took away my sister. Before that, a few Germans went through the barracks and listed the children. They chose the pretty ones, especially those who were blond. My sister had blond curly hair and blue eyes. They didn't list all of them, but specifically those. They didn't take me, I was dark haired. The Germans patted my sister on the head, they really liked her.

They would take my sister away in the morning and bring her back in the evening. She faded more with each passing day. My mother questioned her, but she didn't say anything. Either they were scared, or they were given something, some pills, but she didn't remember anything. Later we learned that they were taking their blood. Apparently they took a lot of their blood, because after a few months my sister died. She died in the morning. When they came again for the children, she was already dead.

I was very fond of my grandmother, because I always stayed with her when papa and mama went to work. We hadn't seen her die and we all hoped she was alive. But my sister died right beside us . . . She lay there as if alive . . . Beautiful . . .

In the barrack next to ours lived women from Orel. They wore fur coats, bell-shaped fur coats; each of them had many children. They drove them out of the barracks, lined them up by six, and forced them to march with their children. The children clung to them. They even played some music . . . If one woman didn't keep pace with the rest, they beat her with a whip. They beat her, and yet she went on, because she knew if she fell, she would be shot and her children would be shot. Something rose in my chest when I saw how they got up and walked. In their heavy fur coats . . .

The adults were sent off to labor. They had to take logs from the Neman River and drag them to the bank. Many died there in the water. Once the commandant grabbed me and put me in the group that was supposed to go to labor. Then an old man ran out of the crowd, pushed me away, and took my place. In the evening, when my mother and I wanted to thank him, we didn't find him. They told us he died in the river.

My mother was a teacher. She said repeatedly, "We must remain human." Even in hell she was trying to keep some habits from home. I don't know where or when she washed them, but I always wore clean, laundered clothes. In winter she washed them with snow. She would take all my clothes off, and I would sit on the bunk under a blanket while she did the laundry. We only had what we were wearing.

Still, we celebrated our holidays . . . We saved something to eat for that day. A piece of boiled beet. Or a carrot. My mother tried to smile on that day. She had faith that our soldiers would come. Thanks to that faith, we survived.

After the war, I went straight into fifth grade, not first grade. I had grown. But I was very reserved, I avoided people for a long time. All my life I've liked solitude. People were a burden to me, I had trouble being with them. I kept something inside that I couldn't share with anyone.

Mama, of course, noticed how I had changed. She tried to distract me. She invented holidays, and never forgot my birthday. We always had guests, her friends. She herself invited my friends. It was hard for me to understand. She was drawn to people. And I didn't realize how much mama loved me.

She still saves me with her love . . .

"I REMEMBER THE BLUE, BLUE SKY . . . AND OUR PLANES IN THAT SKY . . ."

Pyotr Kalinovsky

TWELVE YEARS OLD. NOW A CIVIL ENGINEER.

Before the war . . .

I remember that we studied war. We prepared. We learned to shoot, to throw grenades. Even the girls. Everybody wanted to earn the Voroshilov Sharpshooter badge, we were burning with desire. We sang the song "Granada." The words were beautiful, about a hero going to war "to return their land to the peasants of Granada." To pursue the cause of the revolution. The worldwide revolution! Yes, that was who we were. Those were our dreams.

In childhood I composed stories myself. I learned to read and write early. I was a gifted boy. I think mama wanted me to become an actor, but my dream was to learn to fly, to wear a pilot's uniform. That, too, was a sign of the times. For instance, before the war I never met a boy who didn't dream of becoming a pilot or a sailor. We wanted either the sky or the sea. The whole globe!

Now imagine what it was like for me . . . for our people . . . What it was like for us, when we saw Germans in our own town. On our own streets. I cried. When night fell, people closed their blinds, and they cried behind their closed windows.

Papa joined the partisans . . . Our neighbors across the street put on their white embroidered shirts and greeted the Germans with bread and salt. They were filmed.

When I first saw our people hanged, I ran home: "Mama, our people are hanging in the sky." For the first time I was afraid of the sky. After that incident, my attitude toward the sky changed, I became wary of it. I remember that the people were hanging very high, but maybe it seemed like that because of the fear. Hadn't I seen dead people on the ground? But it didn't frighten me like that.

Soon papa came back for us . . . Then we left together . . .

One partisan post, a second . . . And suddenly we hear Russian songs all through the forest. I recognize the voice of Ruslanova.* The brigade had a gramophone and three or four records completely worn out from frequent playing. I stood there dumbfounded and couldn't believe that I was with the partisans, and they sang songs there. For two years I had lived in a town occupied by Germans. I had forgotten how people sang. I had seen how they died . . . How they were scared . . .

In 1944 I took part in the Minsk partisan parade. I was at the right-hand end of the rank; they put me there so I could see the tribune. "You're not grown up yet," said the partisans. "You'll get lost among us and won't see anything, and you have to remember this day." There was no photographer with us. It's a pity. I can't remember how I looked then. I'd like to know . . . To see my face . . .

I don't remember the tribune. I remember the blue, blue sky. And our planes in that sky. We had been waiting for them, waiting all through the war . . .

---

* Lidia Ruslanova (1900–1973) was a Ukrainian-born singer who became widely popular for her renditions of Russian folk songs and performed all over Russia.

"LIKE RIPE PUMPKINS . . ."

Yakov Kolodinsky

SEVEN YEARS OLD. NOW A TEACHER.

The first bombardment . . .

They began dropping bombs . . . We dragged pillows, clothing into the garden, under the cherry tree; the pillows were big, we couldn't be seen behind them, only our legs stuck out. The planes flew away, and we dragged everything back into the house. And so it went several times a day. Later we already didn't care about anything, our mother just gathered us children, and we left everything else behind.

That day . . . I believe I've added something from what my father told, but I remember most of it myself. In the morning . . . Mist in the garden. The cows had already been taken out. My mother woke me up, gave me a mug of warm milk. It was nearly time to go to the fields. My father was riveting the scythe.

"Volodya." A neighbor knocked at the window, calling my father. He went outside. "We'd better run for it . . . The Germans are going through the village with a list. Somebody reported all the Communists. They've taken the teacher . . ."

They both scrambled through the kitchen gardens into the forest. After a while, two Germans and a *polizei* came into our house.

"Where is the man?"

"He's gone haymaking," answered my mother.

They went through the house, looked around, didn't touch us, and left.

The blue morning haze was still hanging outside. Chilly air. Mama and I watched from behind the gate: a neighbor was pushed out into the street, they were tying his hands, the teacher was taken, too . . . They tied everybody's hands behind their backs and stood them two by two. I had never seen a man tied up. I began to shiver. My mother chased me away: "Go into the house, put on your jacket." I stood there in my shirt, trembling all over, but didn't go into the house.

Our house stood right in the middle of the village. They gathered everybody there. It all happened quickly. The prisoners were standing, their heads bowed. They counted them according to their list, and led them outside the village. There were many village men and the woman teacher.

The women and children ran after them. They were led quickly. We were left behind. We ran up to the last barn and heard gunshots. People started falling, falling and getting back up. They executed them quickly and were about to leave. One German on a motorcycle turned around and drove all over those dead people. He had something heavy in his hands . . . Either a bludgeon or a crank from his motorcycle . . . I don't remember . . . Driving slowly, without getting off of the motorcycle, he smashed all of their heads . . . Another German wanted to finish them off with his gun; but the first one waved his hand as if to say no need. They all drove off, but he didn't drive off until he had smashed everyone's head. I had never heard the sound of cracking human bones . . . I remember that they cracked like ripe pumpkins, when my father split them with an ax and I scraped out the seeds.

I got so scared that I abandoned mama and everybody and ran off somewhere. Alone. I didn't hide in a house, but for some reason in a barn; mother looked for me for a long time. I couldn't utter a word for two days. Not a sound.

I was afraid to go outside. I saw through the window a man carrying a board, a second an ax, and a third a bucket. The boards were trimmed, the smell of freshly planed wood was in every yard, because in almost every yard there was a coffin. Even now I get a lump in my throat from that smell. To this day . . .

In the coffins lay people I knew. None had their heads. Instead of their heads, something wrapped in a white cloth . . . Whatever could be found . . .

. . . My father came back with two partisans. It was a quiet evening, the cows had been brought in. It was time for bed, but my mother prepared us to set out. We put on our suits. I had two other brothers—one was four years old, the other nine months old. I was the biggest. We got to the forges, stopped there, and my father looked back. I also looked back. The village no longer looked like a village, but like a dark, unknown forest.

Mama carried my little brother. My father carried the bundles and my middle brother. And I couldn't keep up with them. A young partisan said, "Put him on my back."

So he carried his machine gun and me . . .

"WE ATE . . . THE PARK . . ."

Anya Grubina

TWELVE YEARS OLD. NOW AN ARTIST.

I lose my voice when I tell about this . . . My voice dies . . .

We arrived in Minsk after the war. But I'm a Leningrad girl. I survived the siege there. The siege of Leningrad . . . When the whole city, my dear and beautiful city, was starving to death. Our papa died . . . Mama saved her children. Before the war, she had been a "firebrand." My little brother Slavik was born in 1941. How old was he when the siege began? Six months, just about six months . . . She saved this little one, too . . . All three of us . . . But we lost our papa. In Leningrad, everybody lost their papa, the papas died sooner, but the mamas stayed alive. I guess they couldn't die. Otherwise who would have been there for us?

When the ring of the siege was broken through, we were taken out on the "road of life" to the Urals, to the city of Karpinsk. The children were saved first. Our entire school was evacuated. On the road, everybody talked constantly about food, about food and parents. In Karpinsk we immediately rushed to the park; we didn't stroll in the park, we ate it. We especially liked larch, its fluffy needles—they're so delicious! We ate the young shoots from small pine trees, we nibbled grass. From the time of the siege, I knew about every kind of edible grass; in the city people ate all that was green. In the parks and the botanical garden, the leaves were already gone in the spring. But in the park of Karpinsk there was a lot of wood sorrel, also called hare cabbage. This was in 1942. In the Urals, too, there was hunger, but not as terrible as in Leningrad.

In the orphanage I was in, which housed only Leningrad children, they weren't able to feed us. For a long time they couldn't feed us enough. We sat in the classroom chewing paper. They fed us sparingly . . . I sat at the table, it was breakfast. And I saw a cat. A live cat . . . I jumped up from the table: "A cat! A cat!" All the children saw it and started chasing it: "A cat! A cat!" The house mistresses were all local, they looked at us like we were crazy. In Leningrad there were no living cats left . . . A living cat—that was a dream. A whole month's worth of food . . . We told them, but they wouldn't believe us. I remember many caresses. Hugs. Nobody raised their voice until our hair grew back after the journey. Before leaving, we were all given a close crop, boys and girls alike, but some lost their hair from starvation. We didn't play, didn't run. We sat and looked. And we ate everything . . .

I don't remember who in the orphanage told us about the German prisoners . . . When I first saw a German . . . I already knew he was a prisoner, they worked outside the city, in the coal mines. To this day I still don't understand why they came rushing to our orphanage, precisely the Leningrad one.

When I saw him . . . that German . . . He didn't say anything. He didn't ask. We had just finished our lunch, and I obviously still smelled of food. He stood next to me and sniffed the air, his jaw involuntarily moving, as if he was chewing something, and he tried to prevent it with his hands. To stop it. But it went on moving. I couldn't look at a hungry person at all. Absolutely not! We all had this sickness . . . I ran and called the girls. Somebody had a leftover piece of bread, and we gave it to him.

He kept thanking us.

"*Danke schön . . . Danke schön . . .*"

The next day he came to us with his comrade. And so it went . . . They walked in their heavy wooden clogs. *Thump-thump . . .* When I heard that thump, I ran outside . . .

We already knew when they would come, we even waited for them. We ran outside with anything we happened to have. When I was on duty in the kitchen, I kept my entire daily piece of bread for them, and in the evening I scraped the pans. All the girls kept something for them; I don't remember if the boys did. Our boys were constantly hungry, they never had enough to eat. The house mistresses scolded us, because the girls also fainted from hunger, but we still secretly kept food for those prisoners.

In 1943 they no longer came to us, in 1943 things were easier. There wasn't as much hunger in the Urals. We had real bread in the orphanage, they gave us plenty of kasha. But to this day, I still can't look at a hungry man. The way he stares . . . He never stares straight, always somewhere to the side . . . Recently they showed refugees on television . . . Somewhere, again, there is war. Shooting. Hungry people standing in lines with empty bowls. With empty eyes. I remember those eyes . . . I ran to the other room, I was in hysterics . . .

In the first year of our evacuation, we paid no attention to nature, everything about nature evoked a single desire—to taste it: is it edible? Only after a year did I notice how beautiful nature was in the Urals. The wild fir trees, tall grass, whole forests of bird cherry. Such sunsets! I began to draw. I had no paint, so I drew with a pencil. I drew postcards. We sent them to our parents in Leningrad. Most of all I loved to draw bird cherry trees. Karpinsk smelled of bird cherry.

For many years now, I've been obsessed with the desire to go there. I have a great wish to see whether our orphanage is still standing . . . It was a wooden building—has it survived in the new life? What has become of the city park? I'd like to go there in the spring, when everything is in bloom. Now I can't imagine eating handfuls of bird cherries, but we did eat them. We even ate them when they were still green. Bitter.

After the siege . . . I know that a man can eat anything. People even ate dirt . . . At the market, we could buy dirt from the destroyed and burned-down Badayev warehouses; dirt with sunflower oil spilled on it was particularly valued, or dirt soaked in burned jam.

Those two were expensive. Our mama could only afford the cheapest dirt, which barrels of herring had stood on. That dirt only smelled of salt, but didn't contain any salt. Only the smell of herring.

To find joy in flowers . . . New grass . . . Simply find joy in them . . . It took me some time to learn . . .

Decades after the war . . .

"WHOEVER CRIES WILL BE SHOT . . ."

Vera Zhdan

FOURTEEN YEARS OLD. NOW A MILKER.

I'm afraid of men . . . I have been ever since the war . . .

They held us at gunpoint and led us into the woods. They found a clearing. "No," says the German, shaking his head. "Not here . . ." They took us farther. The *polizei* say, "It would be a luxury to leave you partisan bandits in such a beautiful place. We'll leave you in the mud."

They chose the lowest spot, where there was always water. They gave my father and brother shovels to dig a pit. My mother and I stood under a tree and watched. We watched how they dug the pit. My brother took one last shovelful and looked at me: "Hi, Verka! . . ." He was sixteen years old . . . barely sixteen . . .

My mother and I watched how they were shot . . . We weren't allowed to turn away or close our eyes. The *polizei* watched us . . . My brother didn't fall into the pit, but bent double from the bullet, stepped forward, and sat down next to the pit. They shoved him with their boots into the pit, into the mud. Most horrible was not that they were shot, but that they were put down into the sticky mud. Into the water. They didn't let us cry, they drove us back to the village. They didn't even throw dirt over them.

For two days we cried, mama and I. We cried quietly, at home. On the third day that same German and two *polizei* came: "Get ready to bury your bandits." We came to that place. They were floating in the pit; it was a well now, not a grave. We had our shovels with us, started digging and crying. And they said, "Whoever cries will be shot. Smile." They forced us to smile . . . I bend down, he comes up to me and looks me in the face: am I smiling or crying?

They stood there . . . All young men, good looking . . . smiling . . . It's not the dead, but these living ones I'm afraid of. Ever since then I've been afraid of young men . . .

I never married. Never knew love. I was afraid: what if I give birth to a boy . . .

"DEAR MAMA AND DEAR PAPA— GOLDEN WORDS . . ."

Ira Mazur

FIVE YEARS OLD. NOW A CONSTRUCTION WORKER.

I should probably tell you about my loneliness. How I learned to be lonely . . .

One girl, Lenochka, had a red blanket, and I had a brown one. And when the German planes flew over, we lay on the ground and covered ourselves with our blankets. First the red one, then my brown one on top. I told the girls that if the pilot saw brown from above, he would think it's a stone . . .

The only memory I have of my mother is how afraid I was to lose her. I knew a girl whose mother had died in a bombing. She cried all the time. My mother took her in her arms and comforted her. Later . . . we buried my mother in the village, some woman and I . . . We washed her. She lay there thin as a girl. I wasn't afraid, I caressed her all the time. Her hair and hands smelled as usual. I didn't notice where she was wounded. Apparently it was a small bullet wound. For some reason I thought that mama's bullet wound was small. I once saw small bullets on the road. And I wondered: how can these small bullets kill such a big person? Or even me—I'm a thousand, a million times bigger than them. For some reason, I remember that million, it seemed to me that it was very, very much, so much it was impossible to count. Mama didn't die immediately. She lay in the grass for a long while and kept opening her eyes: "Ira, I have to tell you . . ."

"Mama, I don't want to . . ." It seemed to me that if she told me what she wanted, she'd die.

When we washed my mother, she lay in a shawl with her big braid. Like a girl . . . That's how I see her today. I'm already twice her age; she was twenty-five. I now have a daughter that age, and she even looks like my mother.

What's left in me from the orphanage? An uncompromising character. I don't know how to be gentle and careful with words. I'm unable to forgive. My family complains that I'm not very affectionate. Can one grow up affectionate without a mother?

At the orphanage, I wanted to have my own personal cup, that would be mine alone. I've always been envious: people have kept some belongings from their childhood, but I don't have any. Nothing of which I could say: "This is from my childhood." I wish I could say that, sometimes I even make it up . . . Other girls grew attached to our house mistresses, but I liked our nannies. They were more like our imaginary mamas. The house mistresses were strict and orderly, but the nannies were always bedraggled and grouchy like at home. They might spank us, but never painfully. Maternally. They washed us, did laundry for us in the bathhouse. We could sit on their laps. They touched our naked bodies—and that only a mama could do, so I understood. They fed us, treated our colds as they knew how, and wiped our tears. When we were in their hands, it wasn't an orphanage anymore, but started to be a home.

I often hear people say, "My mother" or "My father." I don't understand—why mother and father, as if they were strangers? It should only be mama or papa. And if mine were alive, I would call them "dear mama" and "dear papa."

Those are golden words . . .

"THEY BROUGHT HER BACK IN PIECES . . ."

Valya Zmitrovich
ELEVEN YEARS OLD. NOW A WORKER.

I don't want to remember . . . I don't want to, I never want to . . .

We were seven children. Before the war, mama laughed: "The sun is shining, the children are growing." The war began—she cried: "Such an evil hour, and children all over the place like beans . . ." Yusik was seventeen years old, I was eleven, Ivan nine, Nina four, Galya three, Alik two, and Sasha was five months old. A baby, nursing and crying.

At the time I didn't know, only after the war people told me that our parents were connected with the partisans and with our prisoners of war who worked in the dairy plant. My mother's sister worked there, too. I remember one thing: some men were sitting at night in our house, and apparently the light seeped through the window, though it was curtained with a thick blanket. A shot rang out—straight through the window. Mama grabbed the lamp and hid it under the table.

Mama was cooking us something with potatoes. She could do anything with potatoes—as they now say, a hundred dishes. We were preparing for some celebration. I remember it smelled delicious in the house. And my father was cutting clover by the forest. The Germans surrounded the house and ordered, "Come out!" Mama came out with us, three children. They started beating mama. She shouted, "Children, go inside!"

They stood her up against the wall under the window, and we stood in the window.

"Where is your oldest son?"

Mama answered, "Digging peat."

"Let's go there."

They pushed mama into the truck and got in themselves.

Galya ran out of the house and shouted, asking to go with mama. They threw her into the truck along with mama. And mama shouted, "Children, go inside . . ."

Papa came running from the field. Apparently someone had told him. He grabbed some papers and ran after mama. And he also shouted to us, "Children, go inside." As if the house would save us, or mama was there. We waited in the yard . . . In the evening we climbed up, some on the gate, some in the apple tree: aren't our papa and mama, sister and brother coming back? We saw people running from the other end of the village: "Children, leave your house and run away. Your family is gone, and they're coming for you . . ."

We crawled through the potato field to the swamp. We sat there for the night. The sun rose: what should we do? I remembered that we forgot the little one in her crib. We went to the village, took the little one; she was alive, just turned blue from crying. My brother Ivan says, "Feed her." What should I feed her with? I didn't have breasts. But he was afraid she would die, and asked: "Try . . ."

Our neighbor came. "Children, they'll be searching for you. Go to your aunt's."

Our aunt lived in another village. We said, "We'll go and find our aunt, but you tell us, where are our mama and papa, and our sister and brother?"

She told us that they had been shot. They were lying in the woods . . .

"But you mustn't go there, children."

"We'll go to say goodbye on our way out of the village."

"You mustn't, children . . ."

She led us out of the village, but didn't let us go where our family lay.

Many years later, I learned that my mother had had her eyes torn out, her hair pulled out, her breasts cut off. They set German shepherds loose on little Galya, who was hiding under a fir tree and wouldn't come out. They brought her back in pieces. Mama was still alive, she understood everything . . . It was all right in front of her . . .

After the war, I was left with my little sister Nina, just the two of us. I found her with some strangers and took her to live with me. We went to the district committee: "Give us a little room, the two of us will live there." They gave us a corridor in the worker's dormitory. I worked in a factory, Nina studied at school. I never called her by her name, always just "Little Sister." She's all I have. The only one.

I don't want to remember. But I need to tell people about my misfortune. It's hard to weep alone . . .

"THE CHICKS HAD JUST HATCHED . . .
I WAS AFRAID THEY'D BE KILLED . . ."

Alyosha Krivoshey

FOUR YEARS OLD. NOW A RAILROADMAN.

My memory . . . The only one . . . The chicks had just hatched. Small and yellow, they ran around the floor, came to my hands. During the bombing, my grandmother gathered them on a sieve.

"How about that: war—and chicks."

I was afraid the chicks would be killed. I still remember how I cried because of that fear. Bombing . . . Everybody ran to hide in the cellar, but I wouldn't leave the house. I was holding the chicks . . . Grandmother took the sieve with us, then I went. I went and counted: one chick, two, three . . . There were five of them . . .

I counted the bombs. One fell, two . . . seven . . .

That's how I learned to count . . .

"KING OF CLUBS . . . KING OF DIAMONDS . . ."

Galina Matuseeva

SEVEN YEARS OLD. NOW RETIRED.

A man is born . . .

Beside him sit two angels, and they lay out his fortune. They prescribe the years of his life, whether his path will be long or short. And God watches from above. He sent the angels to welcome the new soul. To say that He is there.

My good one . . . I can see from someone's eyes whether the person is happy or not. I won't walk up to just anyone in the street and stop him: "Young, handsome, may I ask you?" People run, run, and I choose one from the crowd, as if I recognize him. I feel something in my chest, I feel warm, and the words appear. The heat of speech. I start speaking . . . I tell his fortune . . . I lay out my cards, and everything is in the cards: what was and what will be, and how the soul will rest, and what it will take with it. It will go back where it came from—to heaven. The cards will show . . . Man is proud, but his fortune is written in the heavens beforehand. There is a text there . . . But each one reads it in his own way . . .

We're Gypsies . . . Free people . . . We have our own laws, Gypsy laws. Our home is where we live, and where our heart is glad. For us anywhere is home. Anywhere under the sky. My father taught me so, and my mother taught me. The *kibitka* sways, shakes along the roads, and mama reads me our prayers. She sings. Gray . . . the color of the road, the color of dust . . . the color of my childhood . . . My good one, have you ever seen a Gypsy tent? Round and high as the sky. I was born in one. In the forest. Under the stars. From the day I was born, I've had no fear of night birds and animals. I learned to dance and sing by the bonfire. You can't imagine the Gypsy life without singing; each of us sings and dances—it's like speaking. The words of our songs are tender. Devastating . . . When I was little I didn't understand them, but I still cried. Such words . . . They creep into the human heart, they tease it. Lull it. Tease it with the road. Freedom. Great love . . . No wonder they say the Russian people die twice: once for the Motherland, the second time from listening to Gypsy songs.

My good one, why do you ask so many questions? I'll tell you myself . . .

I saw happiness in my childhood. Believe me!

In summer we lived in a camp together. One family. We always stopped near a river. Near a forest. In a beautiful place. In the morning, the birds sing, and my mama sings. She wakes me up. And in winter, we sought out people's apartments—back then people were pure gold. Good-hearted. We lived well with them. But for as long as there was snow on the ground, we waited for spring. We took care of our horses. Gypsies look after horses like children. In April . . . At Easter we bowed to the good people and prepared for the road. Sun, wind . . . We live for the day. Today there's happiness—someone hugs you at night, or the children are healthy and well fed—and you're happy. But tomorrow is a new day. Mama's words . . . Mama didn't teach me much. If a child is from God, there's no need to teach him much, he learns on his own.

That's how I grew up . . . My short-term happiness. Gypsy happiness . . .

I woke up one morning from the talking. From the shouting.

"War!"

"What war?"

"With Hitler."

"Let them fight. We're free people. Birds. We live in the woods."

Then the planes came flying. They shot the cows in the field. Smoke rose into the sky . . . In the evening, mama's cards laid themselves out in such a way that she clutched her head and rolled in the grass.

Our camp stood still. Didn't move. I was bored. I liked the road.

One night an old Gypsy woman came to the fire. Wrinkled like dry dirt under the sun. I didn't know her, she was from another camp. From far away.

She told us, "In the morning they surrounded us. On good, well-fed horses. Their manes were shiny, their horseshoes strong. The Germans sat in their saddles, and the *polizei* pulled the Gypsies out of their tents. They pulled off their rings, tore off their earrings. All the women had their ears covered with blood and their fingers dislocated. They stabbed the featherbeds with bayonets. Looking for gold. Afterward, they began to shoot . . .

"One little girl asked them, 'Misters, don't shoot. I'll sing you a Gypsy song.' They laughed. She sang for them, danced, then they shot her . . . The whole camp. The entire camp was wiped out. They set the tents on fire. Only the horses were left. Without people. They took away the horses."

The bonfire burns. The Gypsies are quiet. I'm sitting next to mama.

In the morning—packing up: bundles, pillows, pots fly into the *kibitka*.

"Where are we going?"

"To the city," mama answers.

"Why the city?" I was sorry to leave the river. The sun.

"The Germans ordered it . . ."

We were allowed to live on three streets of Minsk. We had our own ghetto. Once a week the Germans showed up and checked us according to their list: "*Ein Zigeuner . . . Zwei Zigeuner . . .*" My good one . . .

How did we live?

Mama and I went from village to village. We begged. One would give us some wheat, another corn. They all invited us in: "Ah, Gypsy woman, come in. Tell my fortune. My husband is at the front." The war separated people from each other, they all lived apart. Waiting. They wanted to have hope.

Mama told fortunes. I listened . . . King of clubs, king of diamonds . . . A black card—Death. The ace of spades. The seven . . . The white king—burning love. The black king of spades—a military man. The six of diamonds—a future journey . . .

My mother came out of the yard smiling, but on the road she cried. It's terrible to tell people the truth: your husband is dead, your son is no longer among the living. The earth has taken them, they are—there. The cards bear witness . . .

We stayed overnight in a house. I didn't sleep . . . I saw how, at midnight, the women let loose their long braids and told fortunes. Each one opened the window, tossed grain into the dark night, and listened to the wind: if the wind is quiet—the promised one is alive, but if it howls and beats on the window, then don't wait for him, he won't come back. The wind howled and howled. It beat on the windowpane.

People never loved us the way they did during the war. During the hard times. Mama knew spells. She could help men and animals: she saved cows, horses. She spoke to them all in their own language.

There were rumors: one camp was shot up, then another . . . A third was taken to a concentration camp . . .

The war ended, we rejoiced together. You meet someone and embrace him. There were few of us left. But people still told fortunes and read cards. In the house, under the icon, lies a death notice, but the woman still asks, "Oh, Gypsy woman, tell my fortune. What if he's alive? Maybe the clerk made a mistake?"

Mama told her fortune. I listened . . .

For the first time I told the fortune of a girl at the market. She drew "great love." A lucky card. And she gave me a ruble. I had given her happiness, if only for a moment.

My good one, you, too, be happy! May God be with you. Tell people about our Gypsy fate. People know so little . . .

Taves bahtalo . . . God be with you!

"A BIG FAMILY PHOTOGRAPH . . ."

Tolya Chervyakov

FIVE YEARS OLD. NOW A PHOTOGRAPHER.

If something has stayed in my memory, it's like a big family photograph . . .

My father is in the foreground with his rifle, wearing an officer's cap. He wore it even in winter. The cap and the rifle are outlined more clearly than my father's face. I really wanted to have my own cap and rifle. A little boy!

Next to my father—mama. I don't remember her from those years, but instead I remember what she used to do: she was constantly laundering something white; she smelled of medicine. Mama was a nurse in a partisan brigade.

My little brother and I are there somewhere. He was always sick. I remember him—red, his whole body covered with scabs. He and mama both cry at night. He from pain, mama from fear that he will die.

And then, in the big peasant cottage which housed mama's hospital, I see women carrying mugs. The mugs contain milk. They pour the milk into a bucket, and mama bathes my brother in it. My brother doesn't cry that night, he sleeps. For the first night . . . In the morning, mama says to my father, "How will I repay the people?"

A big photograph . . . One big photograph . . .

"AT LEAST LET ME POUR SOME LITTLE POTATOES IN YOUR POCKETS . . ."

Katya Zayats

**TWELVE YEARS OLD. NOW A WORKER
ON THE KLICHEVSKY STATE FARM.**

Grandma chases us away from the windows . . .

But she looks out and tells mama, "They found old Todor in the shed . . . Our wounded soldiers were there . . . He brought them his sons' clothes; he wanted them to change so the Germans wouldn't recognize them. They shot the soldiers in the shed, and brought Todor to his yard and ordered him to dig a pit near the house. He's digging . . ."

Old Todor was our neighbor. Through the window we could see him digging a pit. He finished digging . . . The Germans took away his shovel, yelled something at him in their own language. The old man didn't understand or didn't hear because he had long been deaf. Then they pushed him into the pit and made signs for him to get on his knees. And they buried him alive . . . On his knees . . .

Everyone became frightened. Who are they? Are they even human? The first days of the war . . .

For a long time we avoided old Todor's house. It seemed to everyone that he was shouting from under the ground.

They burned our village so that only dirt was left. Only stones in the yards, and even they were black. There was no grass left in our garden. It was burned up. We lived by charity—my little sister and I went around to other villages, asking people, "Give us something . . ."

Mama was sick. Mama couldn't go with us, she was ashamed.

We would come to a cottage.

"Where are you from, children?"

"From Yadrenaya Sloboda. They burned us out."

They would give us a bowl of barley, a piece of bread, an egg . . . I thank them all, they all gave something.

Another time we'd cross the threshold, the women would wail loudly, "Oh, children, how many are you? This morning two pair came by." Or: "Some people just left. We don't have any more bread, let me at least pour some little potatoes in your pockets."

They wouldn't let us leave the cottage empty-handed. They'd give something, if only a bunch of flax, and by the end of the day we'd have gathered a whole sheaf of flax. Mama spun it herself, she wove it. At the swamp she dyed it black with peat.

My father came home from the front. We started building a cottage. There were just two cows left in the whole village. The cows carried the wood. We did, too. Also on our backs. I couldn't carry logs bigger than myself, but if one was my size, I would drag it.

The war didn't end soon . . . They count it as four years. There was shooting for four years . . . And how many years to forget?

"A IS FOR APPLE, B IS FOR BALL . . ."

Fedya Trutko

**THIRTEEN YEARS OLD. NOW BRANCH DIRECTOR
OF A LIMESTONE FACTORY.**

Here's the story . . .

Just two days before the war, we took mama to the hospital. She was gravely ill. The hospital was in Brest. We never saw our mama again.

Two days later the Germans entered the city. They drove the patients out of the hospital, and those who couldn't walk they took away somewhere. Among them, people told me, was my mother. They were shot somewhere. But where? How? When? I never learned, there was no trace left.

The war found my sister, my father, and me at home in Bereza. My brother Volodya was studying at the school of highway engineering in Brest. My other brother, Alexander, graduated from the Red Navy School in Pinsk and worked there as a mechanic on a steamship.

Our father—Stepan Alekseevich Trutko—was deputy chairman of the Bereza district executive committee. He was given the order to evacuate with documents to Smolensk. He came running home. "Fedya, grab your sister and go to your grandfather's in Ogorodniki . . ."

We arrived at my grandfather's farm in the morning, and that night my brother Volodya knocked on the window. He had walked for two days and nights from Brest. In October, Alexander showed up at the farm. He told us that the steamship on which he was sailing to Dnepropetrovsk had been bombed. All survivors were taken prisoner. Several people escaped, among them our Alexander.

We all rejoiced when the partisans came to my grandfather's—let's go with them! We'll take revenge!

"How many grades have you finished?" asked the commander, when we were brought to him.

"Five."

I heard the order: "Leave him in the family camp."

My brothers were given rifles, and I was given a pencil for schoolwork.

I was already a Young Pioneer by then. It was my best card, that I was a Pioneer. I asked to join a combat unit.

"We have fewer pencils than rifles," laughed the commander.

War was all around, but we studied. Our school was called "the green school." There were no desks, no classrooms, no textbooks; there were only students and teachers. We had one ABC for everybody, one history book, one problem book in arithmetic, and one grammar book. No paper, chalk, ink, or pencils. We cleared a meadow, scattered sand over it, and that was our "blackboard." We wrote on it with little twigs. In place of notebooks, the partisans brought us German leaflets, old wallpaper, and newspapers. They even found us a school bell somewhere. We were very pleased with it. Can it be a real school, if no bell rings? We had red neckerchiefs.

"Air raid!" shouts the sentry. The meadow empties.

And after the bombing, the lesson continues. The first graders write on the sand with their twigs: "A is for apple, B is for ball . . ."

We made a big standing abacus out of sticks and stones. We cut out several wooden alphabet sets. We even had physical education. We equipped the playground with a crossbar, a racetrack, a pole vault, and circles for grenade throwing. I threw grenades the farthest of all.

I finished sixth grade and said firmly that I would go to seventh grade after the war. They gave me a rifle. Later I got hold of a Belgian carbine; it was small and light.

I learned to be a good shot . . . But I forgot my math . . .

"HE GAVE ME AN ASTRAKHAN HAT
WITH A RED RIBBON . . ."

Zoya Vasilyeva

TWELVE YEARS OLD. NOW A PATENT ENGINEER.

There was so much joy in me before the war! Happiness! And that saved me . . .

I enrolled in the dance school at our Opera and Ballet Theater. The school was experimental, they chose the most talented children. And I had a letter of recommendation from the famous Moscow director Galizovsky.* In 1938 there was a parade of athletes in Moscow, and I was in it. We were sent there by the Minsk Palace of Pioneers. Blue and red balloons were released in the sky . . . We walked in a column . . . Galizovsky was the main director of this parade, and he noticed me.

A year later he came to Minsk, found me, and wrote a letter to Zinaida Anatolievna Vasilyeva, a people's artist . . . Our Belarusian celebrity . . . At the time, she was organizing a dance school. I delivered the letter. I really wanted to read what was written in it, but I forbade myself. Zinaida Anatolievna lived in the Hotel Evropa, not far from the conservatory. Since I did it all in secret from my parents, I was in a big hurry when leaving home. I ran down the street bare-

---

* The correct spelling (i.e., pronunciation) is Goleizovsky. Kasyan Goleizovsky (1892–1970) was a Russian ballet dancer and choreographer who made his name in the avant-garde of the 1920s. He had a marked influence on George Balanchine.

foot, and only then put my sandals on. I didn't change clothes. If I had put on something fancy, mama would have asked, "Where are you going?" And my parents didn't want to hear anything about any ballet; they were absolutely against it. Categorically.

I gave the letter to Zinaida Anatolievna, she read it and said, "Get undressed. Let's see your arms and legs." I froze in horror: how can I take off my sandals, when my feet are so dirty? I evidently had such a look on my face that she understood everything. She handed me a towel, pulled up a chair by the sink . . .

They enrolled me in the school. Out of twenty, only five people were kept. A new life began: classics, rhythmics, music . . . I was so happy! Zinaida Anatolievna loved me. And we all loved her. She was our idol, our divinity. No one in the world was as beautiful as she was. In 1941, I already danced in the ballet *The Nightingale,* by Kroshner.* I was assigned to dance the Little Cossack in the second act. We even had time to present it at the Ten Days of Belarusian Art in Moscow. It was a success. I also danced as a little chick in our school premiere, in the ballet *Chicks.* There was a big mother hen, and I was the littlest chick.

After the Ten Days in Moscow, we were awarded passes to go to the Pioneer summer camp near Bobruisk. There, too, we performed our "chicks." As a gift, they promised to bake us a huge cake. They baked it on the 22nd of June . . .

In token of solidarity with Spain, we wore little forage caps, my favorite headpiece. I immediately put it on when the children shouted "War!" On the road to Minsk, I lost my little cap . . .

In Minsk, my mother embraced me on the doorstep, and we ran to the station. We lost each other during a bombardment. I didn't find my mother and sister; I got on the train without them. In the morning, the train stopped at Krupki and didn't go any farther. People went to the village houses, but I felt shy, because I was without my

---

* The composer Mikhail Kroshner (1900–1942) was born in Kiev and studied in Minsk. He composed in many forms. The ballet *The Nightingale* (1939) is his most well-known work.

mother, alone. In the evening, I finally went into a house and asked for something to drink. They gave me milk. I raised my eyes from the cup to the wall and saw—my young mama in a wedding dress. And I shouted, "Mama!" The old man and woman started questioning me: "Where are you from? Who are you?" Such things can only happen in times of war—I found myself at my great-uncle's, the brother of my father's father, whom I had never seen. Of course, he didn't let me go anywhere. Such miracles!

In Minsk I had danced the "chicks," and now I had to guard them, so that the magpies wouldn't snatch them. Chicks are nothing, but I was afraid of geese. I was afraid of everything, I was even afraid of the rooster. I first showed courage when I went herding the geese. The male goose was smart, he realized I was scared of him, he hissed and tried to pull my skirt from behind. I had to playact in front of my new friends, who from their childhood hadn't been afraid either of geese or of the rooster. I was also very scared of thunderstorms. If I saw a thunderstorm coming, I immediately made up some excuse and ran into the first house I found. And there was no scarier sound than the clap of thunder. Though I had already seen bombings . . .

I liked the village people, their kindness; everybody called me "the wee one." I remember I was very interested in the horse. I loved to ride him, and my great-uncle let me. He would snort, wave his tail, and above all he obeyed me: I'd give a tug with my right hand, he knew he had to turn that way, if with the left, then to the left.

I asked my great-uncle, "Take me to mama on the horse."

"Once the war is over, I'll take you." My great-uncle was sullen and strict.

I arranged an escape. A girlfriend of mine led me out of the village.

At the station I climbed into a freight car, but I was chased out. I climbed into some truck and sat to the side. A scary memory: a German man and woman got in, there was a *polizei* with them, and I was there, but they let me be. On the road, they began asking questions, "Where did you study? What grade were you in?"

When I told them I also studied at the ballet school, they didn't believe me. Right there in the truck I showed them my "chick." And had I studied a foreign language?

In fifth grade we had started studying French; it was all still fresh in my memory. The German woman asked me something in French, and I answered. They were amazed that they had picked up a girl in a village who was in fifth grade, studied at a ballet school, and even knew French. They were doctors, as I understood, educated people. They had been told that we were savages. Subhumans.

It seems ridiculous now: I was afraid of a rooster, but when I saw the partisans in their Astrakhan hats, sword belts, with stars and machine guns, I said, "Misters, I'm brave. Take me with you." In the partisan unit, all my dreams were crushed, because I sat in the kitchen peeling potatoes. Can you imagine the mutiny in my soul? For a week I was on duty in the kitchen. Then I went to the unit commander: "I want to be a real fighter." He gave me an Astrakhan hat with a red ribbon, but I just wanted a rifle. I wasn't afraid to die.

I returned to mama with the medal Partisan of the Patriotic War, second degree. I went to school and forgot about everything. I played field hockey with the girls, rode a bike. One time, I fell into a bomb crater on my bike, got hurt, saw the blood, and remembered—not the war, but my ballet school. How am I going to dance now? Zinaida Anatolievna Vasilyeva will return soon, and I have an injured knee . . .

Only I didn't go back to ballet school. I went to work in a factory, I had to help mama. But I wanted to study . . . When my daughter was in the first grade, her mama was in the tenth. At night school.

My husband offered me a ticket to the ballet. I sat and cried through the whole performance . . .

"AND I FIRED INTO THE AIR . . ."

Anya Pavlova

NINE YEARS OLD. NOW A COOK.

Oh, my soul is going to ache . . . To ache again . . .

The Germans dragged me into the barn . . . Mama ran after me, tearing her hair. She screamed, "Do whatever you want with me, just don't touch my child." I had two younger brothers. They shouted, too . . .

We were from the village of Mekhovaya, in the Orel region. From there we were driven on foot to Belarus. From one concentration camp to another . . . When they wanted to take me away to Germany, mama padded her belly and put my little brother in my arms. That's how I survived. I was removed from the list.

Oh! Today my soul won't be still all day and all night. I'm moved, stirred . . .

Dogs tore children apart . . . We sat over a torn-up child waiting for his heart to stop. Then we covered him with snow . . . That would be his grave till spring . . .

In 1945 . . . after the Victory . . . mama was sent to build a health center here in Zhdanovichi. I went with her. And so I stayed here. I've been working in the health center for forty years . . . Since the first stone I've been here; it all rose up before my eyes. They gave me a rifle, ten German prisoners, and I led them to work. The first time I brought them, women surrounded us: one with a stone, another with a shovel, yet another with a stick. And I ran around the prisoners with my rifle and shouted, "Good women! Don't touch them . . . Good women, I signed papers for them. I'll shoot!" And I fired into the air.

The women cried, and I cried. And the Germans stood there. Never raised their eyes.

Mama never once took me to the military museum. One time she saw me looking at a newspaper with photographs of people who had been shot—she took it away and scolded me.

To this day there isn't a single book about the war in our house. And I've been living without mama for a long time now . . .

"MY MOTHER CARRIED ME TO FIRST GRADE IN HER ARMS . . ."

Inna Starovoitova

SEVEN YEARS OLD. NOW AN AGRONOMIST.

Mama kissed us and went away . . .

The four of us were left in the hut: the younger ones—my little brother, my two cousins—and me, the oldest one, seven years old. It wasn't the first time we were left alone, and we had learned not to cry, to behave quietly. We knew our mama was a scout, she had been sent on a mission, and we had to wait for her. Mama had taken us away from the village, and we now lived together with her in a partisan family camp. It had long been our dream! And now—our happiness.

We sit and listen: the trees rustle, women are doing laundry nearby, scolding their children. Suddenly a call: "Germans! Germans!" Everybody runs out of their huts, calling children, fleeing farther into the forest. But where should we run, alone, without mama? What if mama knows that Germans are coming to the camp, and she's running to us? Since I'm the oldest, I order, "All of you keep quiet! It's dark here, and the Germans won't find us."

We lay low. We became completely silent. Someone looked into the hut and said in Russian, "Whoever is in there, come out!"

The voice was calm, and we came out of the hut. I saw a tall man in a green uniform. "You have a papa?" he asked me.

"Yes."

"And where is he?"

"He's far away, at the front," I revealed. I remember the German even laughed.

"And where is your mama?" he asked next.

"Mama left on a mission with the partisans . . ."

Another German came, he was in black. They discussed something, and that one, the one in black, showed us with his hand where to go. There stood the women with children who hadn't managed to escape. The black German pointed his machine gun at us, and I understood what he was about to do. I didn't even have time to shout and embrace the younger ones . . .

I woke up to my mother's crying. Yes, it felt like I'd been sleeping. I got up and saw mama digging a pit and crying. She stood with her back to me, and I didn't have the strength to call to her, I only had the strength to look at her. Mama straightened up to rest, turned her head toward me, and cried out, "Innochka!" She threw herself at me, picked me up. She held me with one arm, and with the other she felt the rest of us: what if one of the other children was alive? No, they were cold . . .

After I was treated, mama and I counted: I had nine bullet wounds. I learned to count: in one shoulder—two bullets, and in the other—two bullets. That made four. In one leg—two bullets, and in the other—two bullets. That made eight. And on the neck—a wound. That made it nine.

The war ended. My mother carried me to first grade in her arms . . .

"MY DEAR DOG, FORGIVE ME . . .
MY DEAR DOG, FORGIVE ME . . ."

Galina Firsova

TEN YEARS OLD. NOW RETIRED.

I had a dream—to catch a sparrow and eat it . . .

Sometimes, but rarely, birds appeared in the city. Even in spring, everybody looked at them and thought of only one thing, the same thing I thought of. The same thing . . . Nobody had strength enough to stop thinking about food. From hunger, I constantly felt cold inside, a terrible inner cold. Even on sunny days. No matter how many clothes I put on, I was cold, I couldn't get warm.

We really wanted to live . . .

I'm telling you about Leningrad, where we lived then. About the siege of Leningrad. They starved us to death, for a long time. Nine hundred days of siege . . . Nine hundred . . . When one day could seem like an eternity. You can't imagine how long a day can seem to a hungry man. Or an hour, a minute . . . The long wait for lunch. Then for dinner. The daily ration during the siege went down to 125 grams of bread. That was for those who didn't work. A dependent's ration. The bread was oozing water . . . It was divided into three pieces—breakfast, lunch, and dinner. We drank only boiled water. Plain boiled water.

In the dark . . . From six in the morning, in the winter (I mostly remember the winter), I stood in line at the bakery. We stood for hours. Long hours. When my turn came, it was dark outside again. A candle burns, and the counterman cuts those pieces. People stand and watch him. His every move . . . with burning, mad eyes . . . And all this in silence.

There were no trams. No water, no heating, no electricity. But the worst thing was the hunger. I saw a man chewing his buttons. Small buttons and big ones. People went crazy from hunger . . .

There was a moment when I stopped hearing. Then we ate the cat . . . I'll tell you how we ate it. Then I went blind . . . They brought us a dog. That saved me.

I can't remember . . . I've forgotten when the idea that we could eat our cat or our dog became normal. Ordinary. It became part of our life. I didn't keep track of that moment . . . After the pigeons and swallows, cats and dogs suddenly started disappearing in the city. We didn't have any, we didn't take one in, because mama believed it was a great responsibility to have a dog, especially a big one, in the house. But my mama's friend couldn't eat her own cat, so she brought it to us. And we ate it. I started hearing again . . . I had lost my hearing unexpectedly. In the morning I could still hear, but in the evening, mama said something and I didn't respond.

Time passed . . . And we started dying again . . . Mama's friend brought us her dog. And we ate it, too. If it weren't for that dog, we wouldn't have survived. We certainly wouldn't have survived. It's obvious. We had started to swell from hunger. My sister didn't want to get up in the morning . . . The dog was big and gentle. For two days, mama couldn't . . . How could she make up her mind? On the third day, she tied the dog to the radiator in the kitchen and sent us outside . . .

I remember those meatballs . . . I remember . . .

We really wanted to live . . .

Often we gathered and sat around papa's photograph. Papa was at the front. We rarely received letters from him. "My dear girls . . ." he wrote to us. We answered, but we tried not to upset him.

Mama kept several pieces of sugar. A small paper bag. It was our golden reserve. One day . . . I couldn't resist, I knew where the sugar was, I climbed up and took a piece. Several days later, another one . . . Then . . . Some time went by—and again . . . Soon there was nothing left in mama's little bag. An empty bag . . .

Mama fell ill . . . She needed glucose. Sugar . . . She couldn't stand up anymore . . . At the family council, we decided to fetch the precious little bag. Our treasure! Well, we had saved it for such a day! Mama would most certainly recover. My older sister went searching, but there was no sugar. We ransacked the entire house. I searched along with everyone.

But in the evening I confessed . . .

My sister beat me. Bit me. Scratched me. And I begged her, "Kill me! Kill me! How can I go on living?!" I wanted to die.

I've told you about a few days. But there were nine hundred.

Nine hundred days like that . . .

Before my eyes a girl stole a bread roll from a woman in the market. A little girl . . .

She was caught and knocked to the ground. They started beating her . . . Beat her terribly. Beat her to death. But she hurried to eat, to swallow the roll. To swallow it before they killed her.

Nine hundred days like that . . .

Our grandfather became so weak that one time he fell down in the street. He had already said goodbye to life. A worker passed by, workers had better ration cards, slightly, but better . . . Anyhow . . . So this worker stopped and poured sunflower oil in my grandfather's mouth—his ration. Grandfather walked back home, told us, and wept: "I don't even know his name!"

Nine hundred . . .

People moved slowly around the city, like shadows. Like in sleep . . . In deep sleep . . . I mean, you see it, but you think you're dreaming. Those slow . . . those floating movements . . . It's like the person isn't walking on the ground, but on water . . .

People's voices changed from hunger. Or disappeared completely. It was impossible to identify people by their voices—a man or a woman? Or by their clothes. Everybody was wrapped in some kind of rags. Our breakfast . . . our breakfast was a piece of wallpaper, old wallpaper, but it still had paste on it. Flour paste. So there was this wallpaper . . . and boiled water . . .

Nine hundred days . . .

I walk home from the bakery . . . I've got my daily ration. Those crumbs, those miserable grams . . . And a dog runs toward me. He comes up to me and sniffs—he smells the bread.

I understood that this was our chance. This dog . . . Our salvation! I'll bring the dog home . . .

I gave him a piece of bread, and he followed after me. Near the house I nipped off another piece. He licked my hand. We went through the entryway. But he went up the stairs reluctantly, he stopped on every floor. I gave him all our bread . . . Piece by piece . . . So we went up to the fourth floor, and our apartment was on the fifth. There he stopped and wouldn't go any farther. He looked at me . . . as if he sensed something. Understood. I hugged him: "My dear dog, forgive me . . . My dear dog, forgive me . . ." I asked him, I begged him. And he went.

We really wanted to live . . .

We heard . . . They said on the radio, "The siege is broken! The siege is broken!" We were the happiest of people. There could be no greater happiness. We had survived! The siege was broken . . .

Our soldiers walked down our street. I ran up to them . . . But I wasn't strong enough to embrace them.

There are many monuments in Leningrad, but one that should be there is missing. We forgot about it. It's a monument to the dogs of the siege.

My dear dog, forgive me . . .

"AND SHE RAN AWAY: 'THAT'S NOT MY DAUGHTER! NOT MI-I-INE!'"

Faina Lyutsko

FIFTEEN YEARS OLD. NOW A CINEMA WORKER.

Every day I remember, but I still live . . . How do I live? Explain to me . . .

I remember that the death squads were all in black, black . . . With tall caps . . . Even their dogs were black. Shiny.

We clung to our mothers . . . They didn't kill everyone, not the whole village. They took those who stood on the right. On the right side. And we were there with mama . . . We were separated: children here, and parents there. We understood that they were about to execute the parents and leave us to ourselves. Mama was there . . . I didn't want to live without mama. I asked to stay with her and cried. Somehow they let me through . . .

As soon as she saw me, she shouted, "That's not my daughter!"

"Mama dear! Ma . . ."

"That's not my daughter! Not my daughter! Not mi-i-ine . . ."

"Mama-a-a!"

Her eyes weren't filled with tears, but with blood. Eyes full of blood . . .

"That's not my daughter!"

They dragged me away somewhere . . . And I saw how they first shot the children. They shot and watched how the parents suffered. My two sisters and my two brothers were shot. Once the children were killed, they began killing the parents. I didn't see my mama any-more . . . Mama probably fell down . . .

A woman stood holding a young baby in her arms; he was sucking at a little bottle of water. They first shot at the bottle, then at the baby . . . Only after that did they kill the mother . . .

I'm surprised that I can live after all that. I survived as a child . . . But how do I live as a grown-up? I've been a grown-up for a long time now . . .

"WERE WE REALLY CHILDREN? WE WERE MEN AND WOMEN . . ."

Victor Leshchinsky

SIX YEARS OLD. NOW DIRECTOR OF AN
ENERGY TECHNICAL SCHOOL.

I went to visit my aunt. She invited me for the summer . . .

We lived in Bykhovo, and my aunt in the village of Kommuna, near Bykhovo. In the center of the village there was a long house, for about twenty families—a communal house. That's all I've managed to remember.

They said "War." I had to go back to my parents. My aunt didn't let me go.

"When the war ends, you can go."

"And will it end soon?"

"Of course."

After some time, my parents came on foot: "The Germans are in Bykhovo. People are fleeing to the villages." We stayed at my aunt's.

In the winter partisans came to the house . . . I asked for a rifle. They were my mother's nephews, my cousins. They laughed and let me hold one. It was heavy.

The house always smelled of leather. And warm glue. My father made boots for the partisans. I asked him to make boots for me. He told me, "Wait, I have a lot of work." And, I remember, I showed him that I needed small boots, I had a small foot. He promised . . .

The last memory I have of my father is of how they led him down the street to a big truck . . . And they hit him on the head with a stick . . .

. . . The war ended, we had no father, and no home. I was eleven, I was the oldest in the family. The other two, my brother and sister, were little. My mother took out a loan. We bought an old house. The roof was in such condition that, if it rained, there was nowhere to hide, it leaked everywhere. The water poured through. At the age of eleven, I repaired the windows myself, covered the roof with straw. I built a shed . . .

How?

The first log I rolled in and placed by myself; with the second one my mother helped. We weren't strong enough to lift them any higher. Here's what I did: I would trim the log on the ground, make a notch, and wait until the women set off for work in the fields. In the morning, they would all grab it together and lift it, I would fit it a bit and set it down in the notch. By evening, I would have trimmed another one. They came back from work in the evening, and lifted . . . And so the little wall grew . . .

There were seventy households in the village, but only two men came back from the front. One on crutches. "Baby! My dear baby!" my mother lamented over me. In the evening I fell asleep wherever I sat down.

Were we really children? By the age of ten or eleven, we were men and women . . .

"DON'T GIVE SOME STRANGER
PAPA'S SUIT . . ."

Valera Nichiporenko

EIGHT YEARS OLD. NOW A BUS DRIVER.

This was already in 1944 . . .

I was probably eight years old. I think I was eight . . . We knew by then that we had no father. Others waited. They had received death notices, but they still waited. But we had a trustworthy sign. A proof. A friend of our father's sent his watch. To his son . . . To me . . . That was my father's request to him before dying. I still have that watch, I cherish it.

The three of us lived on my mother's small salary. We got by on bread and water. My sister fell ill. She was diagnosed with open tuberculosis. The doctors told mama that she needed good food, she needed butter. Honey. And that every day. Butter! For us it was like gold. Solid gold . . . Something unbelievable . . . At market prices mama's salary was enough for three loaves of bread. And for that money you could buy maybe two hundred grams of butter.

We still had my father's suit. A good suit. We took it to the market with mama. We found a buyer, found him quickly. Because the suit was fancy. My father bought it just before the war and hadn't gotten to wear it. The suit had hung in the closet . . . Brandnew . . . The buyer asked the price, bargained, and gave mama the money, and I started yelling for the whole market to hear, "Don't give some stranger papa's suit!" A policeman even came up to us . . .

Who can say after that, that children weren't in the war? Who . . .

"AT NIGHT I CRIED: WHERE IS MY CHEERFUL MAMA? . . ."

Galya Spannovskaya

SEVEN YEARS OLD. NOW A DESIGN TECHNICIAN.

Memories have colors . . .

Everything before the war, I remember in motion: it moves and changes colors. The colors are mostly bright. But the war, the orphanage—it all becomes still. And the colors turn gray.

We were taken to the rear. Only children. Without mamas. We rode for a long time, somehow very long. We ate cookies and cocoa butter; apparently they didn't manage to stock up on anything else for the road. Before the war, I loved cookies and cocoa butter—they're very tasty. But after a month on the road, I stopped liking them forever.

All through the war I kept wishing mama would come soon, and we could go back to Minsk. I dreamed of the streets, the movie theater near our house, I dreamed of the tramway bells. My mother was very nice, very cheerful. We lived together like girlfriends. I don't remember papa, we lost him early.

And then my mother located me and came to the orphanage. It was completely unexpected. What joy! I run to mama . . . I open the door . . . There stands a soldier, in boots, trousers, a cap, and an army shirt. Who is it? And it turns out to be my mama. Pure joy! Mama, and what's more, a soldier!

I don't remember her leaving. I cried a lot, that's obviously why I don't remember.

Again I wait and wait for mama. Three years I waited. This time mama came in a dress. In shoes. The joy of being taken back kept me from seeing anything. There was just mama—and this joy! I looked at mama, but I didn't notice she was missing an eye. Mama—it was such a miracle . . . Nothing could happen to her . . . Mama! But mama came back from the front very sick. She was a different mama now. She seldom smiled, she didn't sing, didn't joke like she used to. She cried a lot.

We went back to Minsk and lived a very hard life. We didn't find our house, which I had loved so much. The movie theater was gone . . . and our streets . . . Instead of it all—stones and more stones . . .

Mama was always sad. She didn't joke and spoke very little. She was mostly silent. At night, I cried: where is my cheerful mama? But in the morning I smiled, so that mama wouldn't guess about my tears . . .

"HE WON'T LET ME FLY AWAY . . ."

Vasya Saulchenko

EIGHT YEARS OLD. NOW A SOCIOLOGIST.

After the war, the same dream tormented me for a long time . . .

A dream about the first German I killed. I killed him myself, I didn't just see him dead. Either I'm flying, and he prevents me. I'm going up . . . flying . . . flying . . . He overtakes me, and we fall together. We fall down into some pit. Or I want to rise, to stand up . . . and he won't let me . . . Because of him I can't fly away . . .

One and the same dream . . . It haunted me for decades . . .

By the time I killed that German, I had already seen a lot . . . I had seen my grandfather being shot in the street, and my grandmother near the well . . . Before my eyes, I saw them beat my mother on the head with a rifle butt . . . Her hair turned red . . . But when I shot at that German, I had no time to think of it. He was wounded . . . I wanted to take away his submachine gun, I had been told to take away his submachine gun. I was ten years old, the partisans had already taken me on missions. I ran up to the German and saw a gun dancing before my eyes. The German had seized it with both hands and was aiming it at my face. But he didn't manage to shoot first. I did . . .

I wasn't frightened that I had killed him . . . And I didn't think about him during the war. There were many dead all around, we lived among the dead. We even got used to it. Only once did I get frightened. We walked into a village that had just been burned down. It had been burned in the morning, and we arrived in the evening. I saw a burned woman . . . She lay, all black, but her hands were white, a living woman's hands. That's when I first felt frightened. I could barely keep from screaming.

No, I wasn't a child. I don't remember myself as a child. Although . . . I wasn't afraid of the dead, but I was afraid of walking through a graveyard at night. The dead on the ground didn't frighten me, but those under the ground did. A child's fear . . . It stayed with me. Though . . . though I don't think children are afraid of anything . . .

Belarus was liberated . . . Dead Germans lay everywhere. We picked up our own people and buried them in mass graves, but those lay there for a long time, especially in winter. Children ran to the field to look at the dead . . . And right there, not far away, they went on playing games of war or "Cops and Robbers."

I was surprised when, many years later, that dream about the dead German appeared . . . I didn't expect it . . .

And that dream haunted me for decades . . .

My son is already a grown-up man. When he was little, I was tormented by the very thought of trying to tell him . . . to tell him about the war . . . He kept asking me, but I avoided the conversation. I liked reading him stories, I wanted him to have a childhood. He grew up, but I still don't want to talk about the war with him. Maybe someday I'll tell him about my dream. Maybe . . . I'm not sure . . .

It would destroy his world. A world without war . . . People who haven't seen a man kill another man are completely different people . . .

"EVERYBODY WANTED TO KISS THE WORD *VICTORY* . . ."

Anya Korzun

TWO YEARS OLD. NOW A ZOOTECHNICIAN.

I remember how the war ended . . . May 9, 1945 . . .

Women came running to the kindergarten.

"Children, it's Victory! Victory-y-y-y!"

Everybody laughed and cried. Cried and laughed.

They all began kissing us. Women we didn't know . . . Kissing us and crying . . . Kissing . . . We turned on the loudspeaker. Everybody listened. But we were little, we didn't understand the words, we understood that joy came from up there, from the black dish of the loudspeaker. The grown-ups picked some of us up . . . the others climbed by themselves . . . they climbed on each other like a ladder, only the third or fourth one reached the black dish and kissed it. Then they traded places . . . Everybody wanted to kiss the word *Victory* . . .

In the evening there were fireworks. The sky lit up. Mama opened the window and burst into tears.

"Little daughter, remember this all your life . . ."

When my father came home from the front, I was scared of him. He would give me candy and ask, "Say 'papa' . . . "

I would take the candy, hide with it under the table, and say, "Mister . . ."

I had no papa during the war. I grew up with mama and grandma. With my aunt. I couldn't imagine what a papa would do in our home.

He'd come with a rifle . . .

"WEARING A SHIRT MADE FROM MY FATHER'S ARMY SHIRT . . ."

Nikolai Berezka

BORN IN 1945. NOW A TAXI DRIVER.

I was born in 1945, but I remember the war. I know the war.

Mother would lock me up in another room . . . or send me outside with the other boys . . . But I still heard how my father screamed. He screamed for a long time. I clung to the crack between the doors: my father held his ailing leg with both hands, rocking it. Or he rolled about, pounding the floor with his fists: "The war! The cursed war!"

When the pain passed, my father took me in his arms. I touched his leg. "It's the war that hurts you? . . ."

"The war! Curse it!" answered my father.

And then this . . . The neighbors had two little boys . . . I was friends with them . . . They were blown up by a mine outside the village. That was probably already in 1949 . . .

Their mother, Auntie Anya, threw herself into their grave. They pulled her out . . . She screamed . . . people don't scream like that . . .

I went to school wearing a shirt made from my father's army shirt. I was so happy! All the boys whose fathers had come back from the war had shirts sewn from their fathers' army shirts.

After the war, my father died from the war. From his wounds.

I don't have to make anything up. I've seen the war. I dream about the war. I cry in my sleep that they will come tomorrow and take my papa away. The house smells of new military cloth . . .

The war! Curse it! . . .

"I DECORATED IT WITH
RED CARNATIONS . . ."

Mariam Yuzefovskaya

BORN IN 1941. NOW AN ENGINEER.

I was born in the war. And I grew up during the war.

And so . . . We're waiting for papa to come back from the war . . .

What did mama not do with me: she shaved my head, rubbed me with kerosene, applied ointments. I hated myself desperately. Felt ashamed. I wouldn't even go out in the yard. Lice and blisters in the first year after the war . . . There was no escaping them . . .

And then the telegram: father is demobilized. We went to meet him at the train station. Mama dressed me up. She tied a red bow to the top of my head. What it was tied to isn't clear. And she kept yanking my arm: "Don't scratch yourself. Don't scratch yourself." But the itching was unbearable! The cursed bow was about to fall off. And there was this buzzing in my head: "What if my father doesn't like me? He hasn't seen me even once."

But what actually happened was even worse. My father saw me and rushed to me first. But right then . . . for a moment, for just a moment—but I felt it at once, with my skin, with my whole little body—it was as if he backed away . . . For a single moment . . . And it was so hurtful. So unbearably bitter. And when he took me in his arms, I pushed him away with all my might. The smell of kerosene suddenly hit my nose. It had been following me everywhere for a year, I had stopped noticing it. I got used to it. But now I smelled it.

Maybe it was because my father had such a nice and unusual smell. He was so handsome compared to me and my exhausted mama. And it stung me to my very soul. I tore off the bow, threw it on the ground, and stepped on it with my foot.

"What are you doing?" my father asked in surprise.

"It's your character," laughed mama, who understood everything. She held my father with both hands, and they walked home like that.

At night I called mama and asked her to take me to bed with her. I had always slept with mama . . . All through the war . . . But mama didn't answer, as if she was asleep. I had no one to tell how hurt I was.

Before falling asleep, I firmly decided to run away to an orphanage . . .

In the morning, my father gave me two dolls. I didn't have real dolls till I was five. Only homemade rag dolls. My grandmother's. The dolls that my father brought had eyes that closed and opened, their arms and legs could move, one of them squeaked a word like *mama*. It seemed magical to me. I treasured them. I was even afraid to take them outside. But I showed them in the window. We lived on the ground floor, all the children in the yard gathered to see my dolls.

I was weak and sickly. I was always unlucky. Either I bruised my forehead, or I cut myself on a nail. Or I would simply fall in a faint. And the children were reluctant to include me in their games. I tried to gain their trust however I could; I invented all sorts of ways. It reached a point where I started fawning on Dusya, the caretaker's daughter. Dusya was strong, cheerful, everybody liked to play with her.

She asked me to bring out my doll, and I couldn't resist. However, not at once. I still refused for a little while.

"I won't play with you," Dusya threatened me.

That worked on me at once.

I brought out the doll that "spoke." But we didn't play for long. We quarreled over something, and it turned into a cock fight. Dusya grabbed my doll by the legs and smashed it against the wall. The doll's head fell off and the speaking button fell from its stomach.

"Dusya, you're crazy," all the children began to cry.

"Why is she giving the orders?" Dusya smeared the tears on her cheeks. "Since she has a papa, she can do anything. Dolls, a papa—all just for her."

Dusya had neither a father nor any dolls . . .

Our first Christmas tree was set up under the table. Back then we lived at my grandfather's. It was pretty cramped. So cramped that the only empty space left was under the big table. That's where we set up the little Christmas tree. I decorated it with red carnations. I remember very well how fresh and clean the tree smelled. Nothing could overcome that smell. Neither the cornmeal mash that my grandmother cooked, nor my grandfather's shoe polish.

I had a glass ball. My treasure. I couldn't find a place for it on the tree. I wanted to hang it in such a way that it shone from wherever you looked at it. I placed it up at the very top. When I went to bed, I took it down and hid it. I was afraid it would disappear . . .

I slept in a washtub. The tub was made of zinc. It had a bluish sheen with frosty veins. No matter how we scrubbed it after doing laundry, the smell of the ashes we used instead of soap, which was a rarity, lingered. I liked it. I liked to press my forehead to the cold edges of the tub, especially when I was sick. I liked to rock it like a cradle. Then its rumbling would betray me, and I would get scolded. We cherished that tub. It was the only thing we had left from our life before the war.

And then suddenly we bought a bed . . . With shiny beads on the headboard . . . All this caused me indescribable excitement! I climbed on it and immediately rolled down on the floor. What? Is it possible? I couldn't believe that anyone could sleep in such a beautiful bed.

Papa saw me on the floor, picked me up, and hugged me tight. And I hugged him . . . I put my arms around his neck the way mama did.

I remember how happily he laughed . . .

"I WAITED A LONG TIME FOR MY FATHER . . . ALL MY LIFE . . ."

Arseny Gutin

BORN IN 1941. NOW AN ELECTRICIAN.

On Victory Day, I turned four . . .

In the morning I started telling everyone that I was already five years old. Not in my fifth year, but five years old. I wanted to grow up. Papa would come back from the war, and I'd already have grown up.

That day the chairman of the kolkhoz summoned the women: "Victory!" He kissed them all. Each one. I was with mama . . . I rejoiced. And mama cried.

All the children gathered . . . Outside the village, we set fire to rubber tires from the German trucks. We shouted "Hurray! Hur-ray! Victory!" We beat on the German helmets that we had gathered earlier in the forest. We beat on them like drums.

We lived in a mud hut . . . I came running to the mud hut . . . Mama was crying. I didn't understand why she was crying and not rejoicing on such a day.

It started to rain. I broke a stick and measured the puddles around our hut.

"What are you doing?" people asked me.

"I'm measuring how deep the puddles are. Because papa may come and fall into them."

The neighbors cried, and mama cried. I didn't understand what "missing in action" meant. I waited a long time for my father . . . All my life . . .

"AT THAT LIMIT . . . THAT BRINK . . ."

Valya Brinskaya

TWELVE YEARS OLD. NOW AN ENGINEER.

Dolls . . . The most beautiful . . . They always remind me of the war . . .

As long as papa was alive, as long as mama was alive, we didn't speak of the war. Now that they're gone, I often think of how nice it is to have old people at home. While they're alive, we are still children. Even after the war we were still children . . .

Our papa was a soldier. We lived near Bielostok. For us, the war started from the first hour, the first minutes. In my sleep I heard some sort of rumbling, like thunderclaps, but of an unusual, uninterrupted sort. I woke up and ran to the window—above the barracks in the village of Grayevo, where my sister and I went to school, the sky was burning.

"Papa, is that a thunderstorm?"

"Stay away from the window," papa replied. "It's war."

Mama prepared his campaign trunk. My father was often called in when the alarm was raised. Nothing seemed unusual . . . I wanted to sleep . . . I fell back in my bed, because I didn't understand anything. My sister and I went to bed late—we had gone to the movies. Before the war, "going to the movies" was quite different than now. Films were brought only before holidays, and there weren't many: *We Are from Kronstadt, Chapaev, If There Is War Tomorrow, Jolly Fellows*. The screening was set up in the Red Army mess hall. We children didn't miss a single show and knew all the films by heart. We even gave the cue to the artists on the screen or skipped ahead and interrupted them. There was no electricity in the village, nor in the army unit; we "rolled" the film with a portable motor. The motor crackled—we dropped everything and ran to take seats in front of the screen, and even brought along our own stools.

Watching movies was lengthy: the first part ends, everybody waits patiently while the projectionist winds the next reel. It's all right if the film is new, but if it's old, it keeps breaking. We wait while they glue it back and the glue dries. Or, even worse, the film would catch fire. When the motor stalled, it was a totally lost cause. Often we didn't have time to watch a movie to the end. The order would be given: "First company—prepare for action! Second company—fall in!"

And if the alarm was raised, the projectionist ran off. When the breaks between the parts were too long, the spectators lost their patience, agitation set in, whistling, shouts . . . My sister would climb on a table and announce, "The concert begins." She herself liked terribly to declaim, as we used to say. She didn't always know the words perfectly, but she climbed on the table fearlessly.

She had been like that ever since kindergarten, when we lived in the military garrison near Gomel. After the poems, my sister and I would sing. For an encore we would sing "Our Armor Is Strong and Our Tanks Are Swift." The windows shook in the mess hall when the soldiers picked up the refrain:

> With fiery thunder, steel armor gleaming,
> The tanks will furiously enter the fray . . .

And so, on June 21, 1941 . . . the night before the war . . . for maybe the tenth time, we watched the movie *If There Is War Tomorrow*. After the movie, we didn't disperse for a long time, father barely managed to herd us home: "So you'll sleep tonight? Tomorrow is a day off . . ."

I woke up finally when there was an explosion nearby and the windows in the kitchen shattered. Mama was wrapping my half-awake little brother Tolik in a blanket. My sister was already dressed. Papa wasn't home.

"Hurry, girls," mama urged us. "There's been a provocation at the border."

We ran to the forest. Mama was out of breath. She was carrying my little brother, and she kept repeating, "Don't fall behind, girls . . . Duck down, girls . . ." For some reason I remember how the sun hit me straight in the eyes. It was very bright. Birds were singing. And there was that piercing roar of airplanes . . .

I trembled, but then I felt ashamed that I was trembling. I had always wanted to be like the brave heroes from the book *Timur and His Gang,* by Arkady Gaidar,* and here I was trembling. I took my little brother in my arms and started rocking him and even singing "And the young girl . . ." There was this love song in the movie *The Goal-keeper.* Mama often sang it, and it perfectly suited my mood and condition in that moment. I was . . . in love! I don't know what science says, what the books about adolescent psychology say, but I was constantly in love. There was a time when I loved several boys at once. But at that moment, I liked only one—Vitya, from the Grayevo garrison. He was in the sixth grade. The sixth graders were in the same classroom with the fifth. Fifth graders in the first row of desks, sixth graders in the second. I can't imagine how the teachers managed to conduct classes. I didn't care about studying. How was it I didn't break my neck staring at Vitya!

I liked everything about him: that he was short—we were well

---

* Arkady Gaidar (1904–1941) was a Soviet writer. The short novel *Timur and His Gang* (1940), his most famous work, was based partly on the life of his own son, Timur Gaidar (1926–1999), who served in the navy, became a rear admiral, and was also a writer and journalist.

matched; that he had blue, blue eyes, like my papa's; and that he was well-read—not like Alka Poddubnyak, who gave painful "flicks" and who liked me. Vitya especially liked Jules Verne! So did I. The Red Army library had his complete works, and I read them all . . .

I don't remember how long we stayed in the forest . . . We stopped hearing explosions. Silence fell. The women sighed with relief: "Our boys fought them off." But then . . . in the midst of that silence . . . suddenly we heard the roar of flying airplanes . . . We ran out to the road. The planes were flying toward the border: "Hur-ray!" But there was something "not ours" about those planes: the wings were not ours, and the sound wasn't ours. They were German bombers, they flew wing to wing, slowly and heavily. It seemed like they left no empty space in the sky. We started counting, but lost track. Later, in the wartime news reports, I saw those planes, but my impression wasn't the same. The filming was done at airplane level. But when you look at them from below, through the thick of the trees, and what's more, with the eyes of an adolescent—it's a scary sight. Afterward I often dreamed about those planes. But the dream went further—the whole of that iron sky slowly fell down on me and crushed me, crushed me, crushed me. I would wake up in a cold sweat, shaking all over. Horrible!

Somebody said that the bridge had been bombed. We got frightened: what about papa? Papa wouldn't be able to swim across, he couldn't swim.

I can't say exactly now . . . But I remember that papa came running to us: "You'll be evacuated by truck." He gave mama the thick photograph album and a warm, quilted blanket: "Muffle up the children, or they'll catch cold." That was all we took with us. In such a hurry. No documents, no passports, not a kopeck of money. We also had a pot of meatballs my mother had prepared for the weekend, and my brother's little shoes. And my sister—a miracle!—grabbed at the last moment a package, which contained mama's crepe de chine dress and her shoes. Somehow. By chance. Maybe she and papa wanted to visit some friends for the weekend? Nobody could remember anymore. Peaceful life instantly disappeared, fell into the background.

That's how we evacuated . . .

We quickly reached the station, but sat there for a long time. Everything trembled and rattled. The lights went out. We lit a fire with paper, newspapers. Somebody found a lantern. Its light cast huge shadows of people sitting—on the walls, on the ceiling. They stood still, then moved. And then my imagination ran away with me: Germans in a fortress, our soldiers taken prisoner. I decided to try and see if I could endure torture or not. I put my fingers between two boxes and crushed them. I howled in pain. Mama got frightened. "What's the matter, dear?"

"I'm afraid I won't be able to endure the torture during the interrogation."

"What do you mean, little fool, what interrogation? Our soldiers won't let the Germans through."

She caressed my head and kissed me.

The train rode under bombs all the time. Whenever they began bombing, mama lay on top of us: "If they kill us, we'll die together. Or else just me . . ." The first dead person I saw was a little boy. He was lying there looking up, and I tried to waken him. To waken him . . . I couldn't understand that he wasn't alive. I had a piece of sugar, I offered him that piece of sugar, hoping he would get up. But he didn't . . .

They were bombing, and my sister whispered to me, "When they stop bombing, I'll obey mama, I'll always obey mama." And indeed, after the war, Toma was very obedient. Mama remembered that before the war, she used to call her a scamp. And our little Tolik . . . Before the war he could already walk well and talk well. And now he stopped talking, he clutched his head all the time.

I saw my sister's hair turn white. She had very long black hair, and it turned white. In one night . . .

The train started. Where is Tamara? She's not in the car. We look.

Tamara is running behind the car with a bouquet of cornflowers. There was a big field, the wheat was taller than us, and there were cornflowers. Her face . . . To this day her face is before my eyes. Her black eyes wide open, she runs, silent. She doesn't even shout "mama." She runs, silent.

Mama went mad . . . She rushed to jump out of the moving train . . . I was holding Tolik, and we both shouted. Then a soldier appeared . . . He pushed mama away from the door, jumped out, caught hold of Tomka, and threw her into the car with all his might. In the morning, we saw she was white. For several days we didn't tell her, we hid our mirror, but then she accidentally looked into someone else's and burst into tears: "Mama, am I already a grand-mother?"

Mama comforted her. "We'll cut your hair, and it will grow back dark."

After this incident mama said, "That's it. Don't leave the car. If they kill us, they kill us. If we stay alive, then it's our destiny!"

When they shouted "Airplanes! Everybody off the train!" she stuffed us under the mattresses, and to those who tried to get her off the train, she said, "The children ran, but I can't go."

I have to say that mama often used that mysterious word *destiny*. I kept asking her, "What is destiny? Is it God?"

"No, not God. I don't believe in God. Destiny is the line of life," mama answered. "I have always believed in your destiny, children."

The bombings frightened me . . . Terribly. Later on, in Siberia, I hated myself for my cowardice. By chance, out of the corner of my eye, I read mama's letter . . . She was writing to papa. We, too, wrote our first letters ever, and I decided to take a peek at what mama was writing. And mama was precisely writing that Tamara is quiet during the bombings, and Valya cries and is frightened. That was too much for me. When papa came to us in the spring of 1944, I couldn't raise my eyes to him—I was ashamed. Terrible! But I'll tell about the re-union with papa later. It's a long way till then . . .

I remember a night air raid . . . Usually there were no raids at night, and the train drove fast. But now there was a raid. A heavy one . . . Bullets drummed on the roof of the car. Roaring planes. Glowing streaks from flying bullets . . . From bombshells . . . Next to me, a woman was killed. I understood only later that she was dead . . . But she didn't fall. There was nowhere to fall, because the car was packed with people. The woman stood among us gasping, her blood flooding my face, warm, viscous. My shirt and pants were already wet with blood. When mama cried, touching me with her hand: "Valya, have they killed you?" I couldn't answer.

That was a turning point for me. I know that after that . . . Yes . . . After that I stopped trembling. I didn't care anymore . . . No fear, no pain, no sorrow. Some kind of stupor, indifference.

I remember that we didn't reach the Urals right away. For some time we stayed in the village of Balanda, in the Saratov region. We were brought there in the evening, and we fell asleep. In the morning, at six o'clock, a herdsman cracked his whip, and all the women jumped up, grabbed their children, and ran outside screaming "Air raid!" They screamed until the kolkhoz chairman came and said that it was a herdsman driving cows. Then they came to their senses . . .

When the grain elevator hummed, our Tolik got scared and trembled. He didn't let anyone go away from him for a second. Only when he fell asleep could we go outside without him. Mama went with us to the military commissariat to find out about father and ask for help. The commissar said, "Show me the documents stating that your husband is a commander in the Red Army."

We didn't have any documents, we only had a photograph of papa, in which he was wearing his uniform. He took it suspiciously.

"Maybe this isn't your husband. How can you prove it?"

Tolik saw that he was holding the photo and not giving it back. "Give papa back . . ."

The commissar laughed. "Well, that's a 'document' I can't help believing."

My sister went around "piebald," so mama cut her hair. We checked every morning whether the new hair would be black or white. Our little brother reassured her, "Don't cwy, Toma . . . Don't cwy . . ." The hair that grew back was white. The boys teased her. Teased her unmercifully. She never took her kerchief off, even in class.

We came back from school. Tolik wasn't at home.

We ran to mama's work: "Where's Tolik?"

"Tolik is in the hospital."

My sister and I are carrying a blue wreath down the street . . . Of snowdrops . . . And our brother's sailor suit. Mama is with us. She said that Tolik had died. Mama stopped outside the mortuary and couldn't go in. Couldn't bring herself to. I went in and recognized little Tolik at once—he lay there naked. I didn't shed a single tear, I turned to wood.

Papa's letter caught up with us in Siberia. Mama cried all night, unable to write to papa that their son was dead. In the morning the three of us took a telegram to the post office: "Girls alive. Toma gray-haired." And papa figured out that Tolik was no more. I had a friend whose father had been killed, and I always wrote at the end of my letters to papa, because she asked me to: "Greetings to you, papa, from me and from my friend Lera." Everybody wanted to have a papa.

Soon we received a letter from papa. He wrote that he had spent a long time in the rear on a special assignment and had fallen ill. They told him in the hospital that he could be cured only by being with his family: once he saw his dear ones, he'd feel better.

We waited several weeks for papa. Mama got her cherished crepe de chine dress and her shoes from the suitcase. We had made a decision not to sell that dress or the pair of shoes, no matter how hard the times would be. It was out of superstition. We were afraid that if we sold them, papa wouldn't come back.

I heard papa's voice outside the window and couldn't believe that it was my papa. We were so used to waiting for him that I couldn't believe I could see him. For us papa was someone you had to wait for and only wait for. That day classes were interrupted—the whole school gathered around our house. They waited for papa to come out. He was the first papa to come back from the war. My sister and I were unable to study for another two days, everybody kept coming to us, asking questions, writing notes: "What is your papa like?" And our papa was special: Anton Petrovich Brinsky, Hero of the Soviet Union . . .

Like our Tolik before, papa didn't want to be alone. He couldn't be. It made him feel bad. He always dragged me with him. Once I heard . . . He told someone about some partisans coming to a village and seeing a lot of freshly dug earth. They stopped and stood on it . . . A boy came running across the field shouting that his whole village had been shot and buried there. All the people.

Papa turned and saw that I had fainted. Never again did he tell about the war in front of us . . .

We talked little about the war. Papa and mama were sure that there would never again be such a terrible war. They believed it for a long time. The only thing the war left in my sister and me was that we kept buying dolls. I don't know why. Probably because we hadn't had enough childhood. Not enough childhood joy. I was already studying at the university, but my sister knew that the best present for me was a doll. My sister gave birth to a daughter. I went to visit.

"What present can I bring you?"

"A doll . . ."

"I'm asking what to give you, not your girl."

"And my answer is—give me a doll."

Our children were growing up, and we kept giving them dolls. We gave dolls to all our acquaintances.

Our marvelous mama was the first to go; then papa followed her.

We sensed, we felt at once that we were the last ones. At that limit . . . that brink . . . We are the last witnesses. Our time is ending. We must speak . . .

Our words will be the last . . .

1978–2004

SVETLANA ALEXIEVICH was born in Ivano-Frankovsk, Ukraine, in 1948 and has spent most of her life in the Soviet Union and present-day Belarus, with prolonged periods of exile in Western Europe. Starting out as a journalist, she developed her own nonfiction genre, which brings together a chorus of voices to describe a specific historical moment. Her works include *The Unwomanly Face of War* (1985), *Last Witnesses* (1985), *Zinky Boys* (1990), *Voices from Chernobyl* (1997), and *Secondhand Time* (2013). She has won many international awards, including the 2015 Nobel Prize in Literature for "her polyphonic writings, a monument to suffering and courage in our time."

Together, RICHARD PEVEAR and LARISSA VOLOKHONSKY
have translated works by Pushkin, Gogol, Dostoevsky,
Tolstoy, Chekhov, Leskov, Bulgakov, and Pasternak.
They have twice received the PEN Book-of-the-Month
Club Translation Prize (in 1991 for *The Brothers Karama-
zov* and in 2002 for *Anna Karenina*). In 2006 they were
awarded the first Efim Etkind International Translation
Prize by the European University of St. Petersburg.
Most recently they have been collaborating with the
playwright Richard Nelson on plays by Turgenev,
Gogol, Chekhov, and Bulgakov.

ABOUT THE TYPE

This book was set in Bembo, a typeface based on an old-style Roman face that was used for Cardinal Pietro Bembo's tract *De Aetna* in 1495. Bembo was cut by Francesco Griffo (1450–1518) in the early sixteenth century for Italian Renaissance printer and publisher Aldus Manutius (1449–1515). The Lanston Monotype Company of Philadelphia brought the well-proportioned letterforms of Bembo to the United States in the 1930s.